THE LIFE AND TIMES OF

WILLIAM
WITHERING

HIS WORK, HIS LEGACY

First published by
Brewin Books Ltd, 56 Alcester Road,
Studley, Warwickshire B80 7LG in 2004
www.brewinbooks.com

ISBN 1 85858 240 7

A Cataloguing in Publication Record
for this title is available from the British Library.

Typeset in Times
Printed in Great Britain by
Alden Press Limited.

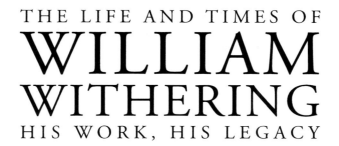

THE LIFE AND TIMES OF
WILLIAM WITHERING
HIS WORK, HIS LEGACY

Peter Sheldon MD FRCP

Senior Lecturer in Immunology, University of Leicester,
Hon. Consultant in Rheumatology, Leicester Royal Infirmary

BREWIN BOOKS

William Withering MD FRS FLS

Preface

Why was this book written? This is a question that I find difficult to answer. Having spent my formative years in Wellington, Shropshire, a town for which I have many fond memories, I then went to Birmingham University to read Medicine. There I learned that the William Withering Chair in Medicine was named after the physician who formally introduced digitalis into medicine, and that he had been born in Wellington. I must admit to a deep seated sense of pride when I discovered this, but did nothing about it until many years later when I thought of retracing his life. (Withering is referred to in the rest of this book, variously as WW, or by his full name). The exercise has been most invigorating, as a consequence of which I have come to learn about many historical events to which I must admit having turned a deaf ear whilst still at school. Perhaps it would have been more interesting if, instead of concentrating on the effects of the French Revolution on the French, we had been taught about the implications in England. The events that took place here included the riots that nearly resulted in Withering losing his Birmingham home, as well as events in Wellington itself - all to be described later in the book.

The Shropshire countryside, so beloved of A.E. Housman, must have been a source of pleasure to Withering, but sadly there is no description of any events during his boyhood days to indicate his knowledge of local beauty spots, or places for a young boy to go fishing. I have therefore resorted to a little imagination, having grown up in the area. Events that were recorded must have been known to him, and with the aid of local history gleaned from the library in Wellington, I have been able to piece together some fragments of the tapestry of the time. Subsequent events have already been most ably described in Peck and Wilkinson's book. However, that book ended with Withering's death in 1799 from presumed tuberculosis. I feel that the impact of digitalis over the subsequent two hundred years, as carefully chronicled by Aronson, has been enormous, and have attempted to sketch this in as his legacy to medicine. William Withering has taught us a lot particularly in regard to careful documentation of the clinical effects of drugs, and not rushing into print before the t's have been crossed and the i's dotted. This almost lost him the accolade that was his due, as others were ready and willing to seize the opportunity.

One problem that is implicit with a book of this nature is deciding to whom it is directed. To the medical profession? To the lay reader with a passing interest in Medicine? To the pharmaceutical historian? The answer is that there is something for all three, notwithstanding the risk of all the pitfalls this entails. Therefore I have tried wherever necessary, to explain in lay terms what is meant, and hope that any physicians reading this book will employ that modicum of patience which their training will have instilled. Where historical events, or snatches of 18th century gossip have intruded, I make no apology for the occasional foray along side tracks, because these lead to the sources of flavour and colour of which this period in time was so rich. Also, for the first time in a book about Withering, his complete MD thesis from the University of

Edinburgh, translated from Latin is included. Likewise, in respect of the technical descriptions in chapter 8, I suggest that the non-technically minded gloss over the details which follow Sydney Smith's description of digoxin, which is the form of digitalis in common use to this day.

Withering lived at a time of tremendous change, both at home and abroad. He was born within five miles of the epicentre of the Industrial Revolution, and during his lifetime an Empire was being created, America was lost, and a Revolution took place in France. He was a great observer, be it of patients, minerals, or plants. He obviously was a proud man who fought his patch tenaciously, and some of his adversaries were formidable people. Despite this, and his own long drawn out illness, his name has prevailed, as has his treatment for the dropsy, at least when accompanied by that irregularity of the heart beat known as atrial fibrillation. In terms of longevity within the doctor's armamentarium, digitalis rivals aspirin. It seems appropriate that more be written about Withering, notwithstanding that there is already an abundance of information but because the legacy of his work would appear to be worthy of exploration. He was a man ahead of his time, innately versed in the art of scientific method. Today, in the climate of evidence-based medicine, it would pass as commonplace, but this only serves to bring home what Medicine, as well as other disciplines requiring experimental rigour, has gained from his writings.

Leicester, August, 2000

Acknowledgements

I am grateful to Dr. Murray Simpson, of Edinburgh University library, and to Dr. S.R Jenkins, Faculty Archivist, University of Birmingham, for their assistance. I am particularly indebted to Dr. John Reader who was employed by the Wellcome Foundation Ltd, for much helpful advice relating to the history and manufacture of digoxin, based on his vast first hand experience, and to GlaxoWellcome for access to the museum and chemical plant at Dartford now owned by GlaxoSmithKline. For information about the resurrected Lunar Society, I am grateful to Ms. Amanda Cadman. For aspects of local history of Wellington, I thank Mr. George Evans. The assistance of the Library of the Royal College of Physicians of London is also gratefully acknowledged.

Finally, I must express my gratitude for the facilities offered at Leicester University, and in particular to Melissa Funnell and Kamlesh Chandarana of the Audiovisual Department, and Mr. Roy Clements, Curator of the Department of Geology.

Foreword

It is a great privilege to have the opportunity of contributing a few words in praise of this fascinating account of the life of William Withering and associated historical events. It is an outstanding account of a man who contributed so much to both medical and pharmaceutical knowledge, which also takes the opportunity of setting these achievements alongside contemporary events of the day, with a fascinating insight into his place in society of the day. I feel particularly privileged to comment on this from my position as the fourth William Withering Professor of Medicine at the University of Birmingham. Full-time clinical professors were introduced in the Medical School in 1946 and at the start of the academic year in 1948 the Faculty handbook records for the first time that the Professor of Medicine (Professor W. Melville Arnott, later Sir Melville Arnott) was now the "William Withering Professor of Medicine." This followed a decision by the Medical School to endow some of the leading chairs with names from the Medical School's past. This scholarly work by Dr. Peter Sheldon adds immeasurably to the heritage associated with William Withering.

Michael C. Sheppard.

William Withering Professor of Medicine

The University of Birmingham

Contents

PART ONE - The Life of William Withering

PART TWO - The Times of William Withering

PART THREE - Withering's Legacy to Medicine

Appendices

Part One

THE LIFE OF WILLIAM WITHERING (WW)

Chapter 1

WELLINGTON, COUNTY OF THE WREKIN
(FORMERLY SALOP, OR SHROPSHIRE)

WITHERING'S EARLY YEARS

WW was born in Wellington, in 1741. His baptism was recorded in the Parish Register, on April 13th 1742. The church is shown in the figure (McCrea 1991).

The old church, Wellington, Shropshire.

This church was demolished in 1789. The church was damaged in 1644 during the Civil War when it was captured by parliamentary forces and a few days later recaptured by the Royalists.

WW's precise address at that time is unknown, as there was no land registry. His father **Edmund Withering** was an apothecary, but owing to a lack of detailed town plans of the time, we do not know the precise location of WW's birthplace. Edmund had married **Sarah Hector** in the village of Shifnal, Shropshire, in 1734. She was the sister of **Dr. Brooke Hector**, a prominent physician from Lichfield.

They were to have three children. Mary was born in 1739, then William in 1741, followed by Sarah in 1750, (see Peck & Wilkinson 1950). William received his education at home from **Henry Wood**, the curate at Ercall Magna (nowadays High Ercall), situated about six miles away. The vicar of Wellington from 1709-1713, was a Henry Wood B.A. (see McCrea 1991). Was he related to WW's tutor? And there was a Henry Wood who was vicar at Ercall Magna, but this was from 1764-1795, by which time WW was a medical student in Edinburgh. It seems most likely that Henry Wood was the curate at Ercall Magna before becoming vicar in 1764.

We know very little about WW's early years. From his son William, in his 'Miscellaneous Tracts of the late William Withering,' of which the first 207 pages are a memoir to his father, we gather that WW's father, Edmund, the apothecary, was possessed of 'agreeable manners and a prepossessing exterior, engaged early in the medical profession, pursuing an extensive practice so successfully as to acquire no inconsiderable reputation in a populous district.' It would have been an immensely interesting exercise to have studied WW the boy, in an attempt to plot the emergence and development of his enormous talent and intellect. Unfortunately, the Memoir gives us painfully little;

'Of anecdotes illustrative of the days of boyhood we have none—At a season when the rational faculties are unfolding, and the intellect is gradually training into full exercise, a defective memory proved an impediment to that progress which might have been expected from assiduity. To strengthen this necessary aid to the acquisition of knowledge, an increasing portion of verse or prose was daily learned by rote; by which habitual effort the retentive powers were so improved as to induce the young student to relinquish the habit of taking notes, which may, in some degree, be regretted; for, relying wholly on the talent thus, as it were, artificially acquired, during the subsequent pressure of urgent engagements, he committed few ideas to paper.'

We are given perhaps a glimpse of his pre-university days in a throw-away remark in the Memoir. It relates to his early days as a medical student at Edinburgh;

'Scarcely inured to such unremitting and sedentary labours, his health began to suffer, till, **in lieu of those rural sports he had formerly enjoyed in Shropshire,** he participated in the national game of golf, which seems to have succeeded to the more noble pastime of archery, but with little pretension to rival that amusement.'

So, one gathers he had been keen on 'rural sports' whilst at home in Shropshire, maybe archery. Most certainly he would have climbed the Wrekin, at whose foot the town of Wellington nestles (see figure).

We do not know precisely whether he became apprenticed to his father, prior to going up to Edinburgh to study medicine. Generally would-be physicians and surgeons of the time would become *pupils* of surgeons or physicians, whereas *apprentices* to apothecaries would eventually become apothecaries. At the same time, he obviously felt a debt of gratitude to Dr. Brooke Hector, his uncle, to whom he dedicated his eventual thesis, as well as to Henry Wood, the curate. His formative years coincided with the great revival of learning in England during the latter half of the eighteenth century. The revival occurred away from the traditional centres, and instead sprung up in the Midlands, several northern cities, and later in Birmingham. Why did he choose

Edinburgh? To answer this, we need to look back into the events of the previous century. But first, a little more on local history.

A contributor to the **Gentleman's Magazine** of 1758 gave an interesting description of Wellington at that time. The parish contained 780 houses and about 4,000 inhabitants. The description continues:

"There are two manors in the parish, those of Dothill and Hadley; the former belongs to **Brooke Forester** Esq., and the latter to Mr. Roe. There is one park belonging to Brooke Forester Esq., about three miles in circumference and well stocked with deer.

The fuel used is coal at 3s 8d per ton. Carriage from London is 9/- per cwt. in winter and 7/- in summer. There are no manufactures carried on in the town, the inhabitants being chiefly engaged in getting coal, lime, and ironstone. There are two furnaces about one and a half miles on the east side of the town, and a steam engine by means of which the water that works the bellows is returned to the pool above. This engine, which is one of the largest in England, consumes upwards of twenty tons of coal every twenty four hours.

The market is kept weekly on Thursdays, and there are three fairs in the year. The chief commodities exposed for sale are horned cattle, sheep, pigs, hempen cloth, all sorts of grain, and butcher's meat. The prices of provisions are very variable, but chiefly as follows- a goose for 2/-, a duck for 10d., a fowl for 8d., a rabbit for 1/-, beef, veal, mutton, lamb, and pork, 3d., butter from 4d. to 7d., and cheese 3d. Labourer's wages 1/- per day; carpenters, bricklayers, and masons, 1/6, and tailors 8d. with victuals.

The best pasture and meadow land lets for 50/- per acre and arable for 20/-. The ploughs now in use were invented by one Lummis, whose name they bear."

The Wrekin, viewed from Cressage.

The parish at this time, and until the 19th century, covered an area six miles east-west, and three and a half miles north-south. It included Wellington, Lawley, Lawley Bank, Arleston, Ketley, Hadley, Horton, Leegomery, Wappenshall, part of Preston, part of Eyton, Walcot, and Aston. Wellington had been a market town since the middle of the 13th century, with a sparse surrounding population. With the industrialization to the south and east, the population increased. Coal had been known to exist locally since Roman times, but owing to transportation difficulties, it had been little used. However, its importance in relation to the locally found iron was being recognized.

The Forester family mentioned above had lived in or around Wellington since 1170, originally possessing thirty acres (or half-virgate) with an annual value of four shillings, but which by 1876 was 14,891 acres with an annual value of £21,046. Sir William was Member of Parliament for Wenlock for many years. A staunch Protestant he refused to serve during the reign of James II, but was returned during the first Parliament of William and Mary in 1689. He held his seat until his death in 1718 during the reign of George I. He was buried at Wellington on 22nd February 1718. He had two sons, the eldest, William, marrying Catharine heiress of William Brooke of Clerkenwell. They had two sons, Brooke and Cecil. In 1734 Brooke Forester married Elizabeth Weld of Willey and lived at Willey Old Hall.

WW may well have had opportunity to visit the beautiful grounds of Willey Old Hall, as did the author surreptitiously whilst a medical student at Birmingham, and at the time in ignorance of the previous existence of WW.

The **Vicars of Wellington** during Withering's life were:

Robert Eyton, 1713-1751
Richard Smith,1751-1773
Thomas Warter, 1773-1778
Stephen Panting, 1778-1782, with the rectory of Eyton attached
John Rocke, 1782-1803, with the rectory of Eyton attached.

Until 1740 there was little wheeled traffic, goods being carried by pack-horse, but in that year was set up a stage waggon plying between Shrewsbury and London, a distance of about 150 miles. This was a cumbersome vehicle with broad wheels drawn by 8 horses, with two more to help it along bad stretches and up hills. It needed 7-9 days for the journey, and was chiefly intended for the carriage of goods, but often accommodated passengers. In 1751, a new vehicle was introduced, called the Caravan. It did the journey in 4 -5 days. It was of lighter construction than the stage waggon, with benches fitted along the sides for 8-10 passengers and was drawn by 6 horses. By 1825, the journey time was down to 18 hours.

In 1753, there appeared the following advertisement:

"SHREWSBURY STAGE COACH
in three days and a half
Sets out from the George and White Hart in Aldersgate Street, London, every Wednesday morning at five o'clock and from the Raven Inn in Shrewsbury every Monday noon at one o'clock. Each passenger to pay one guinea - half at taking their places, the other at entering the coach, children on lap and outside passengers to pay half a guinea each. Each passenger allowed fourteen pounds weight of luggage, all above to pay 2pence halfpenny per pound. Not to be answerable for any jewels, rings, watches, gold, money, or plate.

Performed, if God permit, by John Fowler
Turvil Drayson
John Benson

Places are taken at Mr. Bathers at the Waggon and Horses in Mardell, Shrewsbury."

This was the first of the stage coaches of the kind which later became so numerous; as yet however, none of these vehicles did more than one journey each week. In 1764 a new coach, the "Machine", left Shrewsbury twice a week, taking only two days for the journey in summer and an extra day in winter. This great rapidity earned it the name of the Flying Machine, and in the summer of 1772 the time for the journey was reduced to a day and a half, an improvement made possible mainly by the better roads. By 1788 London could be reached in less than a day:

"LION INN SHREWSBURY
The Royal Mail coach, upon an entire new construction, in 22 hours to London every morning at 7o'clock, through Wolverhampton, Birmingham and Oxford. Performed by Government Authority, with a guard.

Carries for insides only. Fare £2...5...0
The London Fly, in 30 hours, every Monday, Wednesday, and Friday, at 4o'clock. Carries six insides. Fare £1...16...0
Outsides £1."

The introduction of the Royal Mail coaches on this route was largely due to the initiative of a Mr. Lawrence, the proprietor of the Lion Inn at Shrewsbury, a name inseparable from the history of the road during the next half century.

A diagram of the roads around Wellington circa 1770 is appended, together with a current view of the market square, and a plaque on the wall of a cake-shop, possibly the actual birthplace of Withering.

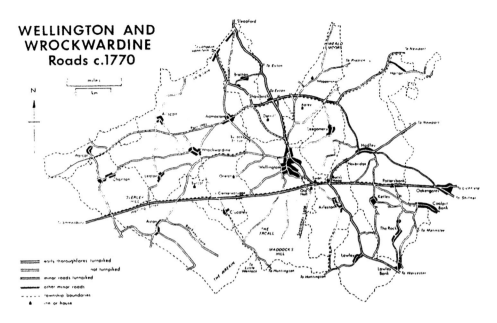

Map of Wellington and Wrockwardine c. 1770.

Wellington, the market square, year 2000.

*The plaque on the wall of the bakery, which is about 30 yards
on the left as viewed in the preceding picture.*

In 1756, when WW was 15 years old, the summer was recorded as being unusually cold and wet. There was a rise in food prices which caused much distress to those of lesser means. Food was so dear and scarce that in the second week of November, a large body of colliers and labourers were visiting market towns in search of cheap provisions. They insisted on paying their own prices. This began in an orderly manner, food being taken and payment being made at the "fair" price. Wheat, priced 8/- a bushel was taken at 5/, butter at fourpence halfpenny instead of the asking 6d. a pound. Eventually, as might have been anticipated, this degenerated into theft and plundering, resistance being met with violence. During one particular week, the mob visited Much Wenlock on Monday, Shifnal on Tuesday, Broseley on Wednesday, and Wellington on Thursday. From a letter dated 12th November 1756 we read:

"Thursday they came to Wellington, it being market day, but here the farmers brought little, being apprehensive of losing what they brought; on this the mob separated into bodies, part plundering many of the inhabitants and part robbing the farmers. They lived at large on the inns, most of which suffered much, and many of the private houses had nothing left at their departure. The gentry had little regard paid them, the middle sort of people less, and the poor were stript of everything. In the dusk of the evening when the main body had left the town, one of the gang snatched a piece of beef from a butcher's stall, on which some of the townspeople ventured to seize him, which occasioned a smart scuffle. The townsmen had the advantage and took three prisoners. This action greatly alarmed the town for now nothing was thought of but that the colliers would return in the night and fire the town, as they had threatened to do on their next visit; others prepared for their defence by keeping armed all night.

..........Little sleep was had that night; hunger and anxiety forbade it in most families. However, our fears were entirely dissipated, for soon after daylight this morning Edward Cludde and Edward Pemberton Esqs. appeared at the head of a large party of their neighbours, tenants, and servants, all pretty well armed........the farmers too for many miles around came in, and a body was formed of nearly 1,500 men. These immediately marched to assist the townsmen who had set forward somewhat earlier to prevent the junction of the colliers now calling together with horns. On the appearance of opposition the rioters dispersed, many of them are taken and much of their pillage brought back."

WW aged 15 must have experienced this frightening experience at first hand, and would again in 1791 be faced with a threatening mob.

Hannah Darby (daughter of Abraham II), wrote to her aunt that year:

"My Dear Aunt,

Being apprehensive that you may hear of the tumult which hath happened here we are willing to inform you of the particulars, as such things generally gains much by carriage - the affair was this; this day week, the 1st Inst. we were somewhat alarm'd in the morning with an account that the Colliers at Brewsley were rose & consternation was greatly increased soon by fresh accounts that the Madely Wood as well as our own colliers had joynd them, and we plainly could hear the dismal sound of blowing of horns which is their signal - their pretended reason for rising was to lower the price of corn so accordingly they went in a body to Wenlock market & there gave the farmers two hours to consider whether they would sell their weat at 5s. pr Bushel or have it took from them, some of them refused the first proposition so they took it, but did not commit any great outrage that day, the next morning they went to Shifnal market & in their way called at an old justice Jourdanns & oblig'd him to ride in the midst of them to the market where they committed great outrages they broke open houses barns etc & took anything they could meet with in this days expedition some of our Dale workmen was with them, the next day was Brewsly market where they were if possible worse than ever; they got into the Baker's shops took some bread & threw it away; here the gentlemen read the Proclamation when they had done the mob gave a loud huzza & told them they neither valued them nor it, & to day they began to visit us both in going and coming; they behaved pretty civil, only asking for meat and drink which we were glad to give them to keep them quiet; they threatened that they would destroy the dale Works if our men would not join them the next day to go to Wellington market - to prevent which my Father gave one of our Clerks twenty guineas to have given the ringleaders had they offered such a thing, but they did not, he also deputed to stand with money in their hands to give them at our lower gate to prevent them coming up to the house for fear of frightening my Mother - where they were to have drink this did with a few but the numbers increased so fast that they all came running up like wild things where we imploy'd several men in carrying them pailfuls of drink this was as they went to Wellington where they became quite Plunderers they not only took from them that sold any thing, but went into private peoples houses & took away money Pewter Silver plate or anything they could meet with, they also Plunder'd farms houses or any out houses they met with, they came back in droves loaded with booty & I believe moste of them called at our house but did not offer any violence - several hundreds had meat & drink this time - we baked bread three days together and sent several miles for it besides, for there was not a bit of bread nor corn nor flower to be had for money, for some miles about - so that the country was in the greatest distress. The mob gave themselves the title of levelers & so they were indeed - this night the gentlemen muster'd up several hundred men, to suppress them, they were all arm'd and marched up our railway they made a formidable appearance, they met with the mob at Ketley & they stood three fires before they fled; that morning they had agreed to Plunder all our houses they intended to have begun with our house & so have gone quite through, but through Divine favour were prevented - they have took many of them prisoners, & we hope its all over, tho we had had several alarms since. I intend to write again soon for cant say more now, we are pretty well all join me in love to you

Post waits

H Darby"

In the spring of 1757, WW being about 16 years old, 37 colliers stood trial at the Assizes. Four had died in gaol whilst awaiting trial, and ten were condemned to death, the judge intending that six of the condemned should be reprieved and that the sentence should be carried out on only four. On the day appointed for execution, no reprieve came from London. It was the duty of the Deputy Sheriff, Mr. Thomas Leeke, of the Vineyard, to see that all ten men were hanged. However, he felt unhappy about this, and, in a step demanding great moral courage, decided to postpone the executions, and meanwhile sent an express letter to London asking for instructions. The reply indicated that his decision was most highly approved. In the event, two men were hanged, but eight lives were saved.

A plea for mercy was made to Earl Gower, by Abraham Darby, in a letter from Coalbrookdale.

"Coalbrookdale
23.8.1757
Shropshire

May it please

Earl Gower

The Riots that we have unfortunately had in this County under pretence of the High price of Corn, made it prudent and necessary for Government to proceed with severity against the Ringleaders & promoters of those disorders for the sake of Example and to prevent the like Tumults for the future; with this view several of the Rioters were prosecuted last year two of whom out of the number of 10 were capitally convicted & have been hanged. The other 8 were reprieved till the last assizes, when they were ordered to be transported for 14 years. In the number to be transported are included Rd Corbett, Wm. Cadman, John Cock, & Saml. Barker who till they were drawn into the said Riots at the Instance and threatenings of others, & perhaps with a view to procure sustenance for their starving families, always behaved as honest Industrious and most laborious Workmen; and as such deserve pity and compassion, and the rather as they are truely sensible of the high offence they have committed and hope his Majesty will extend his Mercy to them for the sake of their distressed Familys.

The characters of these four Men till this unfortunate affair happened, makes me feel greatly for their distress, and solicitous to obtain their pardon, and for that purpose I have presumed to trouble thee with the state of their case, earnestly entreating thee to apply to our king for their pardon.

Examples have been made by hanging two of the said Rioters, and if the King shall be graciously pleased to shew Mercy to the 4 I have mentioned, I am persuaded it will have a good effect upon the minds of the people of this County in general, and be considered as a shining instance of that Humanity Mercy and Compassion which the king always wishes to shew to the moans of his distressed subjects; and thou wilt likewise by thy recommendation of those poor people to the kings Mercy, do a most agreeable act to a great number of thy friends in this County & in particular to with true Submission

Thy Oblig'd Friend

Abraham Darby

As the situation of these unhappy people requires an immediate application I hope thou wilt have the goodness to represent their case to the king in the most favourable light, as soon as possible."

The outcome of this plea is not known, but it reflects the compassion of Darby at a difficult time.

The focal point in Wellington at the time was and is the Market Square, with a Town Hall probably situated on the first floor of the Market House. The Town Hall was licensed as a dissenters' Meeting House, this being recorded in the court of Quarter Sessions, of July 1760.

"The built up area of seventeenth century Wellington probably consisted of the Market Square, the lower end of New Street, Bell St., Crown St., the eastern end of Walker St., Duke St., with present day Mill Bank, High St., Wrekin Rd., Haygate Rd., and Church St. as country roads, and King St. a country lane. It was the earlier phase of the Industrial Revolution, from about 1740 to 1820, that changed Wellington from a village to a town. Miss H. Auden, writing in 'Memoirs of Old Shropshire' described a fine half-timbered old market house at Much Wenlock, then tantalizingly added "Wellington possessed an equally fine Market House as late as 1804, but it has now disappeared.....there are drawings extant of a fine half-timbered Market House of seventeenth century date. Unfortunately these I cannot trace."

It is therefore with extreme gratitude that I acknowledge the highly significant find by Mr. George Evans, local historian of Wellington, which with his kind permission is reproduced, see figure. The Wrekin is seen at the left, the current church on the right. Given that the previous church was demolished in 1789, this means that the illustration depicts Wellington at some time between 1789 and 1800. In the centre is seen a weather vane atop what was almost certainly the Market House mentioned above. To the right of this, equidistant to the Market House and the Parish church, was the eventual site of the railway cutting.

Wellington, an 18th century lithograph.

21st century view of Wellington.

The same view in March 2001, taken from Constitution Hill (in Withering's time, "Belle Vue"), shows the Wrekin in the far distance on the left, with the current Parish Church of All Saints on the right. The centre view is now dominated by the stationmaster's house, testament to an earlier age when express trains ran from Paddington to Birkenhead for Liverpool, and the Cambrian Coast express took thousands of hopefuls to Dolgellau, Barmouth and Pwllheli.

Edmund Withering, WW's father, died in Wellington in 1769. Whether WW was subsequently to visit Wellington to see his mother is not recorded. We know he visited in 1788, in the notorious Houlston case, to be described later.

On a more cheerful note, an advertisement is purported to have appeared as follows:

WELLINGTON JUBILEE 1773

The celebration of the Ancient festival will be as usual on Whitsun Monday the 31st May.

J.Lea	S. Jennings	Stewards
	Thos. Webb	Secretary

There will be a Public Breakfast on the Bowling Green, ordinaries at the principal inns, and a Ball and Card Assembly in the evening. Tickets to be had at the Talbot, Pheasant, and White Lion. (The Talbot, incidentally, was the venue for the Quarter Sessions in

1723, where, as prescribed by Parliament, oaths were taken by Papists and Dissenters, and the Six Bells).

WW by this time however was a practising physician at Stafford, and not very likely to have been tempted (assuming he had any knowledge!) of the aforementioned event.

WW, having chosen a medical career, decided to study in Edinburgh, and for several good reasons, as will become evident.

The Industrial Revolution had its birth on the doorstep of WW's birthplace; Coalbrookdale (the Darby family-iron), Broseley (J.Wilkinson-iron), Bilston (J.Wilkinson-iron), Tipton (Aaron Manby-engineering and shipbuilding; James Keir-chemicals) , Birmingham (Roebuck & Garbett-chemicals; Boulton & Watt-steam engines), Stoke (Wedgwood pottery), all within 30 miles.

Abraham Darby I, a Quaker brass founder, moved to Coalbrookdale in the Severn Gorge in 1708, where he leased an old charcoal furnace from the lord of the manor. However, wood was becoming scarce, and expensive. The furnace, if it were to continue using charcoal, would need 4,000 acres of woodland to support it. Houses, ships and machinery also used wood at this time. It was clear that there was a great need to find an alternative to provide the heat necessary to obtain iron from its ore. Without cheap iron there would have been no Industrial Revolution. And in harnessing the power of fire and steam, the steam engine was the catalyst. The pivotal discoveries in regard to iron smelting and steam engine development were to take place in the region. It is inconceivable to think that WW would not have visited Coalbrookdale at some stage in his boyhood prior to going up to Edinburgh, or that his home town would not have been selling its wares. Indeed, the local ironmonger at the time was an Andrew Shakeshaft, who was a known customer of the company in Coalbrookdale. It is more than likely that WW's home possessed some of the cooking pots, kettles and firebacks made by the company, (known officially as the 'Dale Company' until 1790, then as the 'Coalbrookdale Company' until 1881, when it became a limited company. In 1922 it entered the grouping of Light Castings Ltd., and in recent years has become a member of of the Allied Ironfounders Ltd). Other local ironworks were included, and from mid-18th century these were situated at Ketley and Horsehay, situated 2 and 4 miles respectively from Wellington. Nowadays, the Ketley works manufacture Aga and Rayburn cookers.

Abraham Darby II (1711-1763), and Abraham III (1768-1789) were contemporaries likely to have been names familiar to WW. Abraham I's **achievements using coke instead of charcoal for smelting**, have been described in a letter by Abbiah, second wife of Abraham II, based on information obtained from an old workman and associate of Abraham I. It was written in 1775:

"I now make free to communicate what I have heard my Husband say, and what arises from my own knowledge; also what I am inform'd from a person now living, whose father came here as a workman at the first beginning of these Pit Coal Works.

Then to begin at the original. It was my Husband's Father, whose name he bore (Abraham Darby who was the first that set on foot the Brass Works at or near Bristol) that attempted to mould and cast Iron pots & c., in sand instead of Loam (as they were wont to do, which made it a tedious and more expensive process) in which he succeeded. This first attempt was tryed at an Air Furnace in Bristol. About the year 1709 he came into Shropshire to Coalbrookdale, and with other partners took a lease of the works, which only consisted of an old Blast Furnace and some Forges. He here cast Iron Goods in sand out of the Blast Furnace that blow'd with wood charcoal; for it was not yet thought of to blow with Pit Coal. Sometime after he suggested the thought, that it might be practable to smelt the Iron from the ore in the Blast furnace with Pit Coal: Upon this he first try'd with raw coal as it came out of the Mines, but it did not answer. He not discouraged, had the coal coak'd into Cynder, as is done for drying Malt, and it then succeeded to his satisfaction. But he found that only one sort of pit Coal would suit best for the purpose of making good Iron - These were beneficial discoveries, for the moulding and casting in sand instead of in Loam was of great service, both in respect to expence and expedition. And if we may compare little things with great - as the invention of printing was to writing, so was the moulding and casting in sand to that of Loam. He then erected another Blast furnace, and enlarged the Works. The discovery soon got abroad and became of great utility......"

The exact date when the technique of coke-smelting became satisfactory has not been established, but it does appear to have been included by 1713 (see Smiles S., Industrial Biography, 1863, chap. 5. 'Coalbrookdale Iron-works - the Darbys and Reynoldses.')

During the time of Abraham Darby II, the greatest achievement was in perfecting the technique for producing iron suitable for forging from pig iron obtained from ore that had been coke smelted. This was due to the experiments carried out by the Cranage brothers, who obtained a patent for their method (Pat.no. 815, June 1766, 'Making pig iron or cast iron malleable in a reverberatory furnace or air furnace with pit coal only'). Consequently, the iron was in demand by nailers, locksmiths, chain makers, and other users of wrought iron, who previously would only take bar and rod iron obtained using charcoal smelting. A period of expansion followed with the leasing of coal areas at Ketley Manor, and more furnaces at Horsehay and Ketley in 1755/6. It is certain WW (now aged c. 15) would have observed at first hand, the migration of workers from the land to the furnaces and local mines, and his father Edmund, the apothecary would doubtless have been in demand to treat the numerous medical conditions that arose.

Arthur Young (Annals of Agriculture, 1776, vol.IV, p.168) wrote:

"Coalbrookdale itself is a very romantic spot, it is a winding glen between two immense hills which break into various forms, all thickly covered with wood, forming the most beautiful sheets of hanging wood. Indeed too beautiful to be much in unison with that variety of horrors art has spread at the bottom; the noise of the forges, mills &c., with their vast machinery, the flames bursting from the furnaces with the burning of the coal and the smoak of the lime kilns, are altogether sublime, and would unite well with craggy and bare rocks, like St. Vincent's at Bristol." The artist's impression is shown in the figure below. As the demand for power was steadily increasing it was clear that the time was ripe for some great change in steam engine design or working, if more power were to be available at a reasonable price. **James Watt** improved the design. The existing

Newcomen engine lost heat (and energy) by cooling the cylinder each time it was sprayed with cold water to condense the steam within. This required both fuel and time to re-heat the mass of cylinder (up to 5 tons). Watt's idea was for there to be a separate condenser, thus obviating the cooling of the main cylinder, and this was patented in 1769. 6 years of further experimenting followed, before a steam engine acceptable to industry was achieved. In 1769 the first engine was erected at Kinneil House, in Stirlingshire, but it was not successful due to faults in workmanship. A four-man partnership which included Dr. John Roebuck of the Carron Ironworks, Matthew Boulton, Dr. William Small (a Birmingham physician), and Watt was sought, but a successful working agreement was not obtained. In 1770, Dr. Small tried to secure materials and castings for the new engine, and some were obtained from Coalbrookdale, but were not acceptable to him. It was not until further improvement in the tolerances was obtained by use of John Wilkinson's boring mill, that the Boulton and Watt machine became commercially practicable, much of the pump and pipe work being produced at Coalbrookdale.

On the south side of the Severn, a few miles from Coalbrookdale, in Broseley, clay products (particularly tobacco pipes) were produced from local clay, since the early 1600's. At this site, in 1772, Thomas Turner, late of Worcester, arrived at the Caughley china works. Using Cornish clay, Caughley ware followed, and resembled the current vogue for oriental patterns and colours. Nearby was founded the **Coalport china** works, at the end of the century.

At about this time, other highly significant events were being discussed, the evidence of which is present to this day. 13 business men in Coalbrookdale, including a parson and **Thomas Farnolls Pritchard**, a well known local architect, were of the opinion that a

'Coalbrookdale by Night,' by Philippe Jacques de Loutherbourg, 1801.
(With permission of the Science Museum, London).

*James Watt (1736-1819), improving steam engine design
(With permission of the Science Museum, London).*

bridge connecting the two sides of the Coalbrookdale Gorge, through which flowed the river Severn, would contribute significantly to the future development of the area. The only current option was a much overworked ferry. In February 1776, **Thomas Addenbrooke**, secretary to the bridge consortium, arranged for a petition to be presented to Parliament, in order to obtain an Act permitting the construction of a toll bridge. The Act received the Royal Assent a month later. Various designs for the bridge were considered, and at one time, the consortium either lost its nerve, or else had to be seen to have considered alternative options, but in any case they invited tenders to build the bridge in stone, brick or timber. The replies were disappointing. Pritchard died in October 1777. Eventually, under the leadership of **Abraham Darby III**, construction started in 1778. (This was the year of the notorious scarlet fever outbreak in Birmingham, and may well have affected the inhabitants of Coalbrookdale. An account of this outbreak was published by Withering the following year, q.v.). **It was to be made of cast iron**, which could readily be produced on the doorstep, local expertise being unequalled anywhere. The bridge was opened to the public on 1st January 1781. (This was the same year in which Withering was involved in the Gresley case q.v.) The bridge aroused tremendous interest. People from Shrewsbury travelled through Atcham to Attingham, then across fields to Leighton. This track became a turnpike, and now is the B4380. Withering at this time was aged 40 years, and heavily involved in his work in Birmingham. However, we know that he travelled widely, and he would no doubt have visited **Ironbridge**, the name given to the township situated around the world famous bridge. The bridge remains a major tourist attraction, and is shown below, then and now.

(Artist-William Williams, reproduced by permission of the Ironbridge Gorge Museum).

The cast iron bridge in the 18th century (upper), and today (lower).

Chapter 2

WITHERING THE MEDICAL STUDENT AT EDINBURGH

WW arrived in Edinburgh in 1762 for the purpose of matriculation, having completed four years apprenticeship. Unfortunately there appears to be little record of the medical buildings at the University of Edinburgh in the eighteenth century. **William Cullen** was Professor of Medical Chemistry. He introduced several new remedies into clinical practise, including tartar emetic and henbane, and in 1773 succeeded to the Presidency of the Royal College of Physicians.

WW's first studies comprised anatomy and chemistry. Edinburgh School of Medicine developed early in the eighteenth century when the Town council appointed the first professors. A small area of land was obtained and a herbal garden planted. Subsequently a larger plot was leased. Despite botany flourishing at Edinburgh, there is nothing to suggest that WW's later interest was at any time triggered by his time at Edinburgh University. Linnaeus' great book, **Genera plantarum**, a classification of plants, was published in 1736 in Latin. It was not until 1761 that an enthusiastic botanist obtained the chair - Dr. John Hope, a Fellow of the Royal Society. Perhaps WW's lack of interest at this time was due to the fact that Hope was not inspiring to medical students, and not a very able lecturer. The first Professor of Anatomy was **Alexander Monro** in 1720 at the age of 22. He was very popular, illustrating the lectures by dissections of human and animal bodies. His lectures were so well attended that by 1753 the lecture theatre was too small and he had to give repeat lectures later the same day. His son, **Alexander Monro secundus** graduated MD at Edinburgh in 1755 and after travelling widely returned to Edinburgh and was appointed Associate Professor of Anatomy in 1758. He it was who commenced the campaign for a better anatomy lecture theatre together with his father by petitioning the town council on 5th September 1758. They pointed out that the anatomical theatre in the college was extremely inconvenient both for teachers and students. They pleaded that the theatre be extended before the opening of the 1758-9 session, and attached a plan which they described as "the common model of anatomical schools in other countries." The actual plan of the old anatomy classroom and its intended successor appeared in an article written in the University of Edinburgh Journal in 1966, and the plans are shown on the facing page. The old anatomy classroom is recorded as being 26½ feet long by 18½ feet broad, which is microscopic by today's standards. (Horn 1965. Reproduced by permission of Edinburgh University Library).

There are no records of what ensued, so we cannot say whether WW had to endure the old theatre or was lucky in having the use of the later facility, if in fact it ever came to pass. In 1764, Monro secundus personally approached the Lord Provost, George Drummond. On his advice he lobbied the College Committee of the town council and on 18th June 1764, submitted a formal application to the patrons. It stated that the present theatre was not large enough to contain above two thirds of the students of anatomy necessitating repeating the one and a half hour lectures. Accommodation where students could wait whilst he was lecturing was quite inadequate. His instruments had to be lodged below the seats. Students in the library directly above the lecture theatre frequently disturbed his classes with their noise. In addition, the room was very poorly lit, the only light source being a window on the far side of the table. Monro had tried to get round this by blocking out the daylight and using candles which were placed between the students and the cadaver. However the light was very faint and actually obstructed the students' view, so this idea was abandoned. WW's tutor was Dr. Hay, who not only directed his studies, but also entertained him, and introduced him to Scottish society.

WW became a freemason, joined the Edinburgh students' Medical Society, and gained many friends. WW's certificate of membership is currently in the possession of the Royal Society of Medicine's collection of the Withering letters, and is shown in the figure overleaf.

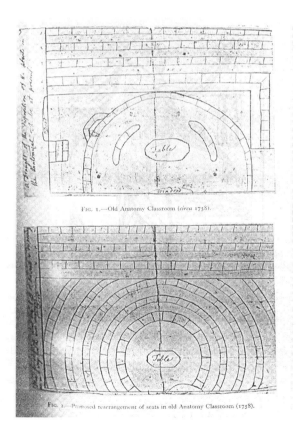

FIG. 1.—Old Anatomy Classroom (*circa* 1758).

FIG. 2.—Proposed rearrangement of seats in old Anatomy Classroom (1758).

The old anatomy classroom at Edinburgh, 1758.

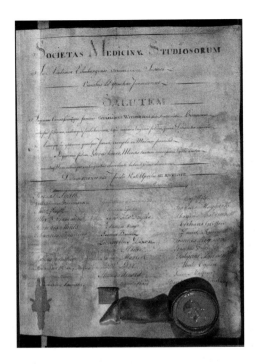

*Withering's certificate of membership of the Society of Medical students
(Reproduced with permission of the Royal Society of Medicine, London).*

Membership of this society, as appears inscribed on the certificate was as follows:

Thomas Smith, Giulielmus Stevenson MD, Mark Smyth, Max[n] Drummond, Johannes Shiels, Johannes Brunius, Jacobus Crowther, Alexander Hamiltonius, Jacobus Blair, Giulielmus Saunders, Giulielmus Bornhead, Johannes Gould, ? Douglas, Andreas Wood, Jacobus Boswell, Leonmellus Dixon, Thomas Mather, Sam Martin, Sam[l] Farr, Thomas Arnold, ? Bard, Benj. Clifton, Johannes Haygarth, Thomas Holdsworth, ? Corbinus Griffin, Daniel Rainey, Joannes Rogerson, Joannes Fyshe ? Dalrimple, Patricius ?, Alex Copland, Francis[s] Balfour, David Saunders - Secretary

Joannes Rogerson was to become the first Physician to the Empress Catherine in Russia. **Thomas Arnold** (1741-1816), MD (1766), FRCP Edin. (1791) was born in or around the same year as WW, and they graduated in Edinburgh the same year. His thesis was on the subject of pneumonia, its general description, post-mortem findings, diagnosis, causation, prognosis and treatment. It ran to 66 pages. Thomas Arnold was born in Leicester, where upon graduation he returned. Unfortunately, subsequent events were none too happy, as a result of a publicized family dispute. It appears that Thomas

Arnold's father William was an unqualified practitioner who specialised in the treatment of the insane. As his assistant, he employed his nephew Robert, who was about eight years senior to Thomas. However, it was William's intention to hand over his practice to his son upon his graduation, which was clearly difficult for Robert to stomach. There was much correspondence in the Leicester and Nottingham Journal between August and October 1768. Thomas Arnold cared for the insane patients in his own house in Bond Street, Leicester, in ten charitable places. In 1782 he published his treatise on "Observations on the Nature, kinds, causes and Prevention of Insanity, Lunacy or Madness," in which he attempted to distinguish between the different kinds of mental illness. Thomas Arnold and his wife Elizabeth née Graham, were to have at least seven children. The second of their three sons was named William Withering Arnold, born in 1775, clearly as a sign of his continued friendship with WW.

About the end of 1762 or in the Spring of 1763, WW became ill. This may have been the first sign of his tuberculosis. In any event, he was sent away for a holiday, during which he attempted the sport of golf. His first long vacation began in July 1763. Together with his friends, he set sail from Leith, to London. Unfortunately there are no details of the happenings of this trip. He then travelled North by coach, calling on his uncle, **Dr. Brooke Hector** in Lichfield before continuing along the Watling Street (nowadays the A5) to Wellington, on the London to Holyhead road, originally constructed by the Romans. On travelling back to Edinburgh, he visited an apothecary named **Fowler**, at York. Fowler eventually took a medical degree at Edinburgh, and practised as a Physician at Stafford, where he introduced a solution of arsenic for the treatment of fevers. This was to be known as **Fowler's solution** and remained in the British Pharmacopoeia until 1932.

In the second year at Edinburgh, WW studied materia medica, theory and practice of medicine, physic and chemistry, and also commenced clinical work. He learned to play the flute and harpsichord, and took up sketching. He was interested in Latin, and formed the **Sodalitium Romanum.** This body assembled weekly for the purpose of acquiring a facility in speaking Latin. According to WW's son, writing in the Memoir,

"—the promptitude of expression thus obtained proved serviceable on various subsequent occasions in promoting an intercourse with learned foreigners."

It was in fact the predecessor of English as the international language of Science. He produced his first essay on **Topical Blood Letting**, and then on **Inflammation of the Pericardium**, which drew praise from Professor Cullen.

In 1765, he visited several London Hospitals, and was of the opinion that too little time was spent there on systematic teaching, whereas in Edinburgh the reverse held true. In his final year, 1766, he wrote his dissertation on malignant putrid sore throat. Thousands of theses are preserved at Edinburgh, and at the time of writing of Peck and Wilkinson's often quoted book on WW, sadly, WW's was missing. Imagine therefore what a pleasant surprise it was, one day in May 1997, whilst enquiring at the Medical Library at Edinburgh University to find that the bound collection of theses had been acquired. Along with WW, there were 16 graduands. The complete list together with the titles of their theses was as follows:

Jacobus Boswell, Scoto-Brit.	**De malo Hysterico**
Marcus Smith, Scoto.	**De Hepatide**
Joannes Fyshe Palmer, Britannus.	**De Vermibus Intestinorum**
Mat. Kirsopp, Anglus.	**De Morbillis**
Ben. Clifton, x Insula St. Christ.	**De Dysenteria epidemica**
Christ. Douglas, Britannus.	**de Dysenteria putrida**
Joan. Mervin Nooth, Brit.	**de Rachitide**
Gul. Mitchell, Brit.	**De Scrophula**
Gul. Withering, Anglo-Brit.	**De Angina gangraenosa**
Jo. Cairnie, Scoto-Brit.	**De Erysipelate**
Tho. Russell, Brit.	**De Phthisi Pulmonali**
Gul. Falconer, Angulus.	**De Nephritide**
Sam. Leeds, Anglo-Brit.	**De Asthmate Spasmodico**
Tho. Lashley, Barbadensis.	**De Colica Pictonum**
Jackobus Mackittrick, Brit.	**De Febre Indiae Occidentalis maligna flava**
Tho. Arnold, Anglo-Brit.	**De Pleuritide**
Galfrid O'Connell, Hibernus.	**de usu et abusa Alimentorum.**

In the summer of 1766, he visited France in the company of a male friend called Townshend, who was fluent in French and knew Paris well. From WW's letters one gathers that he was not too impressed by the Parisians with their exaggerated gestures and grimaces (probably very different from the dour Scots), and he thought the Hôtel Dieu hospital with its 3000 patients somewhat overcrowded.

At this time Mr. Townshend fell ill, became febrile and developed an abscess on his shoulder. This rapidly turned gangrenous, and death followed soon after. WW was not enamoured of the French because after many delays, and legal proceedings their authorities wanted to confiscate his late friend's belongings. Finally, prior to departing Paris he was taken to a fête where he was "entertained" to animal baiting in the company of many elegant spectators, and finally torchlight butchery. On arrival in England he visited Townshend's family, and then travelled to his parents in Wellington in time for Christmas. From his son's Memoir, we learn that at this time he "searched the scriptures comparing the narratives and doctrines of the sacred historians, and inserted annotations in the interleaved copy of the New Testament, till he, by independent and rational conviction, found himself to be a convert, at a time when the stigma of irreligion and contempt of sacred things was being heaped upon professors of the healing art."

One may infer that this had clearly been an issue of great importance to WW. Whilst keen to "go with the flow" of current medical thought, he was nevertheless not keen to abandon the religion whose precepts had doubtless been stressed by his erstwhile tutor, Henry Wood of Ercall.

In 1766, WW presented his thesis in Latin, the cover and first two subsequently printed pages of which are shown in the figure. A typical thesis as presented prior to printing is

A typical thesis as presented in Withering's time.

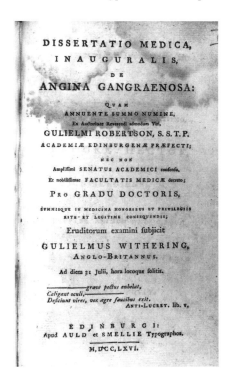

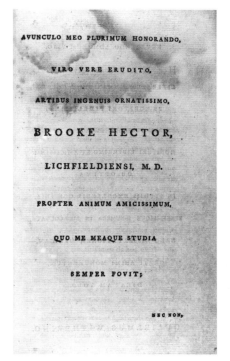

The title page of
Withering's thesis.

Withering's acknowledgement
to Brooke Hector.

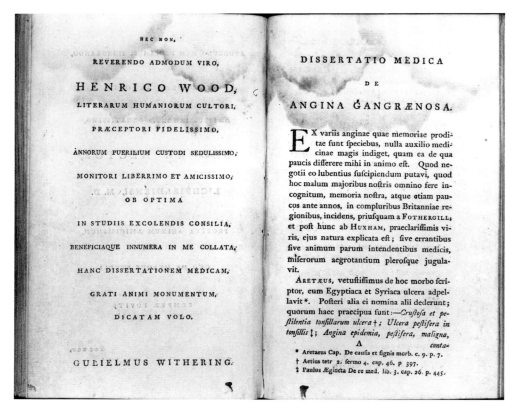

The first page of Withering's thesis and acknowledgement to Henry Wood
(The above four figures are all reproduced by permission
of the University of Edinburgh Library).

also shown, this being someone else's, dated 1783, but in all essential respects likely to have had a similar appearance to Withering's, which unfortunately cannot be traced.

Only a few copies of the thesis were printed. Approximately in 1962, a copy was purchased for the Historical Library at Yale University, and subsequent copies were located at several other universities. The biography on WW by Peck & Wilkinson (1950), suggests that the authors did not see the original thesis, nor a print. Subsequently a translation from Latin of Withering's thesis was carried out by Professor Charles D. O'Malley. This constituted the latter part of the fifth lecture of a ten lecture series known as the Davis Memorial series, from the University of Illinois College of Medicine, in honour of David J. Davis, MD PhD. It was delivered by John F Fulton MD, Sterling Professor of Physiology, Yale University, School of Medicine, in 1948, see appendix (ii). Interestingly, a J. F. Fulton was the William Withering Lecturer at the University of Birmingham, the same year, see appendix (v).

Chapter 3

WITHERING THE PHYSICIAN. STAFFORD AND BIRMINGHAM

WW now had to think about a job. Dr. Buchanan, a physician in Stafford died. Stafford is a mere 20 miles east of Wellington, it was prosperous, with good surrounding country, and it appealed to WW. He moved there in approximately 1766, but did not practice medicine to the exclusion of other interests. He mixed in society, participated in amateur dramatics, and attended the 1769 Shakespearian festival in Stratford upon Avon which was under the direction of **David Garrick** (q.v.)

WW took a leading part in the foundation of the Stafford General Infirmary, and was its first physician. Most prominent among fundraisers was a Mr. John Eld whose portrait hung in the board room of the Stafford infirmary for 120 years before it was realised that it was an original **Gainsborough.** (q.v.) The painting was exhibited in London and Rome, sold for £4,200, to a buyer from Boston and replaced in the board room by a replica. The hospital was completed in 1772, and had 80 beds. It was situated in Foregate Street, but now (1997) is locked up and derelict, the new District General Hospital having replaced it.

In November 1769, Withering's father Edmund died in Wellington. His will, dated 16th February 1765 reads:

'In the name of God amen I, Edmund Withering of Wellington, in the County of Salop, Apothecary and Surgeon Being in Good Health and of sound perfect and disposing mind do give all my freehold messuage lands tenements in the parish of Cheswardine or elsewhere unto my son William.. .'

He also left various sums to his widow and two daughters. Probate was granted to WW at Wellington on January 12th 1770.

It will be noted that he possessed land in Cheswardine, which is situated about 12 miles north of Wellington.

WW was by now interested in botany, and particularly in classification of plants. By this means, he came to meet **Helena Cookes** aged 17 years, who was very skilled at drawing the numerous specimens provided by him. Quite clearly the relationship blossomed, (no pun intended) and they married on September 12th 1772. She was the daughter of an attorney, later Town Clerk of Stafford.

The marriage entry appears in the register of the Parish Church of St. Mary, Stafford:

"William Withering of this parish, doctor of physick, and Helena Cooke, of this parish, spinster, were married in this church by licence this twelfth day of September in the year one thousand seven hundred and seventy two by me

J. DICKENSON, Rector

This marriage was solemnized   WILLIAM WITHERING
between us   HELENA COOKE
In the presence of   JOHN TURTON
      THO. AMERY."

At this time, WW's earnings averaged only £100 per year, and he began to consider a move that would be designed to bring him greater revenue.

He wrote to the Board of the Staffordshire Infirmary informing them of his intention to leave and offering to pay a weekly visit until a successor was appointed. In 1775, Dr. Small, Physician at the Birmingham General Hospital died. **Erasmus Darwin**, physician at Lichfield, wrote to WW, suggesting he apply for the post. This may have been facilitated by the fact that Brooke Hector (WW's uncle), under whose tutelage it seems likely WW served an apprenticeship, was a surgeon at Lichfield. WW did apply, and was successful. Thus WW became one of the founder physicians of this hospital, second in rank to Dr. John Ash (a plaque to Dr. Ash is affixed at the site, currently Rackhams department store). The hospital was formally opened on September 20th 1779. It was situated on a seven acre plot in Summer Lane. It consisted of 40 beds instead of the 116 originally planned (what's new?!). During the first week 10 patients were admitted, 4 nurses were employed at 4 guineas per annum, plus a barber at 10 shillings and six pence per quarter. The other physicians were Dr. Smith and Dr. Edward Johnstone. Consulting Surgeons were Mr. Edmund Hector, (brother of Brooke), Mr. Mynors and Mr. Francis Parrott. Surgeons included Mr. Robert Ward, Mr. George Kennedy, Mr. John Freer, jun., and Mr. Jeremiah Vaux. Dr. John Ash's portrait was painted by Sir Joshua Reynolds, and at least until 1950, hung in the board room. For some reason WW's name always appeared second in the list of physicians after Dr. Ash from 1780-1786. At this time, Dr. Ash resigned on account of a mental disorder and moved to London. He must have made a good recovery, because he went on to become a Fellow of the Royal College of Physicians, Censor, Harveian Orator, Goulstonian, and then Croonian Lecturer. He died at age 75 years in 1798. From 1787, WW's name again appeared second, this time to that of Dr. Thomas Smith, who practised from 23 Newhall Street. Meanwhile WW set up practice at no. 9 Temple Row, where Dr. John Ash had also practised before his move to London.

Here WW saw 2-3000 patients a year. This implied seeing about ten patients at each of five sessions a week. In addition, on one day a week he would travel by coach to Stafford, some thirty miles away, to see patients at the Infirmary. On one such occasion in 1775 he was asked to see a poor old lady with the dropsy (a generalised swelling of the body due to accumulation of fluid). This took place whilst the horses were being changed. He saw her and pronounced a poor prognosis. Several weeks later, when at the same place for the same reason, he happened to enquire of this patient, expecting to be told that she had passed on. To his surprise he was informed that she had made a good recovery. He then saw her again and enquired the reason for her recovery. He was told that it was due to a recipe for a herb tea, previously a secret of an old woman in Shropshire, who had on occasion succeeded where medical practitioners had failed. It was also known that this remedy was not without its problems, in particular violent vomiting and purging. Its diuretic effects (later documented) had gone unnoticed. The medicine was composed of 20 or more herbs, from which WW perceived, from his knowledge of the effects (or lack of effects) of 19 or so, that the only active ingredient must be the foxglove. The story of

Foxgloves growing in the author's garden.
Typical appearance of Digitalis purpurea.

the old woman and her recipe for treating dropsy has perhaps been embellished with the passage of time. There is evidence that digitalis had previously proved helpful in treating the Dean of Brazen nose college Oxford for his dropsy.

The story of Old Mother Hutton selling her secret remedy to Dr. William Withering who paid her in golden sovereigns for the secret of the wayside flower (see figure) derives in fact from the text accompanying a picture by **Will Meade Prince** in 1928 or 1929. This was the 23rd of a series of 250 prints used in advertisements by Parke-Davis, the pharmaceutical company, (now Warner-Lambert), in the late 1920's up till the 1940's. "Old Mother Hutton" was created by a copywriter. The identity of the original lady we will probably never know (Krikler 1985). He depicted WW as an elderly man, at the time of hearing about the recipe, whereas in fact he was in his forties.

(Incidentally, the artist was born in Roanoke, Virginia, and grew up in Chapel Hill. He studied art at the New York School of Fine and Applied Arts. He worked for five years in advertising, and was illustrator for several magazines, including Collier's, The Country Gentleman, and Ladies Home Journal. He also taught illustration and figure drawing at the University of North Carolina, and was head of the Art Department from 1943-1946. He wrote a book about his boyhood in Chapel Hill, called "The Southern Part of Heaven," which was a best seller).

However, long before this, digitalis had been used topically, according to folk medicine, as far back as Celtic times. Galen may have employed it "for cleaning

Old Mother Hutton selling her secret recipe to Withering.

the breath." (Gerard J. 1597. Of foxgloves. The Herball or General Historie of Plantes. J. Norton, London, Book 2, pages 646-647).

Probably the earliest mention is in one of the illustrated herbals derived from the Latin translation of Dioscorides' original Greek text - the Herbarium of Apuleius Platonicus, written at Bury St. Edmunds about 1120 A.D. The plant was known to the **Myddvai**, Welsh physicians of the 13th century. It was applied by inunction as a plaster or ointment, for the treatment of violent headaches, swellings, abscesses, as well as cancerous skin conditions. From the 16th century onwards it began to be extensively applied for the induction of vomiting and catharsis. Thus, like many other currently used drugs, e.g. hormone replacement (oestrogen), nicotine, glyceryl trinitrate, it can be absorbed via the skin, though it has never been commercially marketed in this form.

In 1776, aged 35, WW became ill. It was attributed at first to overwork. He apparently had an irregular fever which lasted three weeks, and sapped all his energy. This was aggravated by the winter in this as well as subsequent years.

In 1779, Withering published his **Account of the Scarlet Fever** as documented in Birmingham the previous year. The title page is reproduced in the accompanying figure. The fact that he apologises in advance for any minor errors and stresses the importance of making it rapidly available as a useful item of information, suggests that in modern times the equivalent would be a "preliminary communication."

The disease in 1778 first appeared in Birmingham in May, and spread rapidly to many towns and villages around. Some cases were preceded by the "true ulcerated sore throat, and accompanied in its course thro' the summer by the chin-cough, the measles, the small pox, and several instances of the true quinsy." All ages between 2 and 50 years were affected, children more so than adults. It occurred with equal frequency amongst male and female children, whereas in adults males were more susceptible.

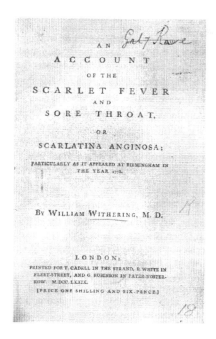

Description of the scarlet fever in Birmingham 1779
(reproduced with permission of the British Library).

Withering went on to give a description of the disease. He mentioned that during the course of the fever, the pulse was quick, small and uncommonly feeble, maybe up to 130 - 140 strokes in a minute.

10 - 15 days after the fever ceased, some cases developed languor, debility, stiffness of the limbs, accelerated pulse, disturbed sleep, loss of appetite and paucity of urine. These symptoms were soon followed by "a universal swelling of the anasarcous kind, and sometimes an ascites. Dropsy.——— In some the dropsy affects the brain, producing coma-vigil, delirium, blindness; with the most enlarged expansion of the iris, which is incapable of contraction in the strongest light. In others, the dropsy falls upon the lungs, and produces every symptom of the true hydrops pectoris———."

Withering went on to give the description of scarlet fever as recorded by others, including **Sydenham**, Dover, and others especially Plenciz, a Viennese physician who also gave an account of the dropsical state found in the disease.

This was followed by a description of the various skin rashes encountered.

"——**petechiae** with fever, where the eruption seldom is found before the fourth day, whereas in scarlet fever the rash is present on the 3rd day, and consists of broad blotches or else one continued redness which spreads over the face and whole body.

In **purpura** with fever, the rash is typified by keeping its colour under pressure, and never appearing early in disease, unlike scarlet fever where the rash appears early."

The end of the paper featured a table comparing and contrasting Scarlatina anginosa and Angina Gangraenosa. At this time, he clearly felt this to be important. To the modern day reader, it will be apparent that he probably witnessed several diseases, including streptococcal sore throat, infectious mononucleosis and glandular fever syndromes, scarlet fever proper, Henoch-Schonlein purpura, and meningococcal septicaemia.

In the preface to the second edition, which appeared in 1793, he stated;

"My chief reason, however, for wishing to establish the difference of the two diseases, was the necessity which I then thought indisputable, for the difference in practice. Had it merely rested as an abstract consideration, it would not have occasioned me a moment's anxiety, but under a persuasion that the welfare of the sick depended on a distinction of the two diseases, I drew up a tabular view, in which I endeavoured to collect the leading symptoms of the ulcerated sore throat on one side, and those of the Scarlatina anginosa on the other. This table is reprinted without any alteration, as it is equally useful whether we consider it as exhibiting a contrasted view of the two distinct diseases or only as pointing out the different aspects of the same disease under different circumstances.

Since the year 1778 our epidemic has frequently presented itself to my observation, both in the town of Birmingham, and its neighbourhood, as well as in several parts of the surrounding counties. From the most assiduous attention to the subject ever since that time, from observing it in every difference of season, exposure, age and temperament, I am now persuaded that the Scarlatina anginosa and the Angina gangraenosa constitute but one species of disease; that they owe their existence to the same specific contagion; that the varieties in their appearance depend upon contingent circumstances, and that the greatest differences are not greater than those of the distinct and confluent smallpox."

Thus, the table in the 1st edition is divided into Scarlatina Anginosa and Anginosa Gangraenosa, whereas in the second edition the overall title is Scarlatina Anginosa with tables headed Inflammatory State and Putrid State. The clue to his eventual thinking is provided in the 1st edition which, under the sub-heading "Nature" describes Scarlatina Anginosa as "Inflammatory" and Angina Gangraenosa as "Putrid."

In regard to the use of blood letting, there appears to have been a difference of opinion between Withering (anti), and Plenciz and Navier (pro). The pro lobby advocated its use "where the inflammatory symptoms run very high."

Withering wrote:

"Indeed, such was the state of the pulse with us during the hot summer months that I never saw an instance of blood being taken away: nor would it be easy to conceive with what view the boldest, or the most ignorant practitioner, would have dared to attempt it; for in those cases where the inflammation upon the surface was very great, the loss of blood could only contribute to the further depletion of the larger vessels, and thereby increase the debility and faintness which already existed in a most alarming degree; for the small vessels accumulating the blood, more in consequence of their own action, than from the pulse of the heart, would not be affected by the usual mode of blood letting; and the extent of the inflammation was much too great to allow us to have recourse to topical bleedings."

The argument here was that there would be no point in bleeding from a large vein when the blood vessels in the skin were causing the inflammation (by vaso-dilatation i.e. widening through relaxation of the vessel wall), rather than by the central action of the heart. Additionally, Withering recognised that the weakness suffered by these patients would be made worse by blood letting. It is interesting here to contrast the attitude of **Benjamin Rush** (q.v.) who was a great believer in bleeding and purging as treatment for yellow fever. Withering's views appear to be based on a consideration of physiological principles, rather than blind faith.

In the preface to the second edition, Withering makes a comment which is of considerable interest bearing in mind the question of his early apprenticeship, prior to going to university. It will be recalled that those training to become apothecaries were generally apprenticed to apothecaries, but that those intending to graduate as physicians, were apprenticed to other physicians. The question in Withering's case was whether he had been apprenticed to Brooke Hector, the physician of Lichfield, or to his father Edmund, the apothecary in Wellington, Withering's birthplace. The preface reads:

"Early in life I had the opportunity of seeing much of the ulcerated Sore Throat, and under the sanction of practitioners, to whom I looked up with deference and respect, I saw it universally treated with port wine, bark, acidulated gargles and anti-septic steams. This mode of practice was not unsuccessful; sooner or later it was very universally adopted, and as the disease never again became so prevalent as I had seen it in my younger days, I felt no inducement to alter the mode of treatment."

The phrase "early in life" would not be likely to refer to his post-qualification days, nor even to his days at Edinburgh university. The phrase "sanction of practitioners" could refer to witnessing his father's provision of care for these cases, under the direction of practitioners whom he treated with "deference and respect." Alternatively it could refer to cases seen whilst apprenticed to his uncle, Dr. Brooke Hector in Lichfield. The subject was clearly of interest to him, and formed the basis for his graduation thesis of 1766. The deciding fact, to the author, is that he dedicated his thesis to Dr. Brooke Hector, making no mention of his father. It would seem to suggest that he had in fact been apprenticed to the former.

Another feature of interest that distinguished the second from the first edition, was in the treatment of the dropsy. Withering's account of the foxglove and its use for treating dropsy was not published till 1785, yet he was already using it in 1778. In the preface to the 2nd edition he states:

"In some cases that resisted the usual remedies, a single grain of Pulv. fol. Digitalis given twice, or at most thrice a day, until its effects became evident, soon effected a cure in a manner highly pleasing to the patient, for it is never necessary to push its doses so far as to occasion nausea, or to produce any other kind of disorder in the system."

What is not explained, is why his record of 156 cases described in 1785, makes no mention of any treated as part of the 1778 outbreak. It is possible that he did not distinguish those cases that were attributable to the scarlet fever outbreak from others, but nevertheless, this remains somewhat puzzling.

In 1783, his friend and senior colleague, Dr. John Ash became very ill. As a consequence, more demands were placed upon WW to attend far and wide, consulting the sick. He even ventured in to Wales on this account. On one occasion, in the autumn of 1781, the control of his carriage horses having been lost, he leaped out, and as a consequence fractured his collar bone and suffered concussion. This led to his indisposition for several weeks. It subsequently affected his ability to consult in the important case of **Mrs. Gresley,** to be described below.

In case we are tempted to entertain the idea that patients or their families seeking to criticise or sue doctors is a new thing, we may be speedily dissuaded. WW clearly had to endure this burden. Fear of loss of earnings was also present in his mind, as will be demonstrated. It is interesting to note from his son's Memoir, that the events of the years 1763-1767, 1772, 1775-1776, 1778, 1782-85, 1787, and 1789-99 were chronicled in some detail. Years 1781, and 1788 were not mentioned. The reason may be the following. Every doctor engaged in clinical practice nowadays has to be covered by malpractice insurance. Settlement of damages can be extremely costly. The other thing to consider was the potential loss of earnings as a result of a tarnished reputation. Withering would not escape this burden. He was to become involved in two notorious cases which threatened both his health and his professional standing.

MEDICAL CASES BROUGHT AGAINST WITHERING

1. The Gresley case.

The first of the two cases to be described was that of a Mrs. Anne Gresley. She was the wife of a surgeon, William Theophilus Gresley of Drakelow. Her father and brother were both rectors. Her husband was a cousin of Sir Nigel Gresley, the sixth baronet. It will be clear that she came from an influential family. At the age of 29yr, she had her first, and only baby. A few days after the birth, on October 5th 1781, a Friday, WW was asked to consult on account of a fever. She was staying at Clifton Campville. WW drove over the same day and, being rather worried about her, reattended on the 7th, a Sunday. 2 days later, whilst driving home from Bilston, WW was involved in the afore-mentioned carriage accident.

He was asked to consult again, but feeling unwell asked that his colleague, Dr. John Ash go instead. Unfortunately, Dr.Ash had been summoned away, and thus could not attend. The drive to Clifton Campville was over 20 miles from Birmingham. However WW reattended on 13th and 17th, requiring the assistance of a companion to help him dress and undress. He stayed the night and saw her again on 18th. He felt too ill for the whole journey back to Birmingham, so instead stayed at Drayton Manor. Mr. Gresley came over to Drayton Manor on Saturday 27th, to update WW on his wife's condition. We are not told what WW did during the 9 days gap. Mr. Gresley was of the opinion that his wife was no worse, but begged that WW visit again. This WW agreed to do, at some future date. Unfortunately, Anne Gresley died that night.

This sad case, probably of puerperal sepsis, with death from unknown cause, perhaps a pulmonary embolism, resulted in a complaint against WW, conveyed to him by a letter from Dr. John Turton FRS of Wolverhampton, physician to the King and to the Prince of Wales. The letter brought notice of a letter to Turton from the late Anne Gresley's husband, the grief-stricken surgeon William Gresley. Turton wrote from Sugnall, on 17th December 1781.

"Doctor Withering,
9, Temple Row,
Birmingham

Sugnall December ye 17th, 1781

Dear Doctor,

.......I purposed writing to you in Consequence of Circumstances that have arisen amongst some of my Friends which very materially injure your Credit as a Physician, and in order to prevent the Progress of ill-founded Accusations and their disagreeable Effects I think it highly necessary that you should be informed of the General Calumny against you that you may if you think proper have an opportunity of doing yourself justice. .....there seemed a very dark Hint thrown out that you had failed in your Duty upon that occasion........I proceed to tell you that you are charged with being the Cause of Mrs. Gresley's Death, that you pronounced her out of danger the day before.........put you properly upon your Guard, I am........confident that no Attention was wanting on your part......

Friend and Servant,

JOHN TURTON"

Before considering WW's reply, it must be said that this writer finds it hard to believe that the patient's health was not in a serious state, taking into account that Mr. Gresley had ridden over to see WW, and begged him to make a visit. We are also told that Mr. Gresley did not think his wife was any worse.

An alternative interpretation would be that he was desperately worried about his wife's condition, that he had been all along, so that when he said he felt she was no worse, he meant no worse than seriously ill, whereas WW interpreted this as no worse than moderately sick. The Physician who constantly is in contact with seriously ill patients has a different attitude to the dead and dying, and at times is mistaken in assuming that a patient is no worse whereas to a close loved one, ominous signs are clear, but conveying these fears is difficult if one is to avoid being regarded as worrying unduly. Why would her husband have taken the trouble to ride over to Drayton Manor if he had not felt his chief purpose was to persuade WW to attend at once, because his wife was not getting better, in fact was dying? Perhaps the contemplation of her death was too terrible for him, and perhaps he subconsciously welcomed WW's interpretation. It was possibly a form of denial. WW was in the process of convalescing from his fractured clavicle.

In WW's reply of 23rd December 1781, he recounts the chronological order of events. And then he seems unwittingly to reveal that the penny has dropped when he says,

'These Sir are all the Facts I know that can influence the Matter - And upon a retrospect I know not how I could have acted otherwise, I might say, that if I was at last mistaken in those assurances, they were founded upon his own representation, and that he must have overlooked some material circumstances.....'

WW goes on to seek reassurance from the fact that two colleagues, a Mr. Lyon and a Mr. Oldershaw were also concerned in the case. 'Mr. Lyon I am told saw her at 11 o'clock the evening preceding her death, and says her pulse was then as good as usual, that she had taken food enough; that she had sat up and walked about the room that afternoon - .....'

Could she on the other hand have truly improved, but the act of re-mobilisation had sent off a fragment of blood clot from a thrombosed vein to the lung?

Subsequently there followed correspondence from the deceased's brother, Rev. John Watkins to Dr. Turton indicating his dissatisfaction regarding WW's handling of the case. This was also communicated to WW by Turton. WW challenged Watkins in a letter to retract or be faced with a tribunal. In this letter he spelled out the circumstances of his handling of the case.

"Birmingham Jan: 1783

Sir_____

Yours of 10th Oct. last now lies before me, and I sincerely ask your pardon for the delay to answer it so long; but a continued series of indispositions has hitherto unfitted me for exertions unless when absolutely necessary. I am now recovering, though slowly, my health and with that my usual activity.

After the written declaration of Dr. Ash..........etc

I remain, Sir,
Yours,

W. Withering"

A few lines of WW's letter to Rev. Watkins, brother of the late Mrs. Gresley are shown over the page.

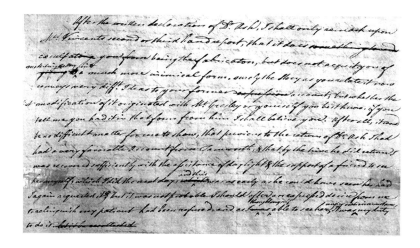

Withering's letter to the Rev. Watkins
(Reproduced by kind permission of the Royal Society of Medicine, London).

"I hope you don't conceive how much this unhappy affair has injured me. It will be sufficient to say, that from that time I have not yet been once called to Tamworth or its neighbourhood that had my principal business lain in that direction, I must have been ruined.————"

Note the many crossings out in another part of the letter. None of the other original letters of WW perused in the Royal Society of Medicine collection contain any such modifications. One wonders whether it was ever sent in that form, or whether it was a draft of the final version. It is also of interest to note that WW's hurt was in no small measure what he perceived to be the damage to his pocket! I think the reader can rest assured, his income from the remainder of the Midlands was more than enough to see him through!

From this it emerged that there had been a misunderstanding by Watkins to the effect that he did not know that Mr. Gresley had reassured WW that he did not perceive any deterioration in his wife, and furthermore, Watkins had been under the misapprehension that WW had sought to dissuade Dr. Ash from attending in his absence. Dr. Ash wrote to Watkins explaining that this was contrary to what had really happened, namely that he had been asked by WW and Mrs. Withering to visit Mrs. Gresley, but had been unable to do so because he had had a call to visit elsewhere in the opposite direction.

Eventually Watkins wrote to WW retracting his complaints. Little seems to have changed in regard to the handling of patients' complaints. What emerges is the value of having the opportunity to express in a calm way the unembroidered facts, particularly when substantiated by a third party, which led, as we have seen to a satisfactory retraction of the complaint.However serious and traumatic to WW and for a while to his reputation, this was small beer to the case that followed in 1788.

2. The Houlston case.

On September 26th 1788, at the end of a busy day, WW received a letter requesting an urgent visit to a Mrs.Houlston, residing in Wellington, Shropshire, the very town in which his birth was registered. The letter was written by an apothecary, Mr. Cartwright. By way of background, we know that the first bookseller's shop in Wellington was opened in 1779 by Edward Houlston, who appears in the list of subscribers to Phillips' History of Shrewsbury, published in 1788, as taking two copies. He was agent for the "Salopian Journal" from its first issue in January 1794. The Houlstons had an 8 years old son, Edward in the year of WW's visit. Edward was to become Wellington's first known printer, with an extremely successful business which became one of the largest provincial publishing houses in the country. The firm's premises in the Market Square were situated immediately to the right of the half-timbered building as viewed in the picture of the market square (see chapter 1). Thus one may even nowadays sense to within a few yards where the drama that was to unfold, was played out (assuming of course that the Houlstons lived on the premises).

WW travelled the same night, a distance of 28 miles. At the time he saw Mrs. Houlston, in the company of Mr. Cartwright, he was not aware that **Dr. Robert Darwin** of Shrewsbury, who he was told had visited her the previous evening, was at the same time actually in Wellington. (As an aside, it is very likely that in travelling from Shrewsbury to Wellington, Darwin would have crossed the Severn at Atcham, where a bridge had been constructed in 1776, and which still stands today, alongside its replacement which opened in 1929, see accompanying figure).

The Houlston's house (?) in Wellington, just off the current town square.

Atcham bridge, opened in 1776. (The current road bridge is seen behind).

However, to return to the Houlston case. This was of great relevance, as WW altered the patient's prescription recommended by Darwin from port and quinine, to calomel. He returned to Birmingham without bothering to communicate with Darwin. WW re-visited on October 8th. Subsequently her condition deteriorated to such an extent that Cartwright feared she would die. He therefore asked Darwin to attend (Shrewsbury being about 12 miles away). On October 17th 1788, Darwin wrote to WW:

"Your ungenteel medical behaviour to me in the case of Mrs. Houlston in not acquainting me that you was there, when you knew I was in the town and had been previously concerned with her, was not very consistent with the character of a gentleman, but the activity with which you have slandered me on this occasion is a matter of much more serious consequence. I understand you told Mr. Houlston that she had no fever when her pulse was 126 in a minute; and that she had an inflammation in her liver when she had neither pain, soreness or fulness in the hepatic region, nor any yellowness of her skin, or any increased evacuation!" He went on to allude to previous alleged mis-diagnoses by WW, and said that if WW should again slander him he would treat him very severely. It is of interest that Darwin was merely 22 years of age at this time, having graduated MD from Edinburgh in 1787, and been made a Fellow of the Royal society the following year. It is insinuated in Peck and Wilkinsons history of WW that the attack on WW may have been the result of antipathy felt by Erasmus Darwin (Robert's father) towards him. Why Erasmus Darwin should feel thus is unknown, and odd given that he it was who had originally written in 1775 inviting WW, then a physician in Stafford, to apply for the late Dr. Small's post in Birmingham. Subsequent events alluded to in the correspondence give clues. Robert Darwin (RD) mentioned other cases in which WW was allegedly mistaken plus "many others which I can produce if necessary."

In any event, the correspondence in relation to the Houlston case was to continue. RD had diagnosed typhus, WW felt Mrs. Houlston had hepatitis, which was a relatively unfamiliar disease, though not to WW who stated that he had attended 12 cases within the previous 6 weeks. RD attributed yellow stools to the rhubarb previously prescribed, WW to bile. WW wrote a long and detailed letter to Mr. Houlston, in an attempt to explain what had transpired. He also mentioned that he did not diagnose typhus on the ground that she never complained of headache in the course of the present illness. It was all to no avail, RD continued writing to WW and others in a vituperative manner. The dispute was broadcast by publication of the first three letters, two from RD and one from WW, after which WW's explanatory letter was published on 31/12/1788, which resulted in RD's response on 6/2/1789. Eventually RD published all the previous correspondence, sent it to local doctors and sent it to the arbitrator, T....F...H. The arbitrator was convinced of the correctness of WW's version and wrote telling him so. WW's son, writing in the Memoir, stated how hurt his father had been as a result of the whole affair. In any event, Mrs. Houlston went on to live a further 20 years, taking over the business from her late husband. Their son Edward added printing to bookselling, including the earliest known examples of Wellington printing, namely the Reverend Henry Gauntlett's "Sermon on Baptism and Confirmation preached 19th May 1805," and the Reverend John Eyton's "Sermon preached on the occasion of the late Naval Victory - 10th November 1805." Under the second Edward Houlston the business achieved remarkable success, becoming one of the largest provincial publishing houses in the country. In 1828, the business re-located to London. The firm's old premises were known to be occupied by Hobsons (booksellers) in 1949, and by personal recollection, into the 1960's. Photographs of these premises are shown, and it seems possible that the building shown was the actual one, or if not, was on the site where the plot for the medical "Battle of Wellington" was enacted.

But who was right from the point of view of the diagnosis? And is the reader inclined to feel, as Peck and Wilkinson would have them, that Withering's behaviour during the whole affair was beyond criticism? Firstly, from the point of view of the correct diagnosis, this has been debated elsewhere (see Posner's 1975 paper "Withering versus the Darwins"). As for Withering's behaviour, Aronson has stated:

"Withering for his part was exceptionally ungracious in his handling of the affair, and his insistence on the correctness of his behaviour in the matter seems only to have inflamed the dispute. A more judicious approach than that which he adopted might have allowed the matter to die down much more quietly. In illustration of his attitude take the letter he sent to Robert Darwin on 30 November 1788:

"Possessed, therefore, as I am of self-satisfaction, of the good opinion of the world at large, and of medical men in particular, your enmity or your friendship, your good or your bad opinion, are to me equally insignificant........" Aronson continues:

"Robert Darwin being only 22 at the time, Withering's handling of the affair betrays his arrogance and self-satisfaction, whether justified or not. ....."

However these events served to mar Withering's professional career, it was between these two celebrated cases, in 1785, that he published the work for which he is best remembered.

An Account of the Foxglove and some of its medical Uses: with practical Remarks on the Dropsy and other Diseases. By W. Withering, M.D., Physician to the General hospital at Birmingham. 8vo. 5s. boards. Robinson 1785.

The original account of the foxglove was printed by M.Swinney, of Birmingham, for G.G.J. & L. Robinson, Paternoster Row, London, see below. It consisted of 207 pages. The coloured frontispiece was taken from the illustration of the foxglove in the Flora Londinensis published in 1777 by William Curtis, botanist to the Society of Apothecaries.

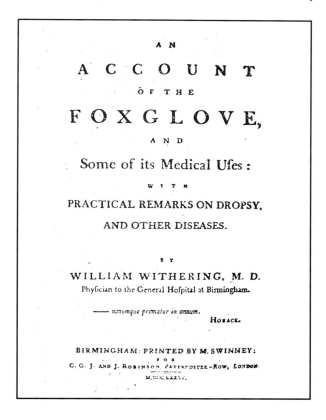

Withering's most celebrated publication
(Reproduced by permission of the British Library).

This is a classic, and the work for which he is best known. Yet from what we know of his many other works, it appears almost as an apology for the fact that, having observed its efficacy, WW was worried lest this most useful drug be incorrectly administered and thus fall into disrepute. Worse still, he was worried about the potential harm it could cause to patients (and possibly to reputations). Therefore, he set about to record in the best way possible, his experience with the drug, with great objectivity. We can observe the fundamentals of scientific observation, of measured conclusion, of careful patient selection, documentation of adverse reactions, of the relation of such reactions to efficacy, and of dose. He realised that other physicians were using it at too high a dose, and wanted to set the record straight.

The book commences with an introduction describing the botanical characteristics of the foxglove as found in Britain. He acknowledges that other species are found on the continent of Europe. The foxglove probably gets its name from "folk's-glove" i.e. fairies' glove. It is known by a variety of names e.g. in Scotland as bloody fingers, dead-men's bells, ladies' thimbles, wild mercury and Scotch mercury. In Ireland, fairy thimble, in Wales *menygellyllon* (elves' gloves), *menygyllwynog* (fox's gloves), *bysedd cochion* (red fingers), and *bysedd y cwn* (dog's fingers). In France – *gants de notre dame*, and *doigts de la Vierge*. The foxglove was originally called **Digitalis** by Fuchsius in 1542, the reason being the resemblance of the blossoms to the fingers (digits) of a glove, **Fingerhut**. Historically, it had a reputation for causing vomiting and purging. Boerhaave judged it to be a poison.

The introduction commences with the remark that foxglove leaves have on occasion been substituted by those of Mullein by those ignorant of the difference. (Mullein is Verbascum, a genus of 300 species, of the Scrophulariaceae family. The species native to this country is **V. thapsus**, which bears yellow flowers. Digitalis, though also belonging to the Scrophulariaceae, is a genus of about 30 species, of which **D. purpurea** produces purple, red or maroon spotted flowers). WW's description is typically detailed and meticulous:

"Our plant is the **Digitalis purpurea*** of Linnaeus. It belongs to the 2nd order of the 14th class, or the DIDYNAMIA ANGIOSPERMIA. The essential characters of the genus are, Cup with 5 divisions. Blossom bell-shaped, bulging. Capsule egg-shaped, 2-celled. _ LINN.

*The trivial name **purpurea** is not a very happy one, for the blossoms though generally purple, are sometimes of a pure white.

DIGITA'LIS **purpu'rea**. Little leaves of the empalement egg-shaped,
sharp. Blossoms blunt; the upper lip entire. LINN.

"Blossom. The bellying part on the inside sprinkled with spots like little eyes. Leaves wrinkled. Linnaeus.

BLOSSOM. Rather tubular than bell-shaped, bulging on the under side, purple; the narrow tubular part at the base, white. Upper lip sometimes slightly cloven.

CHIVES. Threads crooked, white. Tips yellow.

POINTAL. Seed-bud greenish. Honey-cup at its base more yellow. Summit cloven.

S. VESS. Capsule not quite so long as the cup.

ROOT. Knotty and fibrous.

STEM. About 4 feet high; obscurely angular; leafy.

LEAVES. Slightly but irregularly serrated, wrinkled; dark green above, paler underneath. Lower leaves egg-shaped; upper leaves spear-shaped. Leaf-stalks fleshy; bordered.

FLOWERS. Numerous, mostly growing from one side of the stem and hanging down one over another. Floral-leaves fitting, taper-pointed. The numerous purple blossoms hanging down, mottled within; as wide and nearly half as long as the finger of a common-sized glove, are sufficient marks whereby the most ignorant may distinguish this from every other British plant; and the leaves ought not to be gathered for use but when the plant is in blossom.

PLACE. Dry, gravelly or sandy soils; particularly on sloping ground. It is a biennial, and flowers from the middle of June to the end of July."

WW commences his account of the introduction of the foxglove into medical practice by stating that the properties of plants cannot be studied by chemical examination after fire (which he says has proved an immense waste of time), but by observation of the effects on quadrupeds and insects, by analytical deduction based on a knowledge of closely allied plants, or from empirical use and clinical experience. To an extent therefore he was addressing the problem of animal experimentation, chemical analysis (then extremely crude), and clinical observation. He clearly visualized the options, and came down heavily in favour of clinical observation;

"....but the last, as far as it extends, lies within the reach of every one who is open to information, regardless of the source from whence it springs....."

WW was aware of the problem of using the root of a biennial plant, and therefore decided to concentrate his efforts on the leaves. He found great variation in respect of dose depending on which time of the year he took the leaves. He opted therefore to use the leaf only when the plant was in flower, with the intention of maintaining some constancy of effect by this means. For this reason, he discarded the decoction (which required prolonged boiling and which he suspected would inactivate the active ingredient), and instead used an infusion, and subsequently, dried powdered leaf. **He also recognised that the beneficial effect of diuresis did not necessarily require that the patient become nauseated or purged.** In the summer of 1776, he ordered that a quantity of leaves be prepared. In November 1777, WW sent an account of his earlier experiences to a Mr. Russel in Worcester, as an example of how mistaken he (WW) had been, in respect of deducing the optimum dose. Referring to his now discarded view he wrote:

"I generally order it in decoction. Three drams of the dried leaves, collected at the times of the blossoms expanding, boiled in twelve to eight ounces of water. Two spoonfuls of this medicine, given every two hours, will sooner or later excite a nausea. I have sometimes used the green leaves gathered in winter, but then I order three times the weight..........I consider the Foxglove thus given, as the most certain diuretic I know, nor do its diuretic effects depend merely upon the nausea it produces.........and I have, in more than one instance, given the Foxglove in smaller and more distant doses, so that the flow of urine has taken place without any sensible affection of the stomach; ....Sometimes the brain is considerably affected by the medicine, and indistinct vision ensues; but I have never yet found any permanent bad effects from it....

I use it in the Ascites, Anasarca, and Hydrops Pectoris; and so far as the removal of the water will contribute to cure the patient, so far may be expected from the medicine:

but I wish it not to be tried in ascites of female patients, believing that many of these cases are dropsies of the ovaria; and no sensible man will ever expect to see these encysted fluids removed by any medicine...."

In the year 1783, digitalis appeared in the new edition of the Edinburgh Pharmacopoeia. However, WW was sceptical that it would remain included, since it was being used at too high a dose, and especially so in London.

DETAILS OF WITHERING'S 156 DOMICILIARY CASES TREATED BETWEEN 1775 AND 1784

		Age									
Gender	*ns	0-10	11-20	21-30	31-40	41-50	51-60	61-70	71-80	81-90
Male	8	11	0	5	13	25	19	11	2	3
Female	4	1	0	4	11	13	11	7	1	1
Unstated	1	0	1	0	1	2	0	1	0	0

ns = age not stated

The gender alone was unknown in 5 cases. In 12 cases, the age alone was not stated. In 1 case, neither age nor gender were stated (case 140).

Diuresis where mentioned occurred in 44.6% of males, mean age 47 years, and 29.8% of females, mean age 50.3 years. This difference was probably due to 'dropsy' in females including cases of ovarian cyst, which we now know would not respond to digitalis, because the heart is not involved. Withering concluded that they were unsuitable for digitalis treatment since the fluid was encysted. These were cases 12, 17, 61, 130, and 155, though a diuresis did occur in case 17. However, it did not help the patient, whose swelling still needed tapping. The numbers affecting by nausea and/or vomiting are shown in the table below.

The decline in numbers of patients treated in 1783 may be explained by the fact that his tuberculosis was particularly troublesome at the time. The reduction in the proportion of cases with adverse reactions with increasing experience in the use of digitalis will be obvious.

For a detailed summary of these cases in tabular form, see Appendix (iii).

PREPARATIONS AND DOSES OF THE FOXGLOVE
Following on after the communications, WW describes the preparations and doses of the foxglove. He describes the properties of the root, stem, leaves, flowers and seeds.

"Every part of the plant has more or less of the same bitter taste, varying, however, as to strength, and changing with the age of the plant and the season of the year.

ROOT.- This varies greatly with the age of the plant. When the stem has shot up for flowering, which it does the second year of its growth, the root becomes dry, nearly tasteless, and inert.

Some practitioners, who have used the root, and been so happy to cure their patients without exciting sickness, have been pleased to communicate the circumstance to me.

	SIDE EFFECTS	
Year	**No's**	**Nausea or Vomiting**
1775	1	1
1776	4	2
1777	8	3
1778	6	1
1779	8	3
1780	29	2
1781	25	2
1783	15	1
1784	34	6

as an improvement in the use of the plant. I have no doubt of the truth of their remarks, and I thank them. But the case of Dr. Cawley puts this matter beyond dispute. The fact is, they have fortunately happened to use the root in its approach to its inert state, and consequently have not overdosed their patients. I could, if necessary, bring other proof to shew that the root is just as capable as the leaves, of exciting nausea.

STEM.- The stem has more taste than the root has, in the season the stem shoots out, and less taste than the leaves. I do not know that it has been specially selected for use.

LEAVES.- These vary greatly in their efficacy at different seasons of the year, and, perhaps, at different stages of their growth; but I am not certain that this variation keeps pace with the greater or lesser intensity of their bitter taste.

Some who have been habituated to the use of recent leaves, tell me, that they answer their purpose at every season of the year; and I believe them, notwithstanding I myself have found great variations in this respect. The solution of this difficulty is obvious. They have used the leaves in such large proportion, that the doses have been sufficient, or more than sufficient, even in their most inefficacious state. The Leaf-stalks seem, in their sensible properties, to partake of an intermediate state between the leaves and the stem.

FLOWERS.- The petals, the chives, and the pointal have nearly the taste of the leaves, and it has been suggested to me, by a very sensible and judicious friend, that it might be well to fix on the flower for internal use. I see no objection to the proposition; but I have not tried it.

SEEDS.- These I believe are equally untried.

From this view of the different parts of the plant, it is sufficiently obvious why I still continue to prefer the leaves.

These should be gathered after the flowering stem has shot up, and about the time that the blossoms are coming forth.

The leaf-stalk and mid-rib of the leaves should be rejected, and the remaining part should be dried, either in the sun-shine, or on a tin pan or pewter dish before a fire.

If well dried, they readily rub down to a beautiful green powder, which weighs something less than one-fifth of the original weight of the leaves. Care must be taken that the leaves be not scorched in drying, and they should not be dried more than what is requisite to allow of their being readily reduced to powder.

I give to adults, from one to three grains of this powder twice a day. In the reduced state in which physicians generally find dropsical patients, four grains a day are sufficient. I sometimes give the powder alone; sometimes unite it with aromatics, and sometimes form it into pills with a sufficient quantity of soap or gum ammoniac.

If a liquid medicine be preferred, I order a dram of the dried leaves to be infused for four hours in half a pint of boiling water, adding to the strained liquor an ounce of any spirituous water. One ounce of this infusion given twice a day, is a medium dose for an adult patient. If the patient be stronger than usual, or the symptoms very urgent, this dose may be given once in eight hours; and on the contrary in many instances half an ounce at a time will be quite sufficient. About thirty grains of the powder or eight of the infusion, may generally be taken before the nausea commences.

The ingenuity of man has ever been fond of exerting itself to vary the forms and combinations of medicines. Hence we have spirituous, vinous, and acetous tinctures; extracts hard and soft, syrups with sugar or honey, &c. but the more we multiply the forms of any medicine, the longer we shall be in ascertaining its real dose. I have no lasting objection however to any of these formulae except the extract, which, from the nature of its preparation must ever be uncertain in its effects; and a medicine whose fullest dose in substance does not exceed three grains, cannot be supposed to stand in need of condensation.

It appears from several of the cases, that when the Digitalis is disposed to purge, opium may be joined to it advantageously; and when the bowels are too tardy, jalap may be given at the same time, without interfering with its diuretic effects; but I have not found benefit from any other adjunct.

From this view of the doses in which the Digitalis really ought to be exhibited, and from the evidence of many of the cases, in which it appears to have been given in quantities six, eight, ten or even twelve times more than necessary, we must admit as an inference either that this medicine is perfectly safe when given as I advise, or that the medicines in daily use are highly dangerous.

EFFECTS, RULES, AND CAUTIONS

The Foxglove when given in very large and quickly-repeated doses, occasions sickness, vomiting, purging, giddiness, confused vision, objects appearing green or yellow; increased secretion of urine, with frequent motions to part with it, and sometimes inability to retain it; slow pulse, even as low as 35 in a minute, cold sweats, convulsions, syncope, death.

When given in a less violent manner, it produces most of these effects in a lower degree; and it is curious to observe, that the sickness, with a certain dose of the medicine, does not take place for many hours after its exhibition has been discontinued; that the flow of urine will often precede, sometimes accompany, frequently follow the sickness at the distance of some days, and not unfrequently be checked by it. The sickness thus excited, is extremely different from that occasioned by any other medicine; it is peculiarly distressing to the patient; it ceases, it recurs again as violent as before; and thus it will continue to recur for three or four days, at distant and more intervals.

These sufferings of the patient are generally rewarded by a return of the appetite, much greater than what existed before the taking of the medicine.

But these sufferings are not at all necessary; they are the effects of our inexperience, and would in similar circumstances, more or less attend the exhibition of almost every active and powerful medicine we use."

WITHERING'S EVOLVING THOUGHTS ON DOSING
(Type where bold has been modified by this author)

"Perhaps the reader will better understand how it ought to be given, from the following detail of my own improvement, than from precepts peremptorily delivered, and their source veiled in obscurity.

At first I thought it necessary to bring on and continue the sickness, in order to ensure the diuretic effects.

I soon learnt that the nausea being once excited, it was unnecessary to repeat the medicine, as it was certain to recur frequently, at intervals more or less distant.

Therefore my patients were ordered to **persist until the nausea came on, and then to stop.** But it soon appeared that the diuretic effects would often take place first, and sometimes be checked when the sickness or a purging supervened.

The direction was therefore enlarged thus - **Continue the medicine until the urine flows, or sickness or purging take place.**

I found myself safe under this regulation for two or three years; but at length cases occurred in which the pulse would be retarded to an alarming degree, without any other preceding effect.

The directions therefore required an additional attention to the state of the pulse, and it was moreover of consequence not to repeat the doses too quickly, but to allow sufficient time for the effects of each to take place, as it was found very possible to pour in an injurious quantity of the medicine, before any of the signals for forbearance appeared.

Let the medicine therefore be given in the doses, and at the intervals mentioned above:- let it be continued until either it acts on the kidneys, the stomach, the pulse, or the bowels; let it be stopped upon the first appearance of any one of these effects, and I will maintain that the patient will not suffer from its exhibition, nor the practitioner be disappointed in any reasonable expectation.

If it purges, it seldom succeeds well.

The patients should be enjoined to drink very freely during its operation. I mean, they should drink whatever they prefer, and in as great quantity as their appetite for drink demands. This direction is the more necessary, as they are very generally prepossessed with an idea of drying up a dropsy, by abstinence from liquids, and fear to add to the disease, by indulging their inclination to drink.

In cases of ascites and anasarca; when the patients are weak, and the evacuation of the water rapid; the use of proper bandage is indispensably necessary to their safety.

If the water should not be wholly evacuated, it is best left to allow an interval of several days before the medicine be repeated, that food and tonics may be administered; but truth compels me to say, that the usual tonic medicines have in these cases very often deceived my expectations.

From some cases which have occurred in the course of the present year, I am disposed to believe that the Digitalis may be given in small doses, viz. two or three grains a day, so as gradually to remove a dropsy, without any other than mild diuretic effects, and without any interruption to its use until the cure be compleated.

If inadvertently the doses of the Foxglove should be prescribed too largely, exhibited too rapidly, or urged to too great a length; the knowledge of a remedy to counteract its effects would be a desirable thing. Such a remedy may perhaps in time be discovered.* The usual cordials and volatiles are generally rejected from the stomach; aromatics and strong bitters are longer retained; brandy will sometimes remove the sickness when only slight; I have sometimes thought small doses of opium useful, but I am more confident of the advantage from blisters. Mr. Jones (Page 135) in one case, found mint tea to be retained longer than other things.

See Digibind (index)

INFERENCES

I.   That the Digitalis will not universally act as a diuretic.

II.   That it does so more generally than any other medicine.

III.   That it will often produce this effect after every other probable method has been fruitlessly tried.

IV.   That if this fails, there is but little chance of any other medicine succeeding.

V.   That in proper doses, and under the management now pointed out, it is mild in its operation, and gives less disturbance to the system, than squill, or almost any other active medicine.

VI.   That when dropsy is attended by palsy, unsound viscera, great debility, or other complication of disease, neither the Digitalis, nor any other diuretic can do more than obtain a truce to the urgency of the symptoms; unless by gaining time, it may afford opportunity for other medicines to combat and subdue the original disease.

VII.   That the Digitalis may be used with advantage in every species of dropsy, except the encysted.

VIII.   That it may be made subservient to the cure of diseases, unconnected with dropsy.

IX.   **That it has a power over the motion of the heart, to a degree yet unobserved in any other medicine, and that this power may be converted to salutary ends.**

PRACTICAL REMARKS ON DROPSY AND SOME OTHER DISEASES."

In this section, WW comments on various combinations of oedema, under the terms, "anasarca, ascites, hydrothorax" and other clinical conditions including "asthma, epilepsy, hydatid dropsy, hydrocephalus, insanity, nephritis calculosa, ovarium dropsy, phthisis pulmonalis, and puerperal anasarca." Under this varied heading, it is difficult to discern any firm conclusion or advice that has stood the test of time, apart from the statements that:

1. "The true spasmodic asthma, a rare disease - is not relieved by Digitalis."

2. "In the greater part of what are called asthmatical cases, the real disease is anasarca of the lungs, and is generally to be cured by diuretics. This is almost always combined with some swelling of the legs."

3. "This disease (hydrocephalus), ——I believe , originates in inflammation; and that the water found in the ventricles of the brain after death, is the consequence, and not the cause of the illness."

4. "This species of encysted dropsy" (ovarian cyst), "is not without difficulty distinguishable from an ascites; and yet it is necessary to distinguish them, because the two diseases require different treatment and because the probability of a cure is much greater in one than the other."

The second edition of WW's book appeared in 1787, consisting of two volumes, 1149 pages, plus an index of 150 pages. A third volume was added in 1792 with 503 extra pages and 7 new plates. At the end of each volume, three of his previous publications were advertised:

An account of the Scarlet fever and sore throat or Scarlatina Anginosa, Octavo, sewed, price 1/6d.

Outlines of Mineralogy, translated from the original of Sir Torbern Bergman, Knight of the Order of Wasa, Professor of Chemistry at Uppsala etc. Ocatavo, sewed, price 2/6d.

An account of the Foxglove, and some of its medical uses, with practical remarks on Dropsy. Octavo, boards 4/- with the plain, 5/- with the coloured print of the plant.

WW's portrait by C.F. von Breda in 1791 shows the second volume of the second edition open at page 654 where the article on digitalis appears. This picture is reproduced on page 60.

WW's Genera Plantarum went to a second edition eleven years later in 1787, and the references were carried out by a Dr. Jonathan Stokes of Stourbridge. It appears that Stokes subsequently hung on to no fewer than 178 volumes of books the property of WW, as well as a number of WW's letters. WW finally obtained their return by resorting to the law in 1790.

WW used the leaves gathered at the time the blossoms were expanding. They were dried in the sunshine or in front of a fire, from which a powder was obtained. He determined this to be about five times as potent as the fresh leaf. In 1779, Stokes informed some Edinburgh physicians about the use of the foxglove. They were also told about it by Mr. Charles Darwin, a medical student the son of Dr.Erasmus Darwin. This was not the renowned Charles Darwin, who in fact was the grandson of Erasmus, and the son of Robert. However the doses recommended were far too high. The drug had also been recommended in the treatment of TB and epilepsy.

A review of WW's book was published in the **Monthly review**, Vol. 73. Jly-Dec. 1785. Pg. 369. It was very favourable and the last paragraph read:

"We think the Public under great obligations to Dr.Withering for the labour he has bestowed on the subject of this book: and we have only to wish, for the sake of those who may labour under the distressful state of a dropsy, that the practice of other physicians may confirm the result of this gentleman's experience."

It is of interest that a short time before the appearance of Withering's book, the following papers were read at a meeting held at the **Royal College of Physicians**, in Warwick Lane, London, on March 16th 1785. (ref. Medical transactions of the College of Physicians, 1785 (3) 255-286).

1. A letter to Sir George Baker, Baronet, on the successful use of the — of lead in some haemorrhages, by Henry Revell Reynolds M.D., Fellow of the College of Physicians, and the Royal Society, and of the Society of Antiquaries, in London.

2. Some experiments made upon Rum, in order to ascertain the cause of the Colic frequent among the soldiers in the Island of Jamaica, in the years 1781 and 1782; by John Hunter M.D. Physician to the Army. Communicated by Sir George Baker.

3. An Account of a Case of an uncommon disease in the Omentum, and of a double kidney on one side of the Body, with none on the other: by John Hunter, M.D. Physician to the Army, Communicated by the same.

4. An Account of the successful use of Foxglove in some Dropsies, and in the Pulmonary Consumption: by ERASMUS DARWIN M.D. and Fellow of the Royal Society in London. Communicated by the same.

5. An appendix to the preceding paper, by Sir George Baker

6. A sequel to the Case of Mr. Thomas Wood of Billericay, in the County of Essex. By the same.

To judge from the aforegoing, it was obviously a pretty full programme that day. Darwin's contribution, clearly the most prestigious, may have been timed to allow him to recover from the previous day's travel from Derby. He presented an account of his experiences with the use of a decoction of digitalis in several types of case.

1. Dropsies of the Thorax and Limbs.

He commenced by calling attention to a previous pamphlet he had published in 1780 describing half a dozen cases of dropsy treated successfully by decoction of digitalis. He alluded to similar experience with a score of other cases. This was followed by a detailed description of two cases.

2. Dropsies of the abdomen.

A description of the unsuccessful use of digitalis in a case of ovarian cyst was followed by details of three cases with a better outcome.

3. Pulmonary Consumption.

Three cases, one in a young man with dark eyes and hair, who improved after two weeks. Two other cases, with light eyes and hair did not show improvement. Darwin felt there was some significance in this.

4. Scrophulous ulcers.

"I do not pretend, that these two cases any more than that of pulmonary consumption, should raise any expectations of the decoction producing such constant good effect, as in the dropsies of the chest;——"

5. Asthma.

One case, probably of cardiac asthma, was "—much affected and distressed by its operation; but kept some weeks free from the disease—"

6. Melancholia.

A clearly depressed lady aged 30 - 40 years, who took the decoction for two to three days, vomited profusely, had many concomitant medicines, and after a few weeks "the despondency of her mind wore off." (Perhaps concomitant with the disappearance of the side effects?).

It is clear that Darwin recognised the value of digitalis especially in cases where the chest was affected together with dropsy of the limbs. His descriptions were not very detailed, his case numbers were not great, though he mentioned previous experience with about twenty patients. **No mention was made of Withering**. This is especially interesting since we know that he saw a case with Withering, (Withering's case 4), and added it to his late son Charles' Edinburgh thesis. Failure to acknowledge the work of a rival is something not unknown in science even today, especially where competition for research funds is involved.

As an appendix to the preceding paper, Sir George Baker's description of a case is particularly graphic:

The patient was a male aged 60 years, who suffered from ankle swelling by the end of the day, difficulty breathing, especially climbing stairs. He was prescribed quicksilver and squill. After initial improvement, his symptoms returned seven weeks later. Eventually, the disease became resistant to the previously administered medicines. Abdominal swelling appeared, and urine output decreased.

"Being now in the greatest distress, and most imminent danger, he was encouraged by Dr. Darwin's experience to make a trial of a decoction of foxglove—" His pulse was 90 - 120 per minute, and came down to 50 - 60. It was very irregular, and fell to 48 - 56.

The patient's vision became affected, "Everything was seen as though through a fog." However, he eventually improved. A further case was described in which a rapid diuretic effect was obtained.

These descriptions were followed by an account of the exits and entrances of digitalis from the Pharmacopoeias of London, Edinburgh, and Paris. He concluded:

"As a remedy for the dropsy, this plant seems to have been but of late introduction. But at what time, and by whom, it was first given in this disease, it has not, I believe, hitherto been ascertained. Salmon has mentioned dropsy in a list of several chronic diseases, which, according to the testimony of that author, are curable by foxglove. But neither Salmon, nor any other of the old authors, whom I have consulted, has recommended it as a medicine specifically powerful in this malady. Some years since the case of a gentleman of Oxford, who was reported to have been cured of a dropsy by a decoction of the roots of foxglove, became the subject of medical conversation in London; and, in consequence, some trials were made of that decoction in one of our hospitals; but the results of those trials did not, at that time, raise the credit of the medicine. Some of the late experiments in this town have been more successful; and many have failed——"

As a postscript to the appendix, without clearly stated authorship, but presumably by Sir George Baker, the following interesting statement is made: (this author has added the bold text)

"Whilst the last pages of this volume were in the press, Dr. Withering, of Birmingham, (who appears to have adopted foxglove from a family receipt, and to have, for several years, recommended it as a diuretic) published a numerous collection of cases, in which foxglove has been given, and frequently with good success. To these cases the ingenious author has added some instructions respecting the use of this plant, which claim our attention: for a substance possessing so extra-ordinary and peculiar a power over the motion of the heart, if administered by the hand of ignorance and inexperience, is, in its effect, much more likely to be a poison than a remedy."

We can imagine how galling it must have been for Erasmus Darwin, who rather assumed upon himself the mantle of digitalis expert, to have his attempts so thoroughly outshone by the appearance of Withering's book a short time later. It would have rekindled sad memories of his late son Charles, to whose thesis Erasmus had appended some case descriptions of patients treated with digitalis, including case 4 of Withering's series. Three years later, together with his undistinguished son Robert, Physician at Shrewsbury, and father of the great Charles Darwin of Theory of Evolution fame, he would seek his revenge in the renowned Houlston case q.v.

During this time, WW was still naturally in touch with his widowed mother, Sarah. She, like any mother was very proud of his achievements, but also concerned about his health. She wrote thus: (see figure),

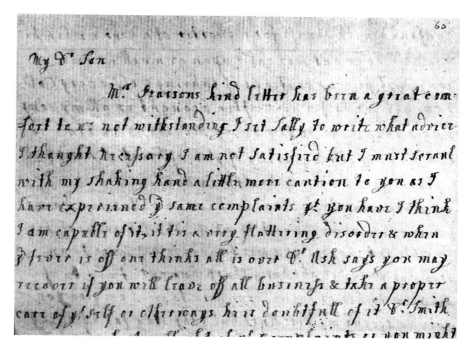

Letter to Withering from his mother 1783
(Reproduced by kind permission of the Royal Society of Medicine, London).

"March 18th 1783

    Dr. Withering
    Thos[n] Pearsons Cottage,
    Tettenhall
    Wolverhampton
    Mr D[r] Son

Mrs. Grassons kind letter has been a great comfort to me notwithstanding I set Sally to write what advice I thought necessary I am not satisfied but I must"..."with my shaking hand a little more caution to you as I have experienced the same complaints"......."Dr Ash says you may recover if you will leave off all business and take a proper care of yr. self or otherwise he it is still doubtful of it. Dr Smith says you make too slight of yr complaints or you might have been well now........
    Yr. most Affec: Mother
    March 8th. S.W."
On the same sheet of paper, WW has added:

"My Mother having tired herself with writing leaves one to say she has tasted the Turkey Coffee but does not think it deserves the name.

I have bought Mrs. Pearson and Mrs. Wood each a pound of the other sort but think they had better know how they like it before they have anymore."

WW received scant recognition in London, Edinburgh, Bristol or elsewhere. WW recognised those cases most likely to benefit from the exhibition of digitalis, namely oedema accompanied by an irregular pulse of the sort nowadays termed atrial fibrillation. No-one at that time knew that this was the consequence of heart failure. But one person was extremely pleased to receive from WW a copy of his work. This was Henry Wood, his old tutor. He wrote:

"Llanyufu, Aug 16th 1785
    Dear Sir,
I received the very kind favour of your Treatise on the Foxglove, accompanied with such friendly remembrances of former Assiduities, as excited pleasing Sensations only to be felt, & not described. And I cannot sufficiently acknowledge the many Favours confer'd on myself, and Family.

I thank you for your accurate analysis of Terra ponderosa, and beg leave to act out of Character by adjoining you not to be too frequent in chimical processes, lest the Effluvia should injure your Constitution, which I fear is not the most robust.

I think the World greatly indebted to you, for your full, accurate, & judicious examinations into the medical virtues of the Fox-Glove, which are ascertained by facts and long experience, the only Criterion of the powers of any Drugs: & every thing relative thereto so plainly, & fully set for the (?) to be level to the common Sense of the Faculty. This neighbourhood was likewise much indebted to you for publishing the truly efficacious Method of treating the sore throat so epidemic 2 or 3 years ago.

My little Granddaughter whom your very judicious prescription restored in less than a Week, is now with me, and the picture of Health. Mrs. Wood and all my Family join in truly respectful Compliments to yourself & Family with Dr: S^n Your sincere Friend & most obliged humble Servt.
    Hen: Wood
P.S. I thank you for your philosophical News. But our new air philosophers like the Air Navigators, rise quick above the Clouds, & out of my sight. They talk much of phlogiston, & I want to know whether it is a simple or a compound Body. Many other Questions I have to ask: which perhaps I may sometime trouble you with__"

This letter was addressed to Dr. Withering, Birmingham, and overstamped Shrewsbury.

At that time, residing in London, was a physician **Dr. John Coakley Lettsom** (q.v.), who was very interested in the use of digitalis, but obtained poor results as a consequence of employing too high a dose and poor patient selection. He founded the London Medical Society in 1773, and in 1778 published his experiences of the use of digitalis. Nevertheless, being a fair minded and objective physician, he was careful in his comments on the results he obtained when treating oedema secondary to alcoholic cirrhosis, and with excessive doses of digitalis. In 1787, he wrote to WW asking permission to propose his name for membership of the London Medical Society. WW accepted, and was duly elected that year. Lettsom then wrote asking WW to write a paper on the subject of digitalis. WW's reply can only be described as truly withering!

"Please accept my thanks for your offer of inserting anything new which I might have to say respecting the Digitalis: but I really have nothing new to observe, nor have I anything to retract of what I have said before. ————Dr. Lettsom has related his unsuccessful attempts with a degree of courage and candour which do the highest honour to his integrity; but no one can compare his choice of patients with my declarations of the fit and the unfit, or the doses he prescribed——with my doses, rules and cautions, without being astonished that he should suppose he had been given this medicine in the manner prescribed by me. I am fully satisfied, that, had I prescribed it in such cases, such forms, such doses and such repetitions as he has done, the effects would in my hands have been equally useless, and equally deleterious. I must, therefore, suppose that he had forgotten what I had written, without being conscious that his memory had deceived him. Had it been otherwise, after perusing the cases I had published——he would hardly have thought it necessary to have published more instances of what I had stigmatised as bad practice"

It would appear that WW was a man who did not mince his words, and who was, perhaps understandably, annoyed when other doctors achieved poor results from their treatment as a consequence of not having read the literature (his literature). An example of the importance of continuing medical education ('CME')?!

Subsequently, on February 4th, 1788, Lettsom read a paper to the Medical Society of London, titled "Of the Digitalis Purpurea in hydropic diseases." This was a description of 8 cases he had treated, almost all unsuccessfully (see appendix 3(b)).

In 1783, WW was ill with a chest infection, probably TB. This forced him to cease practice, and he spent some time with friends in Tettenhall, a pleasant suburb of Wolverhampton.

Again in 1784, the same problem remained, so he stayed at the home of the industrialist, Matthew Boulton in Soho, Birmingham, see illustration page 54.

This house still stands as a memento to its former owner. The house was large and had 300 acres of land. Nearby, Boulton had his "Manufactuary" which was only relocated in 1862. Meetings of the **Lunar Society** were held in Soho house which is now a museum run by Birmingham City Council. Visitors can see the elegant rooms and furnishings. In particular, mention must be made of the dining room, where the distinguished scientists, industrialists, and physicians met. This is shown in the accompanying figure over the page.

Soho House, Handsworth, Birmingham.

The dining room, Soho House, Handsworth, Birmingham.

THE LUNAR SOCIETY

WW was a member of a society of scientists, industrialists, inventors and physicians, called the Lunar Society, started by Matthew Boulton, William Small and Erasmus Darwin in 1765. The society was so named because it met monthly at the time of the full moon in order that members could drive home in moonlight. WW succeeded to Small's seat upon his death in 1775. In the same year James Watt was admitted. Other notable figures included Josiah Wedgwood (1765), Sir William Herschel, Benjamin Franklin, Joseph Priestley, Matthew Boulton, James Keir, and James Watt. This no doubt influenced and broadened the experience of WW's active mind.

Sadly the society disbanded on or around 8th August 1813 at which time lots were drawn for books which had been jointly owned by members. It was therefore very pleasing to learn that the society had risen like a phoenix from the ashes in 1991. It now has nearly 300 members, all of whom are distinguished in their several fields, including Medicine, the Arts and Industry. In an introductory leaflet regarding its purpose it states:

"It (the society) does not itself take positions, but provides a forum for its membership to influence change through focussing debate, linking social, economic, scientific and cultural thinking and catalysing action on issues critical to the future of the city and region as a whole." The society was involved, as a special patron, in the refurbishment of the Lunar Room, now open as a museum commemorating Boulton, the Lunar Society and the region's special place at the forefront of the Industrial Revolution.

Returning to 1784, during this sojourn, WW started preparing the second edition of his **Botanical Arrangement**. He was able to return to practice, though ill health continued to interrupt. The Memoir, written by his son, tells that WW was a physician of the mind as well as the body. His skill and judgment were often sought in difficult and confidential situations.

On July 3rd, 1789, his mother died after a five day illness, in her 81st year. WW wrote:

"Her native good sense, improved by education, made her company for the wise, and the cheerfulness of her declining years rendered her acceptable to the young to the latest period of her life. Both she and my father were examples of the strictest integrity." WW wished his children to witness the death scene, to remove any superstitious dread of death.

In addition, WW was interested in the controversy of the time in regard to the **phlogiston theory**. He collaborated with Priestley in chemical experiments, and in 1788 their correspondence was published in 'Philosophical Transactions of the Royal Society' as follows:

'A letter to Joseph Priestley, LL.D on the principle of acidity, the decomposition of water, and phlogiston' which was appended to Priestley's paper, 'Additional Experiments and Observations Relating to the Principle of Acidity, the Composition of Water, and Phlogiston. With letters to Him on the Subject by Dr. Withering and James Keir.' Phil. Trans. Royal Society, London, 1788; 78: 313-330. WW was frequently visited by learned scientists from abroad and took great delight in showing them the local countryside. Sights included the basaltic columns and rocks of Rowley, limestone caverns near Dudley, and granulated quartz in massive amount at the Lickey Hills in Worcestershire. In 1792, en route to Lisbon, WW fell ill in Malvern, and so occupied his time making observations on the local minerals. In Portugal at last, he investigated the mineral waters at Caldas da Rainhas, the medicinal hot springs situated seventy miles north of the capital. He also made a report on the National Hospital at the Caldas, where the waters were available for the use by the indigent. This report appeared in both languages in 1795.

WW's work in mineralogy (vid. chapter 5) came at a time of change towards more exact chemical methods rather than the purely descriptive methods previously employed. These included the science of crystallography, of which Rene-Just Hauy (1743-1822) was the founder. In 1784, his 'Essai d'une theorie sur la structure des cristaux' appeared. It is perhaps a little odd to reflect that WW almost certainly knew of this work, but never referred to it. He was also interested in horticulture, and in the origin of Stonehenge, about which he corresponded with various authorities at length.

WW was also a man of property. In Cornwall, he had a one thirty second share in Polgouth Mine, which brought him an annual income of £125 in 1781. Within four years of arriving in Birmingham, he acquired the freehold of a piece of land lying between what in 1950 was Corporation St and High St, Union St, and New St in the centre of the city. When purchased only High St and Union St existed. Union St then was a narrow winding lane, known as Corbett's Alley joining Cherry St and High St. The area of the property extended to 3500 square yards. In 1787 he built a house in Corbett's alley, with the intention of using it as his town house, having taken a lease of Edgbaston Hall. It was called the Stone House and is seen below. There is no good evidence that he actually lived at this property. His wife however is known to have lived at the Stone House whilst he and his son were in Portugal in 1793-4. By contrast his out of town house was Edgbaston Hall, also seen below.

The Stone House, in Union Street, formerly Corbett's Alley.
Looking from right to left, is shown the Union Hotel, Withering's house,
and the old library. In 1820, the whole estate was sold by WW junior at auction.
(From Peck & Wilkinson – see Bibliography).

Edgbaston Hall, 1998. Withering's home 1786-1799.
(Currently the headquarters of Edgbaston Golf club).

Edgbaston Hall manor dates back to the Norman Conquest. In the reign of Richard II (1377-99), through the marriage of Isabella de Edgbaston to Thomas Middlemore, the estate passed to the Middlemore family. In 1635, as Roman Catholics, they forfeited their Edgbaston estates to the Crown, but obtained a forty year lease at £100 per year. In 1680, the hall was dismantled to prevent its use as a refuge for the Papists. In 1717, the land was sold to Sir Richard Gough, who erected the hall on its present site. WW obtained the lease on the Hall and Park from Sir Henry Calthorpe in 1786 for 14 years. This was WW's home until a week before his death. It is still owned by the Calthorpe estate.

THE AFTERMATH OF THE FRENCH REVOLUTION

The riots of 1791.

These occurred as a consequence of the powerful emotions engendered by the French Revolution. In 1791, it was intended to call a gathering to commemorate Bastille Day (1789) on 14th July. An advertisement appeared in the Gazette, inviting people to dine at the Hotel in Temple Row, at 3 o'clock. The cost was 5 shillings, including a bottle of wine. Nothing wrong in that, but a handbill appeared on Monday July 11th, addressed to 'My Countrymen', which was a poorly concealed incitement to riot against Parliament, the Church, and the Crown on grounds that Parliament was 'venal', their ministers and clergy 'hypocritical' and 'oppressors' respectively, the reigning family 'extravagant,' and their taxes 'excessive'. They were incited to sacrifice 'public tranquillity' in order to show that the 'Peace of Slavery was worse than the War of Freedom.'

Another handbill quickly appeared seeking to spread the opposite view, and apprise the people of the seditious nature of the preceding one.

On Thursday July 14th, an article appeared in the Birmingham and Stafford Chronicle, offering one hundred guineas reward to anyone revealing the writer, printer, publisher or distributor of the seditious handbill.

WW attended the dinner, and subsequent to the events that followed, wrote an account of what occurred to Sir Henry Calthorpe. It is recited almost verbatim because it is so graphic a description of what happened. It will be recalled that WW would have witnessed the confrontation of rioters and townspeople assisted by farmers in Wellington in 1756 at the age of 15 years, and these memories were doubtless rekindled by the events described.

"21.7.91
Dear Sir,

You will have heard so much of our alarms and our sufferings in the towns in the vicinity of Birmingham that I will not trouble you with particulars the recollection of which is too painful to admit of description by one who has been a witness to these scenes of dreadful devastation. On Thursday 14th about 80 people dined at the Hotel to celebrate the anniversary of the French Revolution. From some inflammatory hand-bills, and some of a more serious and treasonable tendency it was easy to foresee that mischief was intended, but I hardly believed it would take effect. Soon after dinner the company were advised to break up - one of our constables informing them that a mob would insult them. Accordingly they did disperse, and at 5 o'clock not one of the company remained at the Hotel - about eight (o'clock) in my road from Binks Green where I had dined, I saw such a multitude collected in the street in front of the Hotel as I had often seen before on public dining days. My road lay through these people and I passed on. When in the midst of them many pulled off their hats and set up Huzza, to this I answered by bowing to each side. About an hour after this I am informed, the mischief began by the whole of the front windows at the Hotel being broken. The next objects of attack were the two Presbyterian Meeting Houses, which were demolished in the course of the night. In the morning Dr. Priestley's house was plundered and burnt, and here it was supposed the business would end. ....had the military arrived 30 hours later (than they did), I believe there would not have been one good house left within three or four miles of Birmingham. The mob had lists of the order in which the devoted were to be attacked. Their lists were occasionally altered and constantly added to. This house was not in the first, but was in the second list. My gardener .....was employed to mix with the leaders of the mob and occasionally to bring me intelligence.....On Saturday morning about 10 o'clock he brought me positive information that Edgbaston Hall would be burned down on Sunday night. I immediately set about the preparation, removed three carts and two wagon loads of the more valuable property, but about 2 o'clock of the same day I found that a plundering party of about 300 men were coming upon us from Ladywood......250 reached us before the second wagon could get away, which was therefore driven into the hayfield and covered with hay. .....by treating and bribing we got shut of them. ...At night a more determined set of scoundrels took and kept possession of the house and I found did not mean to depart until the mischief was fully effected. But bribes to the most active, strong liquors to those who would get drunk and the assistance of some friends from town once more cleared the house on Sunday morning. Before night the house was completely stripped of both furniture and fixtures, most of which had been deposited in the Church...By a manoeuvre planned and executed by Mr. Alcock the Butler and one of my men, the mob were led from Moseley Hall whose destruction they had accomplished early on the Sunday morning. .....About 8 o'clock this evening the dreaded incendiaries arrived, to the amount of near 300. I was in Birmingham expecting the arrival of the military every hour; and every half hour accounts came to town that the Hall was actually in flames;"

However by plying the mob with alcohol and money with which to repair to The Bell on Worcester Road to spend two guineas...there was left "a mere 30 of the more determined villains who would not go away. The King and Captain, the leaders of the desperate band were attacked" (by WW's party),..."the former was left for dead, the latter was most severely beaten and then locked up in an outhouse. The others after a good deal of hard fighting were completely routed. The king after taking a bribe to depart returned again and swore he would fire the barn before he went, he was carried nearly dead to a cottage by the turnpike from whence the following day he made swift to creep away. ....The sturdy conduct of all my servants deserves the highest applause, women as well as men. Harassed by extreme fatigue, without sleep for several days and nights, they have never once flinched from danger or exertion and we are now busy in replacing fixtures and furniture, and in restoring order. ....I shall keep as accurate an account of the expenses of this distressing business as may be, and I wish Sir for your opinion how far it may be proper to look to the courts for repayment, or whether, and in what proportion we should bear the loss ourselves. As far as I can guess the whole expense of wine, ale, spirits and other provisions may be about £50 or £60. A pipe of Madeira was fortunately saved. ....Mrs. Withering stood the most trying part of the business with much more firmness than I expected, but now she suffers more, and cannot bring herself into a state of mind to revisit Edgbaston, not even in the daytime. I cannot conclude without mentioning our particular obligation to the Commanding and other Officers of the Horse who first came to town for keeping eighteen out of thirty six, the whole number of men then arrived, together with their saddle all the night ready to ride off to Edgbaston at the shortest notice possible. They sat up, as most of us did the greatest part of the night. A march from Nottingham to Birmingham on grass horses in less than 11 hours was a great thing, but a delay of two hours more and the rioters had carried their point. With respectful compliments to Lady Calthorpe, I remain Dear Sir, Your obliged and very humble servant, Wm.Withering".

The mob also burned the New Meeting House in Moor Street, (owned by Dr. Priestley), and at the same time attacked and destroyed the Old Meeting House in Digbeth. They then went off down the Stratford Road to Fairhill (nowadays Sparkbrook), to deal with Dr. Priestley's house. Priestley refused to sanction any organized resistance, and as a consequence the house and its contents, including his laboratory and all its apparatus were destroyed.

It is clear that the measures taken by WW to defend his property and possessions would, in today's political and legal climate, have resulted in numerous counterclaims including grievous bodily harm. He might even have ended up with a custodial sentence which would probably have finished him professionally.

THE DEMISE OF WILLIAM WITHERING

WW's health was becoming more of a problem. In the Spring of 1790 he had a severe attack of pleurisy and fever, in those days called 'peripneumony'. In May 1791, he needed a month off work and took to his bed on account of pleurisy. It was in this year that his portrait was painted by **Carl von Breda**.

This painting is currently in a museum in Stockholm. It shows Withering holding a sheaf of foxglove flowers with his book about the use of the foxglove opened beside him. A copy is in the Postgraduate Medical centre at the Queen Elizabeth hospital, in Birmingham.

Portrait of William Withering, by Carl von Breda, 1791.
(Reproduced with kind permission of the National Museum of Fine Arts, Stockholm).

Carl Frederik von Breda was born in Stockholm in 1759, and died in 1818. He was painter to the Swedish Court. A pupil of Reynolds he became a distinguished portrait painter, being known as the 'Van Dyck' of Sweden. He painted a portrait of King Gustav III in the prevailing Rococo style in 1787, and in the same year visited England, France and Italy. He settled in London for a while, in the studio of Joshua Reynolds, whose portrait he painted in 1791. From 1788 he exhibited annually at the Royal Academy in London. His style was eclectic, displaying the influence of Reynolds and Gainsborough as well as the Italian, Dutch and Baroque masters, especially Rembrandt. He visited Birmingham in the early 1790's, painting portraits of several members of the Lunar Society, including James Watt. In 1795, he visited Paris, and the following year returned to Stockholm, where he was made professor of the Academy. In 1812 he was knighted.

Withering's health meanwhile forced him to resign his post at the General Hospital in 1792, and he had serious thoughts of retiring to a warmer climate. Therefore in September 1792 he set off for Lisbon (France being considered politically unsuitable) together with his daughter Charlotte aged 14 years and friends from Tettenhall. He was quite ill even before leaving these shores, as his letter dated 20th October 1792, written from Falmouth to his wife shows.

"Dear Helena,
I deferred writing until our arrival here which happened on Tuesday evening last, after, to me, a very fatiguing journey, for I did not get the better of the exertions at Plymouth, and became worse and worse every stage, until the fever and inflammation ran so high that I was glad to get instantly to bed here and endeavour to get well speedily by every means in my power. One bleeding and two cuppings have done the business; yesterday I sat up 3 or 4 hours, had very little evening fever, and expect to have none at all today. ....Sunday morning. I go on well; no fever, cough and spitting abating; appetite returning."

In a letter to his son William, dated 11th November, from Lisbon WW stated that he was still very thin, yet eating three times as much as he ever remembered to have done, and always remained hungry. He went on to say that his night sweats had receded, and praised the local climate. On March 1st 1793, he wrote:

"...I cough only in a morning, but my breath is defective under exercise, but attempts to ride a horse have brought back this fever." On 10th April 1793, he says:

"....My cough became almost as bad as it was in November the expectoration and uneasiness in my chest increased, the breath worse, so that I lost the newly acquired faculty of walking up hill;.... June 16th 1793: Dear Helena, ...I said nothing of my health having nothing very good to say. I got through the winter well and nearly lost all cough and oppression; but the unexampled and unexpected cold of March and April at length subjected me to an inflammatory attack which was subdued by bleeding ————."

WW's opinion on the current fashion for advising patients with various illnesses to travel far in search of improvement of their condition, was changed as a result of his personal experience.

"Let those who meditate the removal of a relative or friend from every interesting and tender connection and all the nameless comforts of home pause before they rashly embark upon a foreign expedition which can offer no hope of rescuing the object of their solicitude, but must in all probability greatly aggravate suffering by subjecting the invalid to many inevitable privations."

His final pronouncement on Portugal for tuberculous patients was:

1. The end of phthisical patients is hastened by hot climates.
2. The natives of such climates are far from being exempt from phthisis pulmonalis.
3. Where the tendency is manifest, though the disease not confirmed and Lisbon is to be tried, let the patient leave England in October, and return home or remove to Cintra in April.
4. Invalids should fix their residence in the country, and near the Tagus for the convenience of fine sands, boating and bathing.
5. Lisbon itself is particularly objectionable, the higher parts too exposed, the lower disgustingly dirty and oppressively hot.
6. The sea voyage often proves more beneficial than the country of Portugal.
7. The south coast of England offers prospects at least as good as Portugal to the patient in the incipient stage of the disorder. Especially the Isle of Wight.————"

(The British Tourist Board would have been very grateful to him!).

This trip was successful, his health improved, and he was able to visit the spa town of Caldas da Rainha, where he analysed the spa waters.

From now on WW had frequent attacks of pleurisy, with pneumonia and haemoptysis (coughing up of blood), and he was very breathless. He was unable to continue in medical practice but devoted himself to botany and agricultural pursuits at Edgbaston. He again visited Lisbon in 1794, and on his return enlisted Boulton's aid in order to install a form of air conditioning in Edgbaston Hall. This was accomplished by means of double windows, special flues for heating and elimination of draughts. By this means it was possible to maintain an equitable temperature of 65 degrees throughout the most severe winter.

In 1795, writing to a friend he said:

"Your solicitude about my health is very flattering.....I am reconciled to my fate...At times an exacerbation of feverish or inflammatory attacks on my lungs unhinges me entirely for a week or two....I am happy.....I am busy.."

He was still busy preparing the third edition of Botany to which he devoted 6 to 8 hours a day. By 1797, he was very short of breath. However, thanks to the air conditioning of Edgbaston Hall he survived the severe winter of 1798. But in 1799 Mrs. Withering took ill, which considerably upset WW.

"This sudden and most unexpected seizure threw me into a state of hurry and agitation, a kind of febricula which the hot weather did not suffer me to throw off..."

In 1799, being in a precarious state of health, and Edgbaston Hall being in an exposed position, WW decided not to renew the lease. He purchased a house to the west of the Stratford Road, called "The Larches," with 10 acres of land. It had 10 bedrooms, stabling for seven horses, two coachhouses, a dairy, a piggery, a laundry, and a private pump of good water. It bordered on Joseph Priestley's house. Currently, at 10 Priestley Road, which leads off the Stratford road, there is a mural tablet which is shown below:

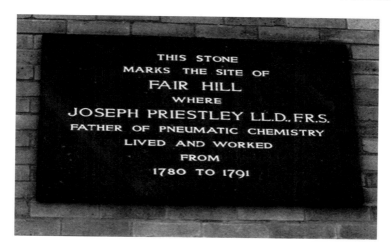

The mural tablet at 10 Priestley Road, Sparkbrook.

In September 1799, he determined to leave Edgbaston Hall for his intended new home, The Larches, at Fairhill nowadays Sparkbrook. Larches Street still exists, a few hundred yards from the Priestley mural tablet.

Mrs. Withering was too ill to accompany him. On Wednesday October 2nd, 1799, he was so ill that his son, home from Glasgow, came over from Edgbaston to be with him. His demise is chronicled by his son in the Memoir:

'The closing scene offers nothing inconsistent with what has already been described. ————As he had on all common occasions displayed the **suaviter in modo**, so on each emergency did he prove himself possessed of the **fortiter in re**: a gentleness of manner engaging affection, combined with a firmness of manner engaging affection, combined with a firmness of mind which served him in every extremity.

In one of the last acute attacks of pleurisy, about eleven o'clock at night, on the 5th July, his surgeon being absent, taking the lancet in his own hand, he performed on himself the operation of venesection with great composure and dexterity.

The desire to repair to a more sheltered spot, increased with the diminished probability of benefit from it, and he informed the agent of Lord Calthorpe of his intention, according to his own expression, not to pass another winter at Edgbaston "unless it were in consecrated ground."

His removal to the Larches was with much hazard effected on the twenty eighth of September.

The circumstances of thus taking possession were rendered peculiarly melancholy by the inability of Mrs. Withering to accompany him. She parted from him under the grievous impression that she should see him no more in this world; though he continued to indulge an expectation of being able shortly to receive her at his new habitation.

Whilst still downstairs, he was prevailed on to give his advice to a young person brought by Lady S___; the last patient for whom he wrote his last regular prescription. On Wednesday, the 2nd of October, the disease seemed to threaten such speedy fatality, that his son was compelled to quit the more lingering malady of his mother, to attend almost entirely on the other sufferer. At this juncture arrived the venerable Lord T__, with an introduction which the Doctor could not altogether neglect, though confined to that bed from which he never arose. The much sought-after physician once more took his pen in his hand, and with extreme difficulty made a few general notes of a plan of treatment; by this act closing his career of medical practice.

As in previous sickness he had been gratified by frequent visits from his brethren in each department of the profession, so now was he sedulously attended; himself becoming a most willing and tractable patient, passively submitting to the suggestions of those in whom he had reason to confide.

On the following night it was found necessary to bring into the sick chamber a waiting man, when an affecting proof of attachment occurred. The faithful domestic, on beholding the traits of death unequivocally depicted in the countenance of his master, instantly swooned away on the floor. The Doctor, with renewed animation, ordered the means to be used for his revival.

On Thursday some of the more painful symptoms subsided, but not in such a way as to afford any well grounded hope of real amendment. In every interval of moderated pain, he became inquisitive for public news, and felt the throb of patriotism strong in death.

Extreme debility and high fever induced a degree of delirium for a few hours——— and on the balance being restored, he returned hearty thanks to God for the divine gift of reason, fervently praying, that however suffering in body, his mind be preserved unshaken.

Towards evening on the fifth, his nearly widowed wife was conveyed to that residence———Early in the morning of Sunday, the 6th of October———Dr. Withering evinced an entire confidence in the goodness of an over-ruling Providence——— Composed and tranquil in himself, he reproved the appearance of grief,———About six o'clock he intreated for two hours of undisturbed repose; but alas! even sleep no longer brought refreshment; for life itself was fast ebbing away. Nevertheless, through the whole forenoon, he engaged in a series of conversations on the most interesting topics. Even his voice in those impressive discourses resumed its natural firmness———On his son and daughter, by his own desire, again drawing near to him in the afternoon, as if to reconcile them to the approaching separation, with a calm and beaming countenance, 'My children,' he said, 'see how easy I lie!'

Dr. Withering had never indulged in that carelessness of personal appearance sometimes observable in the studious. Indeed, he attached so much regard to neatness, as to consider it, in a degree, at least, to the body what virtue is to the soul———Refreshed by an entire renewal of linen, and, perhaps, with a sense of decorum gratified, immediately afterwards, being raised at his own request, he fervently ejaculated, 'Now I am ready!' at the same moment springing forward with an energy that might be deemed almost preternatural, he exhausted the feeble remains of vitality.'

Thus wrote his son William of how he died.

WW had left instructions regarding his interment. On 10th October, his body was taken back to Edgbaston Old Church, not a stone's throw from Edgbaston Hall, see figure, and deposited in a vault by six honest men. His burial is recorded in the register, see accompanying figure.

Edgbaston Old Church.

J. Crane, MD of Crewkerne, wrote:

"Deep in the earth, the debt of nature paid,
The mortal part of WITHERING is laid;
And though he seem to share the common lot,
Of those who perish, and are soon forgot,
His fame will never die! each future age,
Instructed by the labours of his page,
(The faithful page where Nature stands to view,
Displayed in colours ever bright and new,)
Shall hail his honoured name with grateful praise,
And bards his skill record in tuneful lays:
Of Wealth or Power short is the transient state,
Whilst SCIENCE soars above the reach of Fate!"

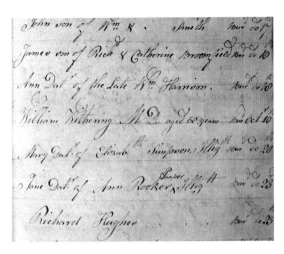

The burial register, recording Withering's burial on October 10th 1799.

A mural monument was erected in the church at Edgbaston, in marble, at the base of which are emblems of Aesculapean art from which extend on the right a representation of the **Digitalis purpurea** (purple foxglove), and on the left, the **Witheringia solanacea**.(see accompanying figure).

The tablet bears the following inscription:
'While heav'n born Genius drops on earth a tear,
And Science, drooping, mourns o'er Withering's bier;
While Pity sighs to find that bosom cold,
Where late she reign'd, dispensing good untold;
While Memory's voice, each virtue telling o'er,
But deeper wounds the peace she would restore,
Hope smiles serene,- her eye upturn'd to Heav'n
Where Virtue's never-fading crown is giv'n,
Shed o'er the weeping sorrowers below
That calm a Christian's grief alone can know.
Yes! on that day, when Nature's ruin'd frame
Shall form a grave for each illustrious name,
And science' star, on earth so seeming bright,
Shall be eclips'd in universal light,
Then shall the sainted sage that bliss receive,
Which here no tongue can paint, no heart conceive,
While Angel choirs, with plaudits justly giv'n,
Proclaim his triumph to the hosts of Heav'n.'

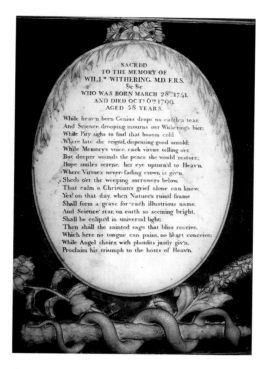

Mural tablet in Edgbaston Old Church (St. Bartholomew's).

WW died at the Larches on October 6th, 1799, and his wife died in 1801. His son William remained in residence there until 1820. Currently there is no remnant of the house in which he spent his last days, though there is a Larches St, abutting onto a park, and which includes a statue to Sir Thomas Attwood, a leading figure in the trade Union movement, who must also have lived in the vicinity. This is sited approximately three hundred yards from where once stood Joseph Priestley's house, and is part of present day Sparkbrook.

From WW's will, it appears he owned an estate in Moddershall, in the secluded hilly country north of Stone, in Staffordshire. By inclosure, he received 21.5 acres from Oulton Heath. He owned four mills, grinding flint, grist, and colour. Although he instructed his wife to sell the estate whilst he was in Portugal, this appears not to have come about, and it was still in his possession at the time of his death.

In the will, which cited his residence as Edgbaston Hall at the time, he bequeathed to his sister Sarah £1200 to include monies owed to her under his Father (Edmund)'s will. Meanwhile, she was to receive £40 twice yearly until she claimed the above sum. To his daughter Charlotte, £3000 was to be paid within 6 months of his wife's decease provided she had reached the age of 21 years. To his son William, £200 from the income of his estates for maintenance and education from the time he be considered to be of proper age to attend University to be followed by an annual income of £50 or £100 when he chose to marry or otherwise settle. The residue of the income of his estate to go to his wife, until her death, and thereafter, all his real estate to his son William and his heirs, but in the event of his death before the age of 21 years, and without an heir, in that event the real estate and residue of the said personal estate to be bequeathed to his daughter Charlotte and her heirs and executors. His will to be executed by his wife and James Watt of Heathfield in the Parish of Handsworth in the County of Stafford. His wife was to be responsible for the tuition and guardianship of their son William and daughter Charlotte, but were she to die before they attained the age of 21 years, then their Guardianship or Tutorship would be the responsibility of Sister Sarah and friends, Thomas Pearson of Tettenhall and the Reverend Augustus Johnson of Kenilworth etc etc.

Chapter 4

WITHERING THE BOTANIST

A few months after WW arrived in Birmingham, he published: **The Botanical Arrangement of all the Vegetables naturally growing in Great Britain.** The work, comprising two volumes, 836 pages and 12 plates in all, was published in May 1776. Prior to that time there had been little attempt to classify plants in a scientific as apart from a romantic manner. A scientific method had been attempted by John Ray (1672-1705) and Robert Morison, first professor of Botany at Oxford. However it was the Swedish botanist **Linnaeus**(1707-1778), a lecturer in Botany at the University of Uppsala who wrote the **Systema naturae**, and later, during a visit to England in 1736, the **Genera plantarum**, the starting point of modern systematic botany.

The Linnaean system sought to classify all plants systematically according to their reproductive organs. Withering's was the first comprehensive **English** publication based on the Linnaean system. In his book he criticised claims for the medicinal value of many plants and vegetables that were the result of superstition rather than observation:

"We shall sooner attain the end proposed if we take up the subject as altogether new, and, rejecting the fables of the ancient herbalist, build only upon the basis of accurate and well considered experiments."

In 1783, a small group of botanists who called themselves the Lichfield Society, and which included Dr. Erasmus Darwin, approached WW with a view to translating Linnaeus' **Genera et Species Plantarum**. WW was visited by a member of the Society, but pointed out that he was too busy to undertake this, but offered to help. At this time WW was working hard on his 2nd edition, and mentioned his own method of accentuation of names so that they would be pronounced properly. He showed his visitor his manuscript. During the summer of 1784, his health again having deteriorated, WW spent several months at the home of **Matthew Boulton** on Washwood Heath, whilst the latter was on holiday in Cornwall, in the hope that the air would be more salubrious than that of the town. WW remained unwell during most of the summer. In 1785 he read in the **Monthly Review**, the announcement of the publication of the **Systema Vegetabilium** in English. The reviewer praised the new mode of accentuation used in the translation, but omitted any reference to WW, although several others were mentioned. WW was somewhat peeved, and wrote a letter to the editor of the Monthly Review.

In 1787, he published his major botanical contribution:

"A BOTANICAL ARRANGEMENT
OF
BRITISH PLANTS;
INCLUDING
THE USES OF EACH SPECIES,
IN
MEDICINE, DIET, RURAL OECONOMY AND THE ARTS,
WITH AN EASY
Introduction to the Study of Botany, &c. &c.
ILLUSTRATED BY COPPER PLATES.
THE SECOND EDITION.
By WILLIAM WITHERING, M.D. F.R.S.
MEMBER OF THE ROYAL MEDICAL SOCIETY OF EDINBURGH, AND
PHYSICIAN TO THE GENERAL HOSPITAL AT BIRMINGHAM.
INCLUDING
A NEW SET OF REFERENCES TO FIGURES.
By JONATHAN STOKES, M.D.
LATE PRESIDENT OF THE ROYAL MEDICAL SOCIETY OF EDINBURGH,
CORRESPONDING MEMBER OF THE SOCIETY OF ANTIQUARIES
OF SCOTLAND; PHYSICIAN AT KIDDERMINSTER.
VOL. I
BIRMINGHAM: PRINTED BY M.SWINNEY;
FOR G.G.J. & J. ROBINSON, PATERNOSTER-ROW,
AND J. ROBSON, NEW BOND-STREET, LONDON;
J. BALFOUR, AND C.ELLIOT,
EDINBURGH.
M.DCC.LXXXVII.

PREFACE

AT length the second Edition of the BOTANICAL ARRANGEMENT makes its appearance. The Author pleads in excuse for its long delay, the multiplicity of his own professional engagements, and the very great improvements, both in the plan, and in the execution of the work. Being conscious of the unavoidable imperfection attendant on a first attempt to naturalize this science, which, in its improved state was new to the English language; he requested the assistance of others. He is happy to have experienced that approbation of his design, which called forth the assistance he sought for; and the effort of naturalising the doctrines of the Linnaean School of Botany, has been crowned with a degree of success beyond his most sanguine expectations.

From the very liberal assistance he has met with, the work is now risen superior to its first institution; aiming at very essential improvements in that branch of Science, which, at first, it only attempted to render more easily accessible. It may therefore be necessary to enumerate some of the more striking features of the present Edition.

The Translation of the Generic and Specific Characters has been compared with REICHARD'S Edition of the Genera and Species plantarum, and the numbers of those editions have been adopted.

The ESSENTIAL GENERIC CHARACTER is subjoined to each Generic description, and the ARTIFICIAL character is retained at the head of the Class.

The particular places of growth of the rarer plants are carefully enumerated, and many new ones are added, which are included between crotchets. This has been done at the request of several friends to the work; their opinion prevailing against the reasons adduced for omitting them in the first Edition*.

The Reader will find in this Edition several species, and many varieties of plants, unnoticed by Linnaeus. The Varieties of preceding authors are marked by Greek letters; those peculiar to this work by Arabic numerals.

The Latin Synonyms of Bauhine, Gerard, Parkinson, and Ray, which occupied so much space in the first edition, are now omitted; partly because they could be of little use to those who do not understand

---

* Mr. Woodward, to whom the readers, as well as myself, are indebted for many improvements, in almost every page of this work, and whose liberality of sentiment is only equalled by his industry and accuracy in botanical investigation, desires me to observe that the Habitats, or native places of growth, in the Northern Counties of England, which stand in his name, belong jointly to himself and Mr. Crowe; the plants having been collected in a journey they took into those Counties, in the summer of 1781.

---

the Latin language, for they who do, may get the references from HUDSON'S Flora Anglica; and partly to make room for a new set of references to figures, which my friend Dr. Stokes undertook to furnish. These references make one of the most valuable parts of the present Edition. Nothing short of his extensive knowledge of the subject, joined to an indefatigable industry, could have effected the reformation required; but the full force of his exertions will only be understood by such as have laboured at the subject themselves, and experienced the difficulty of marshalling error crowded upon error, into regular and beautiful order. These references are expressed in the shortest way possible; the best figures are mentioned first: The abbreviations are explained by the author of the references, in the catalogue of authors sub-joined.

The references to RAY are preserved, so far as the Varieties he furnished rendered them necessary.

The Linnaean names have now taken the lead of the English ones, and to facilitate their adoption, they are accented. In the difficult task of accentuation I had the assistance of my worthy friends Dr. Arnold of Leicester, and the late Revd. Mr. Newling of Birmingham, whose classical attainments, especially in Greek literature, were an ornament to the purity and urbanity of his manners. The English Botanist need not now hesitate to pronounce the Latin names, provided he observe to throw the force of the voice upon that letter which precedes the mark of accentuation*. At the same time, the

English names are still retained, in order to shew that our language is capable of a regular nomenclature; which, except in a few instances, is taken from old established authors, or from the daily use of the inhabitants of our Island.

The 3d. Volume is intended to be published in the course of the ensuing year, and will contain the whole of the Class CRYPTOGAMIA, together with an easy

---

* Further directions for the pronunciation will hereafter be given with the accented Index.

INTRODUCTION to the Study of Botany; the best methods of preparing and preserving a HORTUS SICCUS, or a collection of dried specimens of plants; the GLOSSARY of terms, illustrated by plates; the Rules for ACCENTUATION; and, more humiliating, though not less necessary than these, the table of Errata. The latter may be made more perfect by the observations of others, and the author will be thankful either for such, or for any other communications which can tend to advance a favourite study, or to render more compleat an undertaking which has cost him much labour and some anxiety.

After all, there is nothing farther from the wishes of the Author than, that the botanical student should confine himself to the information which may be obtained within the limits of this work only, for its professed intention is to lead him to other valuable sources of knowledge which are at present inaccessible to the unlearned reader. On this account he has carefully avoided transcribing any thing from Mr. Lightfoot's excellent work on the plants of Scotland, for, although that work is at present of little use to any but the Latin Botanist, as the specific Characters are given in that language; yet the translations in these Volumes will supply that defect, and render the English reader capable of receiving much useful and interesting information, from the valuable descriptions in English, which he has generally subjoined.

BIRMINGHAM,
24th August, 1787."
On the following pages appears a list of contributors. This will be quoted as it will enhance the awareness of Withering's communication with people from many walks of life, and from different localities, in assembling his work.
"A LIST
Of the Names of those Gentlemen who have favoured this Edition with their assistance.
DR. ARNOLD, Fellow of the Royal Medical Society of Edinburgh, Physician at Leicester." (a personal friend and co-graduand of WW).
"Mr. BALLARD, Surgeon, near Malvern Wells, Worcestershire
Dr. BEDDOES, Lecturer in Chemistry, at Oxford.
Dr. BROUGHTON, late President of the Royal Medical Society of Edinburgh, Physician in Kingston, Jamaica.
Mr. BRUNTON, Junr. Perry-hill, near Birmingham.
REV. HENRY BRYANT, M.A. Heydon, Norfolk.
JAMES CROWE, Esq. Tuckswood, near Norwich.

REV. SAMUEL DICKENSON, L.L.B. Rector of Blymhill, Staffordshire.
JOHN FORD, Esq. Surgeon in Bristol.
Mr. HALL, Newton Cartmell, near Ulverstone, Lancashire.
Mr. HAWKES, Birmingham.
T.F.HILL, Esq. late of Ely-Place, Holborn, London; now in Italy
Mr. J.A. HUNTER, Nursery-man, Perry-hill, near Birmingham.
REV. WILLIAM HOLFEAR, A.M. Vicar of Wolvey, near Hinkley, Leicestershire.
Mr. JONES, late Surgeon in Birmingham.
——MARTYN, Esq. Teignmouth.
REV. Mr. NEWBERRY, Fellow of Exeter College, Oxon.
Mr. PITCHFORD, Surgeon, in Norwich.
Mr. SAVILLE, Lichfield.
Dr. J.E.SMITH, Proprietor of the Linnaean Collection.
Dr. STOKES, Member of the Royal Medical Society of Edinburgh, corresponding Member of the Society of Antiquaries of Scotland, Physician at Shrewsbury.
ROBERT STONE Esq. Bungay, Suffolk.
J. Watt Esq. Engineer, Birmingham.
Mr. Whateley, Surgeon, Old Jewry, London.
Mr. WIGG, Schoolmaster, Yarmouth.
REV. MR. WOOD, Leeds, Yorkshire.
THOMAS J. WOODWARD, Esq. L.L.B. Bungay, Suffolk."

This section is followed by a chapter titled "The Design". Some quotations which are very pertinent now follow.

"Notwithstanding the very rapid progress of Science from the middle of the last century, it is only since the beginning of this that the study of Natural history hath attracted the general attention of mankind.

Botanical enquiries in particular have been confined to a few individuals; partly from the difficulties which attended them, and partly from an opinion that they were useful only to the professors of Medicine; but the establishment of the LINNAEAN SYSTEM called forth a number of votaries to cultivate this amiable Science; and the pupils of its admirable author convinced mankind, that the Medical properties of Plants, were far from being the only circumstances worthy their attention."

WW's contribution to Botany will shortly become apparent.

"Still however difficulties remained. An acquaintance with one of the Learned Languages was hardly sufficient to enable us to understand his works. The novelty of the subject compelled him to invent a variety of new terms; and without, or even with the advantages of an Academical education, it was a very laborious task to attain precisely that idea, which he wished them to express.

In this situation of things, what could be done by those, who from nature, or from accident, found themselves possessed with a taste for Botanical knowledge? They studied Botanical plates: but bad plates conveyed false, or insufficient ideas; and good ones were too expensive for general use. If they applied to old voluminous Herbals, the want of method, the deficiencies, and the long continued attention which was requisite, fatigued the most industrious dispositions. If they fought for information in more modern productions, they found such a multiplicity of terms, formed from the Greek and Latin languages, with nothing truly English but the terminations; that they soon began to despair of success, and then relinquished the study in disgust.

A Desire to remove these difficulties, and to render the path in this walk of science, as easy as it is delightful, first gave rise to the present undertaking."

So, we see Withering's desire to make botanical classification more easily understood by those lacking a classical education. He recognised the contribution of people from many walks of life, be they barber-surgeon, man of the cloth, or nursery-man. He also recognised the delicacy required for the descriptive portrayal of gender within the botanical world.

"From an apprehension that Botany in an English dress would become a favourite amusement with the Ladies, many of whom are very considerable proficients in the study, in spite of every difficulty, it was thought proper to drop the sexual distinctions in the titles to the Classes and Orders*, and to adhere only to those of Number, Situation, and Proportion. They who wish to know the curious facts which gave birth to this celebrated system, may consult the Philosophia Botanica, the Sponsalia Plantarum————————"

---

*   The Linnaean titles however, are still preserved on the top of the left hand pages, to accommodate those who have been habituated to use them.

Withering goes on to reveal his adherence to Creationist principle. The theory of evolution would not surface for a further 70 years.

"The structure of every leaf and every flower, exhibits proofs of Divine Wisdom: but we are too apt to pass, without attention, the phaenomena which are daily presented to our eyes. In some parts of the vegetable kingdom, there are however such peculiarities of structure, and such amazing contrivances to answer the wise purposes of the creator, that a total disregard of them would have been unpardonable: These therefore are mentioned in a concise manner, yet sufficiently full to excite the attention of the ingenious————————."

A revealing fact in regard to Withering's thinking on the subject of the usage of drugs for medicinal purposes, was his clear contempt for the concept that foods had medicinal value. He was of the opinion that they had only achieved their reputation for medicinal value because they did not cause harm, and that patients believed what they were told. For medicinal value, he was tempted to go where others feared to tread - namely to examine the use of poisons. He also espoused the principle of carefully thought out and executed experimentation, and all this at a time when others where quick to seize any advantage claimed for untested remedies.

"Many people will be surprized to find so little said upon the Medical Virtues of Plants; but those who are best enabled to judge of this matter, will perhaps think, that the greater part of that little might have been omitted. The superstition of former ages, operating upon the ignorance of mankind, gave rise to miracles of every denomination; and the fashion of combining a great variety of ingredients with a design to answer any particular purpose, rendered the real efficacy of any of them extremely doubtful. The dreadful apprehensions which men formerly entertained of POISONS, made them fearful of employing substances that were capable of doing mischief; and therefore they rejected those which were most likely to do good. A number of Vegetables fit only for food, were supposed capable of producing the greatest alterations in the human body; and at length almost every common Plant was esteemed a cure for almost every disease. In this situation of things, little advantage can be reaped from the experience of former times: we shall sooner attain the end proposed, if we take up the subject as altogether new, and rejecting the fables of the ancient Herbalists, build only upon the basis of experiments well conceived and accurately executed. To facilitate the work as much as possible, the following observations are added.

Certain Plants, capable of producing sudden and remarkably deleterious effects upon Animal Bodies, are called Poisonous: but Poisons in small doses are the best medicines; and useful medicines in too large doses are poisonous. Even the most innocent aliments, in certain quantities, are noxious.............

Different parts of the same Vegetable often manifest very different properties: Thus the leaves of WORMWOOD are bitter, whilst the roots are aromatic. The Seed-vessels, or Heads of POPPIES are narcotic, but the Seeds have no such quality........"

Withering's name was given to a species of Galium. This is a genus of plants of the madder family (Rubiaceae) comprising 250 species of world-wide distribution, mostly slender herbs. Currently included are Asperula odorata (woodruff), one of 200 species of hardy annuals and perennials.

In Withering's 2nd edition, Galium is described as Goosegrass. The following species are mentioned, and described:

procumbens, uliginosum, erectum, spurium, tricorne, anglicum, pusilum, seabrum, verum, Mollugo, boreale, Aparine. Under GALIUM palustre, a dwarf variety, nanum, is mentioned, and stated to have been "Found by Dr. Withering."

In the 6th edition, the number of species described as separate has risen to fifteen, including cruciatum, palustre, Witheringii, procumbens, uliginosum, pusilum, erectum, mullugo, tricorne, scabrum, verum, anglicum, boreale, Aparine, verrucosum,

Under Witheringii we read:

"Leaves strap-spear-shaped, smooth, about 4 or 5 in a whirl; stem feeble, rough: leaves reflected.

PLATE XXVIII

E. bot. 2206

See figure

Of a middle size, between the G. mollugo and G. glaucum. Stem-leaves five in a whirl, bent back. Branch-leaves four in a whirl. Corymbus three cleft; white, purplish on the outside before it expands. Anthers brown. LINN. About eight inches high, not at all branched, except sending off fruit-stalks from the whirls of leaves. Stems feeble, rough.

Leaves five in a whirl; turned back, some so much so, as to point downwards; serrated with hairs, pointed with a hair, not with a rigid bristle or prickle. Blossom purple on the outside whilst young. Anthers red brown. Pistil very short, cloven down to the base. (Rough Heath Bed-straw. G. Witheringii. Fl. Brit. Galium montanum. WITH. Ed. 4. though the author then suspected his plant might prove a new species, distinct from the G. montanum of LINN. which opinion has been confirmed by Dr. SMITH, who has been pleased to name the new plant after its discoverer. E.) On high, but boggy, parts of Handsworth Heath, near Birmingham. (On Bank meadow, Rose Castle, Cumberland, Bishop of Carlisle, in E. bot. Walkington Wood, near Beverley. TEESDALE, in Bot. Guide. E.) July"

The 6th edition (1818), includes a description of the botanical microscope invented by Dr. Withering, see figure .

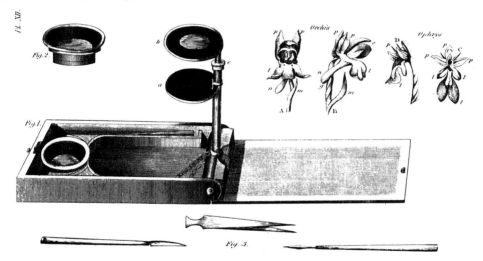

Withering's botanical microscope.

The description was as follows:

"PLATE XII
BOTANICAL MICROSCOPE
FIG. 1. Represents the Botanical Microscope in its present improved state.
FIG. 2. Is a Magnifying Glass, to be held in the hand, and applied close to the eye, whilst the object to be examined is brought immediately under it, at such a distance as shall be found to give the most distinct vision.
FIG. 3. Shews the Dissecting Knife, the Triangular Needle, and a pair of small steel Plyers. These instruments are useful in the dissection of flowers, even when the plants are so large as not to require magnifying.

When the parts in question are very minute, and require a nice and careful dissection, place the miscroscope upon a table, and raise it if necessary, on a book or two, so that the eye may be applied with ease immediately over and close to the glass (b.) Lay the object to be examined on the dark stage (a.) and turn the screw at (c.) until you see the object upon the stage perfectly distinct. With the needle in the left, and the knife in the right hand, the elbows resting on the table, proceed in the dissection at the same time that the eye is applied to the glass (b.)

When the microscope is shut up, the instruments and the hand-glass are to be put into the cells destined to receive them, and the whole forms a shape and size convenient to carry in the pocket"

Clearly with a view to the commercial possibilities, the last page of the fourth volume carried the following advertisement:

"THE
BOTANICAL MICROSCOPE
INVENTED BY
DR. WITHERING

Which is more portable and convenient than any other,
IS NOW MANUFACTURED BY
MR. BEILBY, OPTICIAN, CLARE STREET, BRISTOL;
And may likewise be had of the Publishers of this Work, and of other Booksellers."

In addition to botany, WW's other great interest outside medicine, was in mineralogy, which will now be described.

Chapter 5

WITHERING THE MINERALOGIST

During the winter months, WW diverted his outside interests to chemistry. This involved translations from Latin. WW became interested in the phlogiston theory. As will be recalled, it postulated that combustible bodies lost something when they burned. According to Stahl, it was the material of fire. Metals were composed of a calx, different for each metal, combined with phlogiston, which was the same in all metals, and common to all combustibles. WW devoted a lot of time to considering this theory, in which he did not believe. He passed his papers on the subject to Priestley, who was in favour of the phlogiston theory.

Although WW had a European reputation as a scientific botanist, and chemist, he was also well known as a mineralogist. Whilst at Edinburgh we gather from his diaries that he developed his interest in geological problems and field work. After arriving in Stafford, he studied the different kinds of marl in the county. Marl is a soil in which there is a mixture of clay and calcium carbonate. It is used as a fertilizer. WW studied twelve types, arranging them in tabular form according to their calcium content. He was working on the conversion of local marls into quicklime for agricultural use. After separation of the clay from the calcium carbonate, it was burned in order to see what sort of brick was obtained. Subsequent heating of the solids (calcination) removed the volatile contents for further analysis. He was able to determine which marls were suited to various soils. At the age of 32, his work was published in the "Philosophical Transactions."

Stone workings at Rowley Regis.

William Withering junior, writing in his memoirs states:

'In the south of Staffordshire is a range of hills, the highest of which is near a village called Rowley,' see illustration above.

'The summit of this hill has a craggy broken appearance, and is itself, as well as the fields on each side, to a considerable distance, scattered over with large fragments of the Rag-stone, some of which are sunk deep into the ground. This stone is used for repairing roads, and for paving the streets of Birmingham. It bears an external resemblance to the dark grey masses, the produce of Arthur's Seat, near Edinburgh————To a superficial observer the Rowley Rag exhibits a volcanic appearance, and though Dr. Withering at first imagined that it could not be derived from such an origin, he afterwards became convinced that such was its real nature.' In 1782, his work on "Analysis of two mineral substances, the Rowley-rag-stone and the Toad-stone" was published in the same journal. He sent his results to Priestley together with a covering letter.

"TO DR. PRIESTLEY

SIR, Birmingham.

March 28, 1782

I NOW send you the results of my examination of the Toadstone and Rowley-ragstone, being part of a plan I have long since formed for a chemical analysis of all substances that are known to exist in the earth in large quantity.

Some years ago I transmitted to the Royal Society an analysis of the different marles found in Staffordshire, which they did me the honour to insert in their Transactions; if they think these papers likewise worth their adoption, I shall send them the results of my future enquiries.

In the course of experiments which this subject has led me to, I found it convenient to form some new tables, and to enlarge some that were less completely formed before. These tables will be useful in other branches of chemical enquiry. One of them I subjoin to the present papers. The facts taken from Mr. MACQUER are marked with an M; those with the * are the consequence of my own experiments.

In order to save much repetition in future, it may not be amiss to mention, once for all, a few particulars in the conduct of these processes.

1st, By **water**, is always meant water distilled in glass vessels, or by means of a large tea refrigeratory in Mr. IRWIN'S method.

2dly, Only glass or china vessels are used in the liquid processes.

3dly, By a mortar I mean those excellent ones made by Mr. WEDGWOOD; or, as will be specified at the time, a steel mortar tempered so hard that it will bear the grinding of enamel in it without discolouration.

4thly, Filtres are never employed, it being found impossible to get the quantities accurate where they are used. The powdery parts are allowed to subside until the supernatant liquor becomes clear. This sometimes requires days or weeks; but I am ignorant of a better method. By giving the vessels a circular motion around their axes, I can greatly facilitate the subsiding of the solid contents. If the separating vessels are made like a common tart-dish, with a spreading border, the liquors may be poured off very near, without disturbing the sediments.

5thly, Phlogisticated alkaly means the vegetable fixed alkaly prepared by the deflagration of nitre and crystals of tartar dissolved in water, and boiled with Prussian blue in such quantity that it will not any longer precipitate an earth from an acid.

I remain, &c.

W. WITHERING"

Priestley, writing to Sir Joseph Banks Bart. F.R.S. from Birmingham, October 1st 1781, stated, "I have the pleasure to lay before you an analysis of two mineral substances by Dr. Withering of Birmingham, whose accuracy in processes of this kind will, I doubt not, give you and the members of the Royal Society, great satisfaction.

It may, perhaps, throw some additional light on the subject of these fossils to inform you, that the Rowley-rag appears, by its texture before and after fusion, and also by the quantity and quality of the air which it yields in fusion, to be the same thing with the basaltes with which you have favoured me from Scotland; and that the Toad-stone, treated in the same manner, appears (after the calcareous part has been dissolved out of it) to resemble some of the species of lava, except that it yields much more air. As Dr. WITHERING has sent specimens of the fossils in their natural state, I thought it might not be amiss to present along with them the **glassy substances** into which they are reduced by fusion.

I am, with the greatest respect, &c.

J. PRIESTLEY"

The paper was read to the society, of which Sir Joseph was now President, on May 16th, 1782.

"ROWLEY RAG

THE stone which is the subject of the following experiments forms a range of hills in the southern part of Staffordshire. The lime-stone rocks at Dudley bed up against it, and the coal comes up to the surface against the lime-stone. The highest part of the hills is near the village of Rowley. The summit has a craggy, broken appearance, and the fields on each side to a considerable distance are scattered over with large fragments of the rock, many of which are sunk in the ground. In a quarry near Dudley, where a pretty large opening has been made in order to get materials for mending the roads, the rock appears to be composed of masses of irregular rhomboidal figures: some of these masses inclose rounded pebbles of the same materials. At the distance of four, five, or six miles, as at Bilston, Willenhall, and Wednesbury, the Rag-stone is frequently found some feet below the surface in rhomboidal pieces, forming an horizontal bed of no great depth, and seldom of more than a few yards extent. Over the whole of this tract of country it is used to mend the roads, and lately has been carried to Birmingham to pave the streets. Some people fell it in powder, as a substitute for emery in cutting and polishing.

MORE OBVIOUS PROPERTIES

Its appearance dark grey, with numerous minute shining crystals. When exposed to the weather gets an ochry colour on the outside; strikes fire with steel; cuts glass; melts, though not easily, under the blow-pipe. Heated in an open fire becomes magnetic, and loses about 3 in 100 of its weight."

WW then proceeded to grind smashed up fragments in a Wedgwood china mortar (having weighed the mortar before and after the experiments, because he clearly reasoned that if it lost a substantial amount of weight, it could contaminate the rag-stone, and affect his results). Thereafter, he subjected the powder, after washing, to a series of experiments and weighings, from which he concluded:

"From these experiments it appears, that the Rowley-rag-stone consists of siliceous earth, clay, or earth of allum, and calx of iron. From the latter must be deducted $11\frac{1}{2}$ for the quantity of calciform iron, found by experiment to be contained in the quantity of phlogisticated alkaly made use of, and then the proportions in 100 parts of the stone will be these:

Pure siliceous earth	$47\frac{1}{2}$
Pure clay, free from fixable air	$32\frac{1}{2}$
Iron in a calciform state	20
	100

From this view of the component parts of this stone, it is not improbable, that it might advantageously be used as a flux for calcareous iron ores. The makers of iron are acquainted with such ores; but never could work them to advantage, for want of a cheap and efficacious flux."

With regard to the toadstone:

"TOADSTONE

FROM Derbyshire; sent to me by Mr. WHITEHURST, who has so fully and so accurately described the mode of its stratification, that it is needless to enlarge upon that subject.

MORE OBVIOUS PROPERTIES

Of a dark brownish grey, a granulated texture; with several cavities filled with crystallized spar. It does not strike fire with steel. It melts to a black glass."

As for the rag-stone, WW subjected the ground up powder to a series of experiments, from which he concluded:

"Hence it appears, that 100 parts of this specimen of Toad-stone contained

C.	Siliceous	earth	56
H.	More ditto		$^7/_{10}$ = $63^5/_{10}$
D.	Calciform	iron	16
F.K.	Calcareous	earth	$7^5/_{10}$
G.H.	Earth of	allum	$14^8/_{10}$
			$101^8/_{10}$

From the addition of 13/10 of weight it is probable, that the substances capable of uniting with fixable air were not in the specimen used fully saturated with it, as they would be after their precipitation by the mild alkaly.

Upon repeating these experiments with different portions of the Toadstone, the quantities of the calcareous earth were found to differ a little; but nothing further appeared to invalidate the general conclusions."

Rag stones are also used for honing tools and abrading steel. The commonest variety is sandstone, next ragstone which gives a much finer edge.

In 1783 WW published an annotated translation of the "Sciagraphia regni mineralis" of Sir Torbern Bergman, titled "Outlines of Mineralogy." WW's additions included new mineral species, a table of metals, an index and other notes. He corrected Bergman's definition of salts, substituting that of Cullen (his erstwhile Edinburgh teacher), also on the difference between Devonshire pipe clay and that used in porcelain manufacture, on the difference between amber and ambergris (of which the latter had been stated by a Dr. Swediaur, in a presentation to the Royal Society, to be composed of the indurated faeces of whales, since it contained cuttlefish beaks). A new mineral from Anglesey which WW differentiated as lead sulphate but on account of a faulty analysis did not receive recognition, instead was later named "Anglesite" by Beudant 33 years after WW's death. Bergman went on to state that "terra ponderosa united to the aerial acid has not yet been found." WW's annotation here is significant and says, "I have lately discovered a specimen of terra ponderosa aerata got out of a mine in this kingdom. It is very fine and in a large mass. As this substance is a new acquisition to mineralogy and may be turned to useful purposes in Chemistry, I intend shortly to present a more particular account to the Royal Society. W.' This was the first announcement that WW had differentiated 'terra ponderosa aerata' (barium carbonate), from 'terra ponderosa vitriolata' (barium sulphate). The following year, on April 22nd 1784, sponsored by Richard Kirwan, an Irish mineralogist, WW read his paper titled 'Experiments and Observations on the Terra Ponderosa' to the Royal Society. A sponsor was required since WW was not yet a Fellow. However he was duly elected the following year. He described its properties and the methodology used in his quantitative analysis. In the following discussion, he indicated that marine acid (hydrochloric acid) when contaminated with vitriolic acid (sulphuric acid), could by means of the salt of terra ponderosa (barium chloride), be purified as a consequence of the precipitation of barium sulphate.

'Whether we use the terra ponderosa dissolved in water or as marine acid; in either case the acid of the vitriol immediately seizes upon it and subsides with it on form of an insoluble powder.' This test for sulphates was credited to WW by Fowles. (Fowles G., quoted by Roddis LH; 'William Withering, the Introduction of Digitalis into Medical Practice'. New York, Paul B. Hoeber, 1936). The name 'Witherite' was given to barium carbonate, by the celebrated German mineralogist, A.G. Werner. The first illustration of crystalline barium carbonate, with the appellation 'carbonate of barytes' appeared in Sowerby's 'British Mineralogy or Coloured Figures Intended to Elucidate the Mineralogy of Great Britain', volume one (of five). (Sowerby J., 'British Mineralogy,' or Coloured Figures Intended to Elucidate the Mineralogy of Great Britain. Vol.1, London, 1804.)

Barium carbonate crystals – "Witherite"
(With kind permission of the Department of Geology, University of Leicester).

Witherite occurs as a low-temperature mineral in hydrothermal vein deposits. It occurs in the United States as large crystals at the Minerva no. 1 mine at Rosiclare, Illinois; in Kentucky, Montana, Arizona and California. It is also found in the north of England, and superb crystal groups occur near Hexham, Northumberland, as well as Cumberland, and Durham.

Withering's position in mineralogy has been critically reviewed by Zeman, in his address to the American Association of the History of Medicine, given at the 23rd annual meeting in Boston on May 22nd, 1950:

"Withering is an outstanding example of the eighteenth century scientist, often a physician, occasionally a gifted amateur, whose keen intelligence led to observation, analysis, and theorizing as to the basis of all kinds of natural phenomena, unimpeded by the barriers set up by increasing specialization in the first half of the next century. Today, trained as we have been not to poach upon the sacred preserves of other scientific disciplines, we cannot but marvel at the broad attainments of Withering, at the intensity of his curiosity, and at his expertness in diverse fields, all the while carrying on an extensive medical practice. Nor, in view of the foregoing, is it surprising that the fundamental observations of *An Account of the Foxglove* have never been contradicted and that increasing knowledge has confirmed rather than overthrown the opinions expressed in this masterpiece of clinical research. Looking back over one hundred and fifty years we see in William Withering the embodiment of our present-day ideal, the physician who is equally at home in the laboratory and at the bedside."

Appendix (i)

WILLIAM WITHERING: CHRONOLOGY
OF MAJOR EVENTS IN WITHERING'S LIFE, AND GENEALOGY

17-3-1741 Birth of William Withering, in Wellington, Shropshire. Baptized 13th April 1742

12-2-1750 Birth of younger sister, Sarah

1758 Apprenticeship - probably to his uncle, Dr.Brooke Hector, a surgeon at Lichfield, or possibly to his father 'Apothecary and Surgeon' at Wellington

1762 Matriculated at Edinburgh University Medical School

1766 Graduated, MD at Edinburgh. His dissertation was titled - "De Angina Gangraenosa"

1767 Commenced practice at Stafford Royal Infirmary. Met Helena Cookes

1769 Edmund, Withering's father, died of contagious fever, buried 7th November

1772 Married Helena Cookes, 12th September, in Stafford

1775 Moved to Birmingham, worked at the General Hospital. Member of the Lunar Society. First child, born 1775, died 10th March 1776.

1776 Published "Botanical Arrangement of all the vegetables naturally growing in Great Britain" (The Botany). Developed symptoms of TB. A son (William) was born

1778 Outbreak of scarlet fever in Birmingham. Daughter (Charlotte) born

1779 "An Account of the Scarlet Fever….." was published. Appointed Honorary Physician at the General Hospital in September.

1781 Involved in a carriage accident, fractured his clavicle and suffered concussion. At this time was involved with the Gresely case.

1783 Very ill with TB (self diagnosed)

1784   Discovered barium carbonate, which he differentiated from barium sulphate. Later, this was named 'Witherite'.

1785   Elected Fellow of the Royal Society (FRS), 8th July. Published 'An Account of the Foxglove,' the work for which he is best known.

1786   Took lease on Edgbaston Hall (now Edgbaston Golf Club), from Sir Henry Calthorpe

1787   'The Botany' appeared in its second edition. Was elected to the London Medical Society. **Witheringia solanacea** was named after him by L'Heritier de Brutelle.

1788   The debacle with Robert Darwin in the Houlston case

1789   Fellowship of the Linnean Society. His mother died on the 3rd July.

1791   July; the Birmingham riots. Joseph Priestley's house at Fairhill (now Sparkbrook), destroyed.

1792   Famous portrait by Carl Frederik von Breda. Third edition of the 'Botany'. June- resigned as physician from the General Hospital on account of ill health. Travelled to Portugal for the winter.

1793   Again spent winter in Portugal. Analysed the chemical content of the waters at Caldas da Rainha. 2nd edition of the account of the scarlet fever.

1795   Elected Foreign Corresponding Member of the Portuguese Academy of Science

1799   Moved to 'The Larches' in Fairhill (Larches Road still exists at Sparkbrook).

Died after a few days, on 6th October. Entombed at Edgbaston Old Church, in the close vicinity of Edgbaston Hall, 10th October.

GENEALOGY OF WILLIAM WITHERING
(from Peck & Wilkinson)

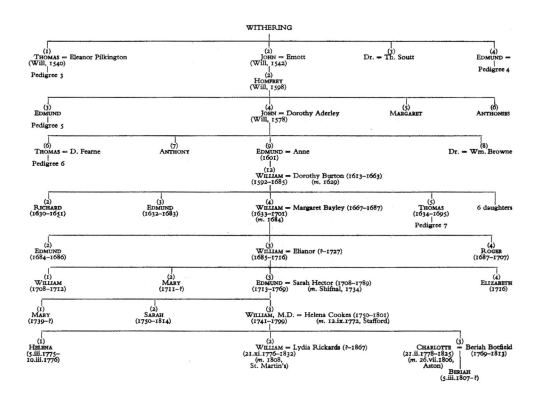

Appendix (ii)

WILLIAM WITHERING'S MD THESIS

UNIVERSITY OF EDINBURGH, 1766.
Translated from Latin by Prof. Charles D. O'Malley

"AN INAUGURAL MEDICAL DISSERTATION
CONCERNING GANGRENOUS ANGINA

which with the Approval of Divine Power and on the Authority of the Very Reverend Man, William Robertson, S.S.T.P, Prefect of the University of Edinburgh, as well as with the Consent of the greatly esteemed Senate of the University and by the Decree of the very noble Faculty of Medicine is presented for the consideration of the learned for the Degree of Doctor and in pursuance properly and lawfully of the Highest Honours and Privileges in Medicine by William Withering, Englishman, on the 31st day of July, at the accustomed hour and place.

.....heavily falls the breast
Blinded are the eyes
Strength is lacking and scarcely does the
voice escape the throat
Anti-Lucret. Bk.V.

Edinburgh
Auld & Smellie, Printers
M D CC LXVI

In greatest honour of my uncle, a truly learned man, greatly distinguished by the liberal arts: Brooke Hector of Lichfield, M.D.

for the sake of his very friendly regard by which he has always encouraged me and my studies. As well as the very reverend man Henry Wood, Promoter of humane letters, most faithful preceptor, very sedulous protector of youthful years, very liberal and friendly Counsellor: for the very best advice in the pursuit of studies and countless kindnesses offered to me, I wish this Medical Dissertation to be the record of a grateful mind.

William Withering

A Medical Dissertation Concerning Gangrenous Angina

Of the various sorts of angina of which accounts have been given, none requires the aid of medicine more than that of which it is my intention to present a brief account. I have the more readily believed that the task ought to be undertaken because this disease, although almost entirely unknown to our forbears, has occurred in our times, as well as a few years before, in many regions of Britain. Moreover, before its nature was explained by those very distinguished men, Fothergill, and after him, Huxham, the disease had killed many of its unfortunate victims, although whether through error or because physicians paid little attention to it.

Aretaeus, the most ancient writer on this disease, called it Egyptian or Syriac ulcers.[1] Later writers gave it now one name, now another, of which these are the most common: Crusted and pestilential ulcers of the tonsils;[2] pestiferous ulcers in the tonsils;[3] Epidemic angina; Pestiferous, malignant and contagious epidemic angina;[4] Strangling and lethal ulcers of the pharynx and throat;[5] Pestilential angina;[6] Garrotillo;[7] Epidemic angina of children;[8] Epidemic Neapolitan angina;[9] Crusted fever;[10] Suffocating affection, Strangling carbuncle, Strangling phlegmon, Pestilential and child strangling abscess disease of the throat, Pestilential tonsils, Malignant aphthae, Strangling disease, Noose of the throat, Epidemic plague of the throat;[11] Gangrenous angina;[12] Sore throat attended with ulcers;[13] Malignant ulcerous sore throat;[14] Pelham sore throat; Cancerous angina.[15] These names, however much they differ, all denote the same disease. For although they may seem to differ in certain things, yet those differences ought to be regarded as based upon the different nature of regions, different kinds of diet and different opinions and ways of speaking among mankind, rather than to the nature of the disease itself, since the important indications are always the same.

DEFINITION

There is nothing more desirable in the arts, or in any part of the discipline of letters, than that he who is about to present in literary form anything worthy of consideration should be able, on the threshold of the work, to encompass it in a few words and disclose to others what its nature is. But since our present knowledge is uncertain and as yet inconclusive, the definition of the problem, always difficult to present, often cannot be completely accomplished. Furthermore, while such definition is of use to the art of medicine, yet the most highly skilled and learned authors and professors often dare not even attempt this difficult thing; wherefore much less should I hope that I will achieve a successful result in a matter of such difficulty. Hence, since it is necessary that diseases be distinguished one from another by certain signs and differences, yet, if we err in defining "Inflammation of the surface of the pharynx very frequently attended as well by ulcers and contagious putrid fever," I do not doubt that the readers will grant me their indulgence.

AN ACCOUNT OF THE DISEASE

Gangrenous angina usually occurs before middle age. It begins with lassitude and dizziness such as usually precede faintness; then to this succeed a slight chill and shivering which soon give place to high fever. Thus chills and fever alternately succeed one another for several hours until finally the fevers conquer. Acute headache is felt and in some who are affected gravely, pain in the back and joints as well. A degree of plenitude is perceived, and in the sicker patients more than merely a soreness of the throat. The patient coughs a little and becomes a little stiff; the muscles of the neck and shoulders, when they are frequently moved, are sore; inquietude and an inexplicable anxiety, faintness, heaviness around the diaphragm and frequent sighs are complained of. Nausea, vomiting, and diarrhoea torment the patient, but in children vomiting and bowel movements occur more often, and often simultaneously. In many, the face becomes flushed and swollen, but in some, pallid and drawn. The eyes appear dull, bloodshot, and moist as from weeping. In a few hours after the onset of the disease, and in some directly from the beginning, the uvula and tonsils are observed to be swollen and inflamed. Those parts, such as the soft palate, each buccal cavity near the entrance to the pharynx, or rather the rear of the pharynx, become very reddish, or may possibly be of a scarlet colour. Through the uvula, tonsils, soft palate, and the rear of the pharynx many whitish or ashen spots are distributed, of which the bordering areas become reddish. These spots are often of great number and size, although in some patients they are otherwise, whether you inspect the number, size, or finally their position. The parotid glands and those of the jaws are much swollen, hardened, and painful to the touch. The face, neck, chest, arms, and hands frequently take on the colour, more or less, of erysipelas (i.e.reddish) and become swollen. Through the same places very reddish, narrow, lentil-like bodies appear, whereupon the nausea almost immediately ends and the vomiting and diarrhoea come to a halt. The end of the tongue is whitish and moist, and thick, yellowish, or brownish crust covers the posterior part. There is not much thirst, but the patient complains of a putrid odour in the throat and nostrils; breathing is bothered by those things present. The interior of the tonsils becomes very reddish or almost livid; or very often blood flows from the nostrils, from the mouth, and in women, by no means rarely from the uterus. Yet the throat under consideration swallows things more easily than you might believe, and solid things descend through the throat less painfully than liquids. The skin is hot, dry, roughened, and covered with a mild sweat. At the onset of the disease the urine is palish and resembles the watery part of milk, and especially in many adult patients it issues forth in small quantities and of deep colour. In many the arteries have a weak and swift pulse; in some the beat is heavy and fluctuates. The blood is of a shiny, reddish colour, and when the thick part has been separated, it is a very yellowish serum. Feverishness is much increased at night, and delirium affects some in the evening. With daylight, sweat breaks forth and there is some alleviation; this usually occurs throughout the course of the disease.

With the advance of the disease, inquietude and anxiety, together with difficulty in swallowing, are much increased. For some are wakeful and tormented by constant frenzy, others lie so stupefied that although from time to time starting up they take no notice of it. With the curbing of the diarrhoea, they usually become constipated, although if the disease is severe the diarrhoea remains to the end. The face is swollen, yellowish and shiny, the neck very swollen and oedematous; the eyes appear to have lost their animated quality and take on the appearance of a dead glassiness. The crusts of the throat increasing in number and size run together and form a single, large one of darkish colour, or rather the surrounding parts now become more livid. The skin of many is covered with petechiae and purplish macules. Now the breath is bad and the odour intolerable. A thin discharge flows from the mouth and nostrils, and it is so sharp that it corrodes the parts which it touches and gives rise to blisters on the face, hands and arms of the patient as well as of the nurse. In children, sneezes, diarrhoea, griping, a false urge to defaecation, and corrosion of the nates and anus occur. There is a great amount of purulent matter, in some tinted with blood, in others completely livid and of loathesome odour. At this time breathing is much more difficult and is a stridulous rasp, the voice hoarse as if carried from the chest; the urine, more coloured, is yellowish as if mixed with bile. The arteries pulsate very swiftly and with a thin beat; in some the stroke is intermittent and completely irregular.

In young children the disease is almost completed in the space of five or six days. In adolescents, or those who have passed those years, sometimes death occurs on the second or third day, but some draw out their miserable life to the tenth or twelfth day.

INSPECTION OF CADAVERS

The dissection and inspection of cadavers, which greatly assist disclosure of disease, lay bare things never suspected and illustrate on a more solid foundation the knowledge of causes, places, and our reasons and considerations. Hitherto it has been too much neglected. And even now although much has been essayed, yet more remains which must be attempted and investigated. It is regrettable that in what pertains to this disease, the keen ability of Morgagni is not available for careful exploration of the interior parts of all the cadavers.

Since public cadavers were lacking and since some private ones had been obtained by that very capable, learned, and especially lovable youth, my friend Nooth"* "who seeks with me the laureate of medicine, I shall present those things which have been observed in two dissected cadavers."

(*Nooth is listed as a co-graduand, see page 22)

"A woman in the space of three months after parturition was involved in gangrenous angina; with the advance of the disease, exanthemata appeared on her chest; her bowel yielded a slimy substance, with griping; on the eighth day she died. When the cadaver was opened, the membrane lining the pharynx and superior part of the oesophagus was found to be thicker than normal and strewn with crusts of tawny colour. These were easily removed and the underlying parts appeared eaten away just as if something had been removed from there. The pharynx had lost the reddishness which it possessed when she was alive. The interior membrane of the larynx was thicker than usual and more reddish, and the stomach and intestines contained slimy matter. Around the throat the lymphatic glands were enlarged, but the salivary glands under the tongue seemed not at all affected. The lymphatic gland situated immediately above the extension of the parotid was greatly swollen, but the parotid gland itself, not at all. Hence the swellings which were thought to have arisen from the affections of the parotid and salivary glands in the jaws were, in truth, of the lymphatic glands, and affected because they received the sharp matter from the ulcers of the pharynx. It is probable then that the salivary glands are affected only by the remaining swollen parts. It seems desirable to add to what has been said above, that upon the removal of fourteen ounces of blood, this woman's arteries had fluttered very weakly; but her strength was wholly broken, and although assistance normally very helpful was employed, she was unable to regain her former strength and health.

Likewise a youth, a boy, five years old, died of this disease, and when the cadaver was examined, it displayed a much thickened membrane lining the pharynx, not encrusted, but with ulcers and livid macules creeping through and covering a large part of the oesophagus, the larynx free of the disease, and the pituitous membrane of the nose remarkably swollen. This boy when alive had lacked exanthemata; but the bowel having been loosened, he was distressed through the whole course of the disease.

In certain cadavers dissected by our distinguished Monro the Father, the interior part of the larynx was found to be lined by such sort of tunic as occurs in stridulous suffocation. This, to be sure, does not occur in all, and the cadavers of those who were so affected when alive breathed during the time of the disease in the manner of those affected by stridulous suffocation.[16]

Also it can happen that gangrenous angina and stridulous suffocation produce the same at the same time. And the more so since the distinguished Whytt who recently taught medicine in this university, demonstrated that, in addition to stridulous suffocation with inflammation, another species of the same disease occurs at the same time, which he called putrid and malignant.[17] To be sure, these species are scarcely ever conjoined in the southern part of England, for Huxham testifies that not even once has he perceived in gangrenous angina that acute barking sound which is often heard in angina with inflammation.[18]

OF EXANTHEMATA

Frequently on the second or third day of the disease a great quantity of pustules which Greek are called ἐξανθ'ηματα arise throughout the upper portions of the body. The back of the neck, neck, chest, arms, and hands are of reddish colour and have a certain degree of swelling, and through these parts many papules, small and more reddish than the surrounding parts, are scattered. The same things occur larger in those patients and in those same parts where the reddishness is less.[19] In some they are very conspicuous, but in others they are so small that they are realized more by touch than by sight. If the swelling is great, the arms, hands, and fingers become stiff and slightly painful.[20]

Reddishness and exanthemata constantly remain on the surface of the skin not so much at this stage of the gangrenous angina as when it appeared.[21] For in some, the exanthemata mark the skin before the angina, but very severe angina attacks others, especially adult patients, without exanthemata. These thereafter convalescing are afflicted with severe itching and abscesses of the epidermis (cuticula).[22]

The pustules of this disease, when Ramazzini first observed it, were so noticeable that he thereafter called it crusted fever, and it may be learned from that author that their surface, just as now, varied in appearance.[23]

Indeed, in Italy they were often completely absent, which is very probable since many Italian writers make no mention of them.

PROGNOSIS

After the end of the first day of the disease some are convalescent. In many the following signs of health appear on the third, fourth, or finally fifth day: remittance of excessive faintness, which is a favourable omen; gradually the reddishness of the surface of the skin decreases; the fever is lessened and a gentle, light sweat breaks forth equally through all the members; the arteries pulsate more slowly, strongly, and evenly, and breathing is gentler and easier; some quality of animation and firmness returns to the eyes;[24] the crusts of the pharynx gently and mildly disappear, and the clean, florid ulcers seem to turn into flesh; the soft swelling of the neck decreases; sleep is not disturbed, wakefulness is tranquil, and the appetite returns. The urine is turbid, and in it is a sediment in the form of meal. The diarrhoea ends a little earlier. Some expectorate much from the chest, others very little or not at all. Exanthemata appearing swiftly and speedily frequently promise a joyous conclusion; and the more so if a considerable peeling of the epidermis (cuticula) follows.

On the other hand, with rigor supervening, and the exanthemata either suddenly vanishing or turning to a darkish and livid colour; the pulse of the arteries very slight, swift, agitated and uneven; the skin hot with dryness, breathing more difficult; continued anxiety; the pharynx very reddish, nearly livid, and drying with a kind of sheen signify that the affliction has become highly perilous. Truly, dull and opaque eyes; pallid and limpid urine; approaching frenzy or coma, with stupor of the countenance and sweat in the extremities; danger of gasping or suffocation; and with this a particular kind of convulsion of the muscles of the throat; sudden relaxing of the bowel, producing a kind of liquid matter of foul odour in the patient; the back of the neck, neck, and countenance turgid as if inflated, and appearing cadaverous, the whole body gently swelling - all declare the approach of death.

The age of childhood usually suffers more than the older in this disease. For in addition to the fact that suitable remedies cannot be administered to children, because they do not understand that acrid things and crusts separating from the throat should be coughed up, and these having been swallowed, corrode the stomach and intestines; likewise, the sickness of the whole body, the gripings, inflammation, gangrene, and blood slime which greatly corrodes, and the odours of the bowel, which are very foul, cause them great suffering.

PREDISPOSING CAUSES

Patients who have loose and humid bodily constitutions are more endangered by gangrenous angina than others,[25] children more than adults,[26] girls more than boys, women more than men and those usually suffering from other diseases more than the robust and healthy.[27]

Whatever things weaken the body, in that way expose it to this disease; these are grief,[28] humours immoderately excreted,[29] and similar things. In addition to the weakening of the strength, the following affect the humours by sharp putridity and are very potent for the disease: putrid fevers,[30] smallpox,[31] scurvy, and dysentery.[32] Finally, angina with inflammation makes a pathway for gangrenous angina. For lately with a disease incipient, within two or three days the nature of it has been changed in almost all the indications of it, and by no means rarely it is observed to end as this one.

OPPORTUNE CAUSES

Special causes directly arousing disease are recounted by writers as a rainy and hot region,[33] southerly winds,[34] and dampness of places.[35] These act perhaps in a double way; for they can be joined with the causes mentioned above and cause the disease, or remaining for a long time, and affecting the body badly, finally render it suitable for this disease. But since I have already spoken above of this action, now I shall speak only of the latter. Aretaeus, when he saw that beyond other disease gangrenous angina attacked Egyptians,[36] conjectured that this occurred because they fed on roots, vegetables, and pungent shoots and obtained their drinking water from the Nile. I do not completely agree with this conjecture; truly, unless I am deceived, the reason must very probably be drawn from the particular site of the region, suffering the inundations of the Nile, so that the natives are carried off by the vapours thus produced, and by the heat of the region, by the river regaining its channel, and by the stinking of what is exposed. This man deserving the very best from the fosterers of medicine, and among the most diligent, considered the dry air as a cause; yet I believe that for once he fell into error, for it ought not to be believed that the air of such a hot region with so great a land surface, so often and so long stagnant, could be dry.

IMMEDIATE CAUSE

In all the evidence which appears in this disease, I agree with the distinguished man Fothergill that the immediate cause of it is the putrid slime, or as he says "its miasma." But whether the seed of this disease originates within the conjoined action of antecedent causes, whether it is carried from some bodies to others by touch or by some medium, is a question difficult to investigate. I shall speak a little of this when first I have investigated what will be very worthy of note, whether or not gangrenous angina is contagious. And since the matter has been based on the diligent and faithful observations of those who are experienced in observing this thing, I shall combine their testimonies into one. Severinus says[37] "What pertains to contagion is comprised in this common agreement of all as well as being approved by reason." Zacutus Lusitanus says "In those parts (that is to say, the pharynx) carbuncular inflammations arise from the virulent fluxion of the humour which in the form of a fearful pestilence, or a very quick poison, seizes upon children and adults by a kind of contagion and, attended by severe and very evil symptoms, usually brings very swift death."[38] These are the words of Moreau: "Those who depart along separate paths will agree on one point, that is, it is a pernicious affection, both epidemic and contagious."[39] Wedelius states: "Infantile angina is contagious."[40] When to these the testimony of Fothergill[41] and Wall[42] is added, it will by no means be doubted that gangrenous angina is contagious.

There remains another question to be investigated in the same way: that is, whether this disease is transferred from some bodies to others by touch, or by an interposed medium? Mercatus asserts that either of these things can occur, whose testimony is written below: "Remarkable to say! there was a fearful condition of the humour, so pernicious, powerful and contagious, that it stung the index finger of a father, with which he extracted that humour from the mouth of his son, and it became reddish and painful; thereafter the father complained of difficulty in breathing and swallowing, with pain and swelling of the pharynx, and its colour deepened and glands appeared outward near the chin. From these things on the second day his expelled breath had a foul odour, so that you can rightly gather that the father had been affected by the contagion of the son."[43]

Anyone who has received only the breath of one suffering from this disease will certainly have to confess that as far as he is concerned, the contagion can be transmitted through the air into neighbouring bodies. Dr. Fothergill testified that when this disease arises in a family, unless the healthy are moved away from the sick, it goes through all the children; and also of those of adult years who spend much time among them, and receive the exhalation of a nearby breath, few escape the sickness in some degree. Likewise, he judged that thing to occur because "the putrid virus or its miasma through contagion penetrated into the body."

DIAGNOSIS

Since I have already defined what gangrenous angina is, it may seem of no value to explain the certain differences which distinguish it from other diseases, which in Greek is called διαγνοσιν. But although a definition may briefly do the same thing, yet it is often worthwhile to examine certain special things and discuss at greater length in what ways the disease which you are considering differs from others close to it, and in what ways it agrees. Therefore as there are three ailments similar to this, aphthae, angina accompanied by inflammation, and lues venerea, I shall demonstrate in order some signs by which they are distinguished from gangrenous angina. No noxious thing infests the pharynx more similar to gangrenous angina than aphthae, for common causes give rise to both, many affections are common to both, and the method of treatment is not dissimilar. These are the distinctions: the ulcers of gangrenous angina are contained in the pharynx, tonsils, soft palate and uvula; on the other hand, aphthae affect not only the pharynx, oesophagus, and those things nearest to them, but attack the interior of the cheeks, the gums, palate, and tongue.[44] The ulcers of the former creep laterally and are of unequal shapes; the latter appear small and round,[45] and sometimes lack fever. On the other hand, gangrenous angina always has fever,[46] and it is contagious; apthae are not contagious. The former in colour more or less resembles erysipelas; in the latter no such colour is observed. More distinctions could be presented if more were required.

Since it is very important from the beginning to distinguish gangrenous angina from that which has inflammation, I shall attempt to gather and indicate those signs in which there is some difference. A common shivering is found at the first onset of each, which is incorrectly called by many "bristling of the hair"; in gangrenous angina it is suddenly replaced by fever. The greatest anxiety, faintness, heaviness around the diaphragm, sighs, unusual lassitude, and loss of spirits are special to it. In angina with inflammation, the arteries pulsate rapidly, fully and strongly; in gangrenous, likewise rapidly, but feebly and unevenly. In the former the swelling of the pharynx is great, and the colour similar to phlegmonic inflammations; in the latter the swelling increases more slowly and is very scarlet in colour which is such a noteworthy indication that he who has once seen gangrenous angina, thereafter only briefly seen, cannot fail to know it. Angina accompanied by inflammation has acute and pulsating pain of the pharynx; in gangrenous, not so much pain as fever and illness are felt. The latter begins with vomiting and frequent bowel movements, the former, never. Finally, when the ulcers appear, then at last the nature of the illness is sufficiently apparent, and doubt is no longer possible. But the mouth and throat must always be gargled before the physician inspects them. When this had not been done, I myself saw the mucus covering the tonsils and the pillars considered to be the crusts of ulcers. Finally, he will hold complete distinctions of each who considers that angina which has inflammation assails those who are healthy, flourishing and robust; the gangrenous, those who are invalids, weak, infirm, women rather than men, and children than both; that one without contagion strikes in spring; that with it, more in autumn.[47]

Lues venerea, which sometimes attacks the throat with small ulcers, alone of other diseases may be mistaken for gangrenous angina, and the similarity between the two affections supports this error. If the patient talks much to the physician, as often occurs, he hides the true cause from him; the latter will consider that lues venerea has a minimum of inflammation of the throat; through this the ulceration proceeds more slowly, and the putrid fever always associated with the gangrenous angina is absent.

ADVICE ON TREATMENT

Whatever things ought to be done in treatment can be referred to some one of these things; first, that the oppressive indications be alleviated; then that the sharp matter be gently expelled; then, that the strength of the patient be preserved; and finally, the remains of the disease removed. Of these common advices I shall consider the method so that I may follow the order of the affections as they display themselves, and thus I shall teach the remedies as proper for the physician attending the patient.

Therefore, with the onset of the disease, if the patient is nauseated or desires to vomit, it will be necessary that this desire be assisted for the sake of gentle vomiting, by an infusion of green tea, centaurea benedicta, matricaria (**flores Chammaemeli**), or a few grains of ipecac. For thus that suffering is best relieved, and anxiety and depression much alleviated. If after vomiting nausea, anxiety, and heaviness around the diaphragm remain, frequent potions of infused mint to which has been added a little port wine or that which is called Claret should be given, more or less according to the age and nature of the patient and the severity of the affections. Likewise a saline draught may be given with a cardiac confection each hour on the second, third, or fourth day. If the bowel is obstinate, a liquor of milk, salt and sugar, or a common concoction may be introduced into it. On the other hand, if the bowel is overactive, although nausea and suffering have been relieved, one must resort to Campeche wood, electuary of scordium, the decoction of Fracastoro, of Fuller, or a powder composed of bole with or without opium,[48] and of strength according to the affections. One or another of these remedies, according to the different nature of the disease, ought to be employed. But none is nicer than the powder composed of bole with an admixture of a little cinnamon water; none more potent than the decoction of Fracastoro. So long as only the pharynx is inflamed, the vapours of vinegar, myrrh and honey, mixed hot, and given each third or fourth hour will be enough. But as soon as macules appear, Peruvian bark must be called into assistance. Of the various preparations of it none is more suitable for the sufferers, or more efficacious for health, than the decoction; for the various tinctures of the bark have less power; powders often display harmfulness for the stomach; of the extracts, there is danger of the strength being lessened while they are being prepared, and unless they are prepared carefully, they do not possess all the strength of the medicine; the simple infusion has not yet been found to be beneficial in acute and dangerous diseases; small children who are unable to take the decoction often take the extract dissolved in a little cinnamon water. The vapours already mentioned must be introduced onto the throat; furthermore, often on this day it ought to be washed with tincture of roses or a medicament composed of a pectoral decoction, and honey, vinegar, and tincture of myrrh should be gargled. The distinguished Fothergill considered that a medicinal gargle ought to be injected through a siphon,[49] which precept the outstanding Pringle greatly praised.[50] If the swelling of the glands is very painful, it is useful to rub them twice a day with a volatile liniment. Around this period of the disease, it is by no means rare for blood to burst forth from the nostrils, mouth, or uterus. If this flow weakens the patient and the pulse of the arteries, as it usually does, as soon as possible it must be stemmed by giving elixir of vitriol, or tinctura Japonica with Peruvian bark, and by introducing the vapours of vinegar into the suffering part or placing upon it a linen thread which has been soaked in vinegar.

If the beginnings of the disease have been neglected, the strength of the patient having been consumed, or the spirits downcast, there is much aid in alexipharmaca with Peruvian bark, of which sort are powdered contrayerva and Virginia snake root and liberal use of port wine. When the flow of the bowel lasts longer than usual, and those things passed through it more corrosive than usual, so that the anus and nates having been corroded, produce great stress for the patient, mild applications for the distressed part, or more often viscous liquors introduced into the bowel, usually greatly alleviate the evil.

Vesicants have been given in aid of depressed spirits, and for opposing or employment against faintness; on the other hand Mercatus condemns their use,[51] and Ramazzini says "Vesicants seem more conducive to the estimation of the physician among the common people, lest anything had not been dared or attempted, than to the health of the sick."[52] If these things possess no common usefulness, perhaps they are beneficial for a soft swelling of the neck and the back of the neck, and ought to be applied across the throat.

From the beginning of the disease, the sufferer, as much as possible, ought to be kept in bed; for thus the troublesome heat of the skin is best tempered; the pores of the skin are kept open, and by a slight movement of the sweat profuse flow of the bowel is often blocked. Likewise, the bedroom ought to be airy, otherwise the patient will have to breathe in again and again the same putrid air, and those in attendance will be moving about in the greatest danger of the disease. His diet ought to be of sago, panade, broth in which either a fowl or beef has been boiled, whey separated out of milk by wine, and red wine diluted with hot water to which a roasted Seville orange is added. If, as is useful to many after the second or third day of the disease, the patient desires more sumptuous and savoury foods and much undiluted wine, it should not be denied him. And always, before he swallows foods or medicaments, it must be seen that the mouth has been washed out, and that he has gargled and that through the whole course of the disease that he expectorates saliva rather than swallows it.

After the crusts have been separated, the ulcers healed, the fever dissipated, and the epidermis (cuticula) begun to peel, the bowel ought to be purged with rhubarb, and this ought to be done again several days later. If the swelling of the glands does not decrease, they ought to be rubbed with a mercurial ointment and a few grains of calomel given with rhubarb. Finally, some have a poor convalescence, aversion to food, dullness of mind, a hectic fever rising and falling, melting sweats. When this is the case, a rural region should be sought, ass's milk drunk and tincture of Peruvian bark, or the same decocted, and elixir of vitriol, should be employed.

CONCERNING EVACUATIONS

To those things said above a few ought to be added on bloodletting and purgation of the bowel.

First, it is remarkable how much the force of opinion, contrary to the manifest testimony of the senses, removes men from the truth. For although it is not true that angina with inflammation may be better treated than by letting blood and purging the bowel, yet physicians discerning in gangrenous angina little difference from the other, after it had begun to rage through Europe, decided that it must be treated by the same remedies. And so they extracted blood, relaxed the bowel, and slew the sufferers! Nor yet, while they attributed this either to the violence of the disease, or aid brought too late, or believed enough of the humours to have perished, did they desist from their sad beginning and persevered in the deadly error. Not only men of former times, but also those who were and are of our age, have followed the same manner of treatment with the same harmfulness to the many as well as those things even less worthy of pardon. These have been ignored because it is useless and unpleasant to name them, and I shall cross over to a more pleasant subject and indicate those who removed such abominable error from our minds. Joannes Weyer was among the first who dared to assert that "Venesections cause more damage than usefulness to the sick"; nor did he permit any humour to be led forth except from the veins under the tongue.[53] Mercatus, only on the first day of the disease, "before the fluxion contained in the parts enters putridity, he permitted the vein to be opened." These are his further words; "For then, if you bring forth blood, you will do great harm (which is the reason that many physicians seeing this damage, decline to let blood); because the strength is greatly dissipated, and you will extract nothing of that humour which has putrefied, nor by revulsion," &c.[54] The learned and intelligent Severinus proposes "to combat" this disease "in its irregularity, not its excesses of plenitude."[55] Yet the same one, considering treatment, so departed from authority that he permits six or eight ounces of blood to be withdrawn "in whatever way the patient may bear it," adding this caution, that he "does not desire, of course, dejection of the strength and native vigour."[56] The ingenious and thorough Ramazzini said "the results of venesection are so unfortunate that all the sick are terrified as often as bloodletting is proposed."[57] If we read Fothergill, Huxham, and Wall, we shall find that extraction of humours has no more beneficial results in England than on the Continent. From all these it is clear that bloodletting and purgation of the bowel are often harmful and rarely beneficial.

Wherefore the correct conclusion seems to me to be that purgation of the bowel at the beginning of gangrenous angina is entirely unsuitable, and bloodletting is beneficial only in those in whom, at the beginning of the ailment, the swelling of the pharynx is so great that suffocation threatens; and even then only the veins under the tongue are to be opened.

REFERENCES

1. Aretaeus Cap. De causis et signis morb. c.9 p.7.
2. Aetius tetr.2 sermo 4. cap.46. p.397.
3. Paulus Aegineta De re med. lib. 3. cap. 26. p. 449.
4. Petri Foresti Observat. med.2 scholia, p. 190.
5. D. Ludov. Mercati oper. tom. 5. consult. 24, p. 134.
6. Joannis Wieri opera, p. 910.
7. Zacutus Lusitanus De praxi medica admiranda, lib. I, observ.92, p. 73.
8. Libello Thomae Bartholini De ang. pueror.
9. Thomae Bartholini Epist. med. cent. I. p. 340.
10. Bernard. Ramaz. Constit. epidem. obs. 17. p. 110.
11. Cortesii miscellanea medica, 696. Severin. et Moreau Epist. ad Th. Barth. De laryng.
12. Mead's Monita medica.
13. Fothergill's Account, & c.
14. Huxham's Dissertation.
15. Nova acta eruditorum, anno 1758.
16. "There ought to be added that which was found by the celebrated professor of anatomy and surgery, Roland Martin, in one of the victims of the epidemic which attacked Stockholm at that time. In the presence of and with the very eminent and learned assistance of the doctors Strandberg and Darelius of the Royal College of Medicine, he dissected a child which had died of this disease. He observed the trachea internally to be everywhere covered by a very thick membrane. It was found to be greyish and filled with putridity in that part of the tube where it adhered to the walls; the exterior, a bloody-purplish colour. In the bronchi concealed by the lung, the cartilages had made notable impressions in it. The farther he descended, the less reddish it was, and wholly whitish in the branches of the bronchi where it displayed the sort of membrane which internally lines the shell of an egg; and whenever it was extended it was able to be distinguished clearly from the special membrane of the bronchi. The lungs were not inflamed, nor injured in any way, so that it was clear that the child had died from suffocation." See Diss. med. inaug. de Angina Infantum, H.C.D. Wilcke, p. 6.
17. In Praelectionibus clinicis.
18. Huxh. diss. p. 280.
19. Foth. acc. p. 33.
20. Huxh. diss. p. 282.
21. Dr. Wall's letter. Gent. Mag. 1751. p. 499.
22. Huxh. diss. p. 281.
23. They were varied and of diverse colour, in accordance with the varied and diverse constitutions of the patients; some were red, others pallid, others of a darkish colour; some small, some broad, some raised, some flat so that one might observe them only by directing his gaze horizontally (i.e. across the plane of the area). This last kind of pustule was very ominous. Bern. Ramazz. constit. epidem. obs. 19. p. 111.

24. Aetius Cletus Signinus de morb. strangulat. cap. I, p. 6.
25. Severinus De recondita natura abscess. p. 547.
26. Aetius Cletus Signinus de morbo strangulatorio, cap. I. p. 6.
27. Foth. diss. p. 49. Aetii Tetr. 2. Sermo. 4. p. 398.
28. Idem. p. 43.
29. Idem.
30. Dr. Wall's letter. Gent. Mag. Ann. 1751. p. 501.
31. Idem.
32. Van Swieten comment. Para 811. p. 683.
33. Van Swiet. comment. Para 811. p. 683. Humid and hot air especially cause putrefaction; this ought to be understood also of humid and hot bodies (such sort as are infantile), of which the temper is harmed more than any others by putrefaction. Becher. Physica subterranea, I. i. Para 5.
34. Huxh. diss. p. 273. Foth. acc. p. 31.
35. Aret. Capp. cap. p. 7. Gent. mag. in the place sited above.
36. De causis et signis morborum, cap. 9. p. 7.
37. De recondita abscessuum natura, p. 530.
38. Zacut. Lusitan. De prax. med. admir. lib. I. obs. 92. p. 73.
39. Epist. R. Moreau ad calcem tractuli Thom. Barth. de Angina pueror. epidem. p. 128.
40. Wedelius De morbis infantuum, cap. 20. p. 77.
41. Foth. Acc. p. 71.
42. Gent. Mag. ann. 1751, p. 497.
43. Opera, tom. 5. consultat. 24. p. 139.
44. Boerhaavii Aphorism. Para 981.
45. Idem, Para 979.
46. Van Swiet. Commentat. Para 983. p. 201.
47. After the month of February the disease so desists that no one is any longer bothered by it. H.C.D. Wilcke De angina infantum, p. 6.
48. Foth.Account, p. 56.
49. Foth. Acc. p.66.
50. Even in the angina maligna, or ulcerous sore throat, I lay chief stress of the cure upon gargling in this manner. In all cases I direct five or six syringe-fulls to be injected, one after another, as far into the throat as the patient can bear, and to repeat the medicine three times a day. Diseases of the army, p. 143.
51. Opera tom. 5. consult. 24. p. 142.
52. Constit. epidem. obs. 30. p. 113.
53. Opera, p. 912.
54. Opera, tom. 5. p. 138.
54. De recond. abscess, natur. p. 539.
56. Idem, p. 542.
57. Const. epidem. p. 112.

Appendix (iii) (a)

WILLIAM WITHERING'S DESCRIPTION OF 156 CASES TREATED WITH DIGITALIS BY HIM BETWEEN 1775 AND 1784

The details given are part para-phrased, part quoted (where stated). Statements regarding the characteristics of the pulse are given following the description of the series of patients.

Abbreviations used. N=nausea, V=vomiting, D=diuresis UNK=unknown

CASE	SEX	AGE	PRESENTATION	N/V	D	OUTCOME
1775						
1	M	50	ASTHMA	+	+	IMPROVED
1776						
2	M	?	ANASARCA, ASCITES	-	+	IMPROVED
3	M	9	? ASCITES	-	+	IMPROVED
4	F	40-50	DYSPNOEA, COUGH IRREGULAR PULSE ORTHOPNOEA, OEDEMA	+	+	IMPROVED
5	F	35	ASCITES, ANASARCA 'INTEMPERATE LIVING'	+	+	IMPROVED
1777						
6	F	45	ASCITES, ANASARCA	?	?	DIED

(Didn't receive medication. Dried leaves finished, so fresh ones left. But too much snow, so the apothecary was not able to procure the fresh leaves)

CASE	SEX	AGE	PRESENTATION	N/V	D	OUTCOME
7	M	61	HYDROTHORAX, ASCITES ANASARCA, 'HARD DRINKER' (winter leaves used of uncertain strength)	+	+	DIED
8	F	32	POST-PARTUM SWELLING	?	+	CURED. RECURRED AFTER 5 WEEKS. AGAIN RESPONDED
9	M	47	ASTHMA, DROPSY	?	?	UNCHANGED
10	?	70	ASTHMA, ANASARCA	+	+	CURED
11	M	54	ASCITES, ANASARCA	+	+	CURED. RECURRED 1½ YEARS LATER NO RESPONSE
12	F	48	OVARIAN DROPSY	?	?	REDUCED ANASARCOUS SWELLINGS. ABDOMEN UNCHANGED
13	F	40	OVARIAN DROPSY	?	?	NO EFFECT

CASE	SEX	AGE	PRESENTATION	N/V	D	OUTCOME
1778						
14	M	?	JAUNDICE, ASCITES SWOLLEN LEGS & THIGHS	?	?	DIED
15	M	54	ASTHMA, DROPSY, PULSE VERY SMALL	?	?	RELIEF BUT SYMPTOMS RETURNED AND HE DIED THREE MONTHS LATER
16	M	33	PULMONARY CONSUMPTION & DROPSY	?	?	FAILED. DIED AFTER TWO MONTHS
17	F	50	OVARIAN DROPSY	?	+	INEFFECTIVE, RESPONDED TO TAPPING
18	?	33	ASCITES, ANASARCA	?	+	RESOLVED EXCEPT SLIGHT ANKLE OEDEMA (*urine output meticulously recorded*)
19	M	60	ASCITES, ANASARCA	+	+	NO EFFECT OTHER THAN TO MAKE HIM SICK
1779						
20	M	?	HYDROPS PECTORIS	?	+	RELAPSED AFTER THREE MONTHS. AGAIN RESPONDED
21	F	69	HYDROTHORAX, ASCITES, ANASARCA	+	+	VERY LANGUID RECURRENCES AFTER 5 AND 9 MONTHS. AGAIN RESPONDED
22	M	59	ASCITES, ANASARCA	?	?	PATIENT DIED SUDDENLY ON DAY 2. (Digitalis had been withheld pending WW's return. Drug not actually administered)

(*Comment by WW - "...how sudden and unexpected the death of dropsical patients sometimes happen, and how cautious we should be in assigning causes for effects."*)

CASE	SEX	AGE	PRESENTATION	N/V	D	OUTCOME
23	M	57	JAUNDICE, ASCITES	?	?	"Removed all his urgent symptoms and he recovered a pretty good state of health"
24	M	63	INSANITY, ORTHOPNOEA	+	+	RATIONAL, NOT ORTHOPNOEIC
25	M	50	DROPSY	?	?	DIED NEXT MORNING
26	F	30	POST-PARTUM OEDEMA	-	+	IMPROVED. SLIGHT RESIDUAL SWELLING
27	M	?	DEFORMED SPINE, THORAX DYSPNOEA	+	-	SOME RELIEF BY ABDOMINAL PARACENTESIS

(*4 months later, relief occurred after vomiting. This caused WW to repeat this when required some months afterwards, again with resulting benefit*)

CASE	SEX	AGE	PRESENTATION	N/V	D	OUTCOME
1780						
28	M	42	BROWNISH YELLOW EMACIATION, FULLNESS OF STOMACH,LEGS & THIGHS GREATLY SWOLLEN	-	+	"Ate a pretty good dinner. Next day suddenly stooped forward, from chair, died instantly"

(A sea captain, "drinking whilst conversing very freely, particularly rum in large quantity")

CASE	SEX	AGE	PRESENTATION	N/V	D	OUTCOME
29	M	63	WATER IN CHEST BELLY & LEGS, & GOUT	?	?	IMPROVED BUT RECURRED WITHIN 1 MONTH
30	M	50	ASCITES, ANASARCA SIGNS OF PHTHISIS	?	?	CURED DROPSY BUT DIED OF CONSUMPTION
31	F	?	POST-PARTUM. LEGS AND THIGHS SWOLLEN. PULSE SMALL & SLOW	-	+	RECOVERED PERFECTLY

(Had already been started on digitalis)

CASE	SEX	AGE	PRESENTATION	N/V	D	OUTCOME
32	M	70	STROKE SOME WEEKS BEFORE. DYSPNOEA, ANASARCA ASCITES, ORTHOPNOEA	+	+	RECOVERED. LIVED OVER 2 YEARS
33	F	5	HYDROCEPHALUS	?	?	NO EFFECT
34	F	?	POST-PARTUM INSANITY SWOLLEN LEGS, THIGHS AND BELLY	?	?	DROPSY & INSANITY DISAPPEARED
35	M	32	HYDROTHORAX RELAPSED 2 MONTHS LATER AGAIN RESPONDED	-	+	CURED
36	F	40	ASTHMA & EFFUSION	?	?	RELIEVED VERY CONSIDERABLY
37	?	12	SCROPHULAR CONSUMPTIVE ANASARCA, NAUSEA	+	-	DIED
38	F	49	ASCITES, ANASARCA	?	-	"Nearly removed the dropsy in a few days...died a few weeks later"

("..seen by another very celebrated physician")

CASE	SEX	AGE	PRESENTATION	N/V	D	OUTCOME
39	M	35	HAEMOPTYSIS,ASCITES ANASARCA, HEAVY DRINKER	?	-	DIED AFTER A FEW MONTHS
40	M	37	ASTHMA, GRADUALLY INCREASING OVER FOUR YEARS	?	+	BREATHING EASIER. DIED A YEAR LATER OF CONSUMPTION

CASE	SEX	AGE	PRESENTATION	N/V	D	OUTCOME
41	M	57	HYDROTHORAX, ANASARCA	?	?	NO APPEARANCE OF DISEASE WITHIN 7 DAYS
42	F	39	PHTHISIS PULMONALIS END STAGE	?	?	DIED
43	F	70	EXERTIONAL DYSPNOEA SWELLING OF LEGS 1 YEAR, FULLNESS OF STOMACH.RECEIVED 8 DOSES 1780-1782	-	+	WELL, BUT SYMPTOMS AND SIGNS RETURNED AND WERE AMENABLE TO TREATMENT ON ALL OCCASIONS. EVENTUALLY DIED,PROBABLY OF DIARRHOEA
44	M	60	DROPSY & "FREE LIVING"	-	?	NO RELIEF
45	M	49	HYDROTHORAX, ANASARCA	?	+	RESTORED TO HEALTH
46	M	35	ASCITES, ANASARCA	?	+*	REMOVED ALL TRACES OF DROPSY
47	F	86	ASTHMA, INCIPIENT ANASARCA	+	?	WELL
48	?	46	JAUNDICE, DROPSY HARDNESS IN THE LIVER REGION	-	+	"...carried off all the effusion"
49 (also case 23)	M	58	BLACKISH HUE PREVIOUSLY JAUNDICED DROPSY	-	-	DIED
50	M	39	ANASARCA, HYDROTHORAX "..consequent to a tertian ague.."	-	+	RECOVERED
51	M	27	ASCITES AND SWELLED LEGS, VERY FREE LIVING	-	+	RECOVERED WITHIN 6 DAYS
52	M	45	QUICK FEEBLE PULSE SALLOW COMPLEXION, EMACIATION IRREGULAR GOUT,OBSCURE DIAGNOSIS? LEAD POISONING DYSPNOEA, PALE SWELLING OF LEGS	?	?	EASED HIS BREATHING

(2 yrs. later, WW spoke to a pump maker who recalled having replaced the lead pump at this house 3 yrs previously because the lead was very thin and eaten away and full of holes)

CASE	SEX	AGE	PRESENTATION	N/V	D	OUTCOME
53	M	70	ASCITES, ANASARCA LEGS & THIGHS, DIMINISHED STRENGTH & APPETITE	?	-	NO GOOD EFFECT "..as had been prognosticated"

* presumed

CASE	SEX	AGE	PRESENTATION	N/V	D	OUTCOME
54	M	57	HYDROTHORAX, SWOLLEN LEGS	?	+	CURED
55	M	42	ALE DRINKER, DIMINISHED APPETITE, INCREASED SHORTNESS OF BREATH,TIGHTNESS OF ABDOMEN, SWOLLEN LEGS, PULSE SLENDER & FEEBLE	+	-	DIED
56	M	47	TERMINAL PHTHISIS DYSPNOEA, ANASARCA	?	?	PURGED, OPIUM HELPED OTHER SYMPTOMS EASED
57	F	53	EPILEPSY, SWOLLEN LEGS & THIGHS "..water in the abdomen"	?	+	RECOVERED, EPILEPSY CEASED
58	F	62	ASCITES, VERY HARD LEGS	?	-	DIED
59	F	53	ASCITES, ANASARCA JAUNDICE	?	+	DIED AFTER 1 MONTH
60	M	?	JAUNDICE, ASCITES GREAT INTEMPERANCE EMACIATION	?	?	FAILED, DIED
61	F	?	DROPSY, EMACIATION DROPSY ENCYSTED DIAGNOSED AS OVARIAN DROPSY	?	?	DIED
62	F	52	DROPSY	?	-	FAILED
63	F	47	LEGS SWOLLEN	?	+	CURED
64	M	?	PULMONARY CONSUMPTION END STAGE	?	-	NO GOOD EFFECT
65	M	63	ASTHMA, DROPSY JAUNDICE, ASCITES, ANASARCA	?	+	CURED
66	M	60	CORPULENT, BLADDER STONE, ASTHMA, FITS DYSPNOEA, ANASARCA, ASCITES ORTHOPNOEA	?	+	RESOLVED, RECURRENCE BUT RESPONDED TO REPEAT DIGITALIS INFUSION
67	M	57	ASTHMA. ANASARCA JAUNDICE, DROPSY, DYSPNOEA	?	+*	SYMPTOMS RESOLVED
68	F	42	PHTHISIS PULMONALIS ANASARCA LEGS & THIGHS	?	-	NO BENEFIT
69	M	6	HYDROCEPHALUS INTERNUS	?	+	RECOVERED
70	F	59	ASCITES, ANASARCA	?	+*	REMOVED THE DROPSY

* presumed

CASE	SEX	AGE	PRESENTATION	N/V	D	OUTCOME
71	M	48	SHORT OF BREATH LEGS SWOLLEN TOWARDS EVENING PASSED LITTLE URINE INTEMPERATE LIVING	?	+	CURED
72	M	50	ASCITES, ANASARCA JAUNDICE, INTEMPERATE LIVING	+	?	DIED 2 MONTHS LATER (treatment produced nausea and slow pulse)
73	M	60	ASTHMA, JAUNDICE DROPSY, HARD DRINKER	?	+	RESOLVED, BUT 6 MONTHS LATER DYSPNOEA RETURNED. NO RETURN OF ASCITES
74	M	58	JAUNDICE, ASCITES ANASARCA	?	+	DYSNOEA EASED. ABLE TO DESCEND STAIRS. LOSS OF APPETITE & JAUNDICE REMAINED. DIED 2 MONTHS LATER
75	F	46	MUCH DEFORMED, ASTHMA LEGS SWOLLEN, FULLNESS OF STOMACH, ORTHOPNOIEC (also received opium)	?	-	DIED 1 MONTH LATER
76	M	65	RETURN OF INSANITY (Same patient as case 24)	?	?	NO EFFECT
77	M	47	ASCITES, SWOLLEN LEGS	-	-*	LOWERED PULSE RATE, NEEDED TAPPING, DIED A FEW HOURS LATER
78	M	63	PAINFUL SWELLINGS IN LIMBS, BED-RIDDEN 6 MONTHS SWELLINGS WERE UNIFORM, TENSE & RESISTING SKIN NOT DISCOLOURED, NOT EASY TO SAY WHAT THE DISEASE WAS	?	+	OUTCOME NOT KNOWN BECAUSE PATIENT LIVED AT A DISTANCE
79	M	42	ASCITES & ANASARCA OF LEGS (Patient was "..a very sensible surgeon at B-, in Staffordshire")	+*	+	DROPSY REMOVED
80	F	42	ENLARGED LIVER	?	-	DIED (AUTOPSY DETAILS GIVEN)
81	M	33	DROPSY, LARGE BELLY GROSS SWELLING OF LEGS & THIGHS	?	+	RESOLVED WITHIN 10 DAYS

* presumed

CASE	SEX	AGE	PRESENTATION	N/V	D	OUTCOME
82 **1782**	M	49	ASTHMA, ANASARCA	?	+	RESOLVED WITHIN DAYS
83	M	74	DROPSY 3 MONTHS BLADDER STONE, DYSURIA	-	?	RESOLVED
84	M	86	DROPSY, DYSPNOEA ORTHOPNOEA, OLIGURIA	?	?	TEMPORARY RELIEF BUT DID NOT SURVIVE LONG
85	M	35	ASCITES, ANASARCA HAEMOPTYSIS (Publican, hard drinker)	?	+	RESOLVED
86	F	53	PALPITATIONS, ANASARCA OF LEGS	?	-	DIED AFTER 10 MONTHS
87	M	81	DYSPNOEA, ORTHOPNOEA SWOLLEN LEGS FOLLOWING SEVERE COLD AND COUGH	?	+*	RELIEVED AFTER 4 DAYS THEN TREATMENT STOPPED RECURRED IN 1 MONTH. AGAIN RESPONDED
88	F	67	CHRONIC LEG ULCERS RECENT DYSPNOEA FEEBLE PULSE	?	-	DIED AFTER 1 MONTH
89	M	73	UNIVERSAL DROPSY	?	-	NO GOOD EFFECT
90	M	10	EPILEPSY OF SOME YEARS CONTINUANCE	?	-*	NO BENEFIT AFTER SEVERAL YEARS
91	M	62	ASCITES, ANASARCA APPEARANCE OF A DISEASED LIVER (A hard drinker)	+	-	DIED
92	F	40	SPASMODIC ASTHMA MANY YEARS	?	?	WORSE
93	M	61	HEMIPLEGIA, DROPSY OF LEGS, THIGHS AND ARMS ON AFFECTED SIDE	?	+*	SWELLINGS GRADUALLY SUBSIDED
94	M	28	ASCITES, VERY LARGE LEGS, FULLNESS OF STOMACH (For 2 months had been under the care of a 'very celebrated physician')	?	+	RELIEVED GREATLY
95	F	36	PULMONARY CONSUMPTION LATE STAGE	?	?	NO BENEFIT
96	M	43	PERIPNEUMONY IN THE PREVIOUS YEAR, HYDROTHORAX	+	+	CURED
97	F	35	POST-PARTUM (3 MONTHS) SWOLLEN LEG	?	?	CURED

* presumed

CASE	SEX	AGE	PRESENTATION	N/V	D	OUTCOME
98	M	60	SICKNESS AFTER EATING & VOMITING, WEIGHT LOSS GOOD APPETITE, NAUSEA	?	?	IMPROVED, RECOVERED STRENGTH AND FLESH
99	F	38	HYDROTHORAX, ANASARCA DEFORMED CHEST	?	+*	CURED
100	M	47	HYDROTHORAX, ANASARCA	?	+*	"THIS PLAN SUCCEEDED PERFECTLY"
101	F	60	ASCITES, ANASARCA	?	?	NAUSEA, LANGUOR NO BENEFIT
102	M	41	LEGS & BELLY SWOLLEN DECREASED APPETITE COUNTENANCE YELLOW, COUGH (Publican, hard drinker)	?	+*	CURED WITHIN A WEEK JAUNDICE DISAPPEARED DIED SOON AFTERWARDS
103	M	39	DROPSY & RHEUMATIC PAINS	?	?	LEG SWELLING AND ABDOMINAL FULLNESS RESOLVED IN EIGHT DAYS "RHEUMATIC PAINS WERE CURED BY THE USUAL METHODS"
104	M	3	ASCITES & UNIVERSAL ANASARCA	?	+	CURED
105 (case 47)	M	88	AS IN CASE 47	?	?	CURED IN A SHORT TIME. RECURRED AFTER 17 MONTHS, HELPED BUT DIED, AGED 90
106	M	61	HYDROTHORAX & SWELLED LEGS. BREATHING BAD, PULSE FEEBLE, COLD EXTREMITIES	+	+	OBTAINED RELIEF BUT CONTINUED DOSING HIMSELF AFTER THE DIURESIS PULSE LESS THAN 40 PER MINUTE OBJECTS APPEARED GREEN RECOVERED AFTER 2 MONTHS
107 **1783**	M	7	ASCITES, ANASARCA	_	+*	PERFECT CURE
108	F	57	DROPSY FOR 2 MONTHS	?	?	NO BENEFIT AFTER 4 DAYS
109	F	72	ANASARCA LEGS & THIGHS REDUCED APPETITE, THIN	?	?	DIED AFTER A FEW WEEKS

* presumed

CASE	SEX	AGE	PRESENTATION	N/V	D	OUTCOME
110	F	?	"MARY BOWEN, OVARIAN DROPSY. A POOR GIRL AT HAGLEY"	?	?	NO EFFECT ON HER BIG BELLY, BUT OTHERWISE VERY WELL
111	M	28	PULMONARY CONSUMPTION END STAGE, SCROPHULOUS KIND	?	?	NO ADVANTAGE
112	M	27	LAST STAGE PHTHISIS PULMONALIS, DROPSY	?	?	NO BENEFIT
113	M	6	UNIVERSAL ANASARCA COUGH	?	?	DROPSY CURED,COUGH CONTINUED. DIED TABID SOME WEEKS AFTER
114	F	28	DROPSY, LATE STAGE PHTHISIS	?	?	NO BENEFIT
115	F	46	ANASARCA, ORTHOPNOEA	-	+	SYMPTOMS CLEARED WITHIN A WEEK
116	F	40	PUERPERAL FEVER SWOLLEN LEGS & THIGHS	?	-	FEVER CONTINUED, THEN DIARRHOEA AND DEATH
117	M	48	DROPSY, DYSPNOEA, COUGH TOTAL LOSS OF APPETITE	?	-	DIED

(Digitalis prescribed late. WW did not expect it to work, based on previous cases of "tense fibre")

CASE	SEX	AGE	PRESENTATION	N/V	D	OUTCOME
118	M	47	PHTHIS PULMONALIS JAUNDICE, ASCITES, SWOLLEN LEGS, NAUSEA	?	+	LIFE PROLONGED A FEW WEEKS
119	F	60	ASCITES, ANASARCA PAUCITY OF URINE, TOTAL APPETITE LOSS	+	+	PATIENT TOOK DOUBLE THE PRESCRIBED DOSE AFTER INITIAL SUCCESS! BECAME LANGUID
120	F	36	FAINTNESS, ANASARCA DYSPNOEA, COUGH, CHILLS NIGHT SWEATS, DIARRHOEA	?	+	ALL COMPLAINTS WENT EXCEPT COUGH WHICH GRADUALLY DISAPPEARED

(WW was surprised at this success, because he thought the patient was probably suffering from TB)

CASE	SEX	AGE	PRESENTATION	N/V	D	OUTCOME
121	?	50	BELLY VERY TENSE SWOLLEN FLUCTUANT CIRCUMSCRIBED SWELLING PULSE 132	?	-	NEEDED TAPPING PULSE CAME DOWN TO 96 SWELLING RESOLVED

(This patient was under the care of WW's very worthy friend, Dr.Ash)

CASE	SEX	AGE	PRESENTATION	N/V	D	OUTCOME
122	M	43	GOUTY ATTACKS JAUNDICE, ASCITES, ANASARCA	?	+	DID NOT RECOVER

(WW considered that the jaundice associated with loss of appetite and diseased viscera made recovery impossible)

1784

CASE	SEX	AGE	PRESENTATION	N/V	D	OUTCOME
123	F	54	FULLNESS OF THE STOMACH SHORTNESS OF BREATH, COUGH, LOSS OF APPETITE, PAUCITY OF URINE, BROWNISH, YELLOW TINGE OF SKIN AND EYES	?	-	DIED
124	F	60	LOSS OF APPETITE DEBILITY, DIFFICULT COUGH SPUTUM, PAUCITY OF URINE	?	+	LESS SHORT OF BREATH SOME RETURN OF APPETITE LATER PURULENT SPUTUM AND DEATH WITHIN A FEW WEEKS
125	F	61	ASTHMA, PURULENT SPUTUM FEVER, SWOLLEN LEGS, DROPSY IN THE CHEST	?	?	GREAT RELIEF, APPETITE RETURNED. TRAVELLED ON 50 MILES TO HER HOME 1 MONTH LATER
126	M	59	ASTHMA, SWOLLEN LEGS ABDOMINAL FULLNESS, COUGH, DIMINISHED APPETITE, THIRST, REDUCED URINE OUTPUT, ORTHOPNOEA DROPSY IN THE CHEST	?	+	FREE FROM ALL COMPLAINTS BY DAY 10
127	F	8	AGUE, DROPSY, LARGE BELLY	?	?	DIMINISHED SWELLING OF APPETITE LOSS, NAUSEA BELLY SOON RESTORED TO HEALTH

(2 other children in the family had died, probably of the same cause. The parents were of the opinion that an ague in springtime was not to be stopped. WW felt that digitalis was a desperate remedy under the circumstances)

CASE	SEX	AGE	PRESENTATION	N/V	D	OUTCOME
128	M	45	EX-DRINKER, DIFFICULT BREATHING FOR 3 MONTHS SWOLLEN LEGS AND FULL BELLY, THIRST, NO APPETITE COMPLEXION BROWNISH YELLOW	?	+	ALL RESOLVED WITHIN 10-12 DAYS NO RELAPSE

CASE	SEX	AGE	PRESENTATION	N/V	D	OUTCOME
129	M	54	ASTHMA FOR YEARS INTERMITTENT PULSE	?	?	"THE EFFECT OF THIS PLAN WAS PERFECT TO OUR WISHES AND IN A SHORT TIME HE RECOVERED HIS USUAL HEALTH. ABOUT HALF A YEAR LATER HE DIED APOPLECTIC"
130	F	"YOUNG"	OVARIAN DROPSY	?	-	UNCHANGED
131	F	56	DROPSY, ORTHOPNOEA COULDN'T WALK, SWOLLEN LEGS, SHORT OF BREATH	?	?	BREATHING MUCH EASIER
132	M	31	TERTIAN AGUE OF 12 MONTHS, PAIN IN HYPOCHONDRIAC REGION, SHORT OF BREATH SWOLLEN LEGS, POOR APPETITE ORTHOPNOEA, SWOLLEN BELLY THIGHS & LEGS, COLD HANDS & FEET, NAILS ALMOST BLACK. PULSE 160, CAROTID PULSE VISIBLE TO THE EYES,IN EFFECT SHAKING HIS HEAD, GREAT THIRST, URINE DIMINISHED IN QUANTITY	?	+	NO LONGER ORTHOPNOIEC FURTHER DOSES NEEDED RETURNED HOME AFTER 2 MONTHS PERFECTLY WELL
133	M	29	PULMONARY CONSUMPTION DROPSY	?	?	INEFFECTIVE
134	M	37	HYDROTHORAX	-	+	DOSED NIGHTLY FOR 3 WEEKS. CURED
135	M	42	ASTHMA, ANASARCA BECAUSE OF "FREE LIVING" WHICH HAD EXPOSED HIM TO DRINK TOO MUCH	?	?	IMPROVED WITHIN A WEEK. CHANGED HIS JOB
136	M	44	ASCITES, ANASARCA PRECEDED BY EPILEPSY	?	?	COMPLAINTS SOON RESPONDED
137	F	55	ANASARCA OF LEG SCIATICA	?	+	PAIN & SWELLING OF LIMB EASED

CASE	SEX	AGE	PRESENTATION	N/V	D	OUTCOME
138	F	78	SHORT OF BREATH DEBILITY, LOSS OF APPETITE EFFUSION OF THORAX SWELLING OF LEGS	?	?	CAUSED PURGING, EASED HER BREATHING, COULD NOW LIE DOWN, APPETITE RETURNED AFTER A MONTH. TREATMENT NEEDED REPEATING. AGAIN FAVOURABLE NO RETURN OF DROPSY
139	F	50	(No details given. "For a particular account of this patient, see Mr. Yonge's second case")			
140	?	?	SPASMODIC ASTHMA FOR MANY YEARS	?	?	NO BENEFIT
141	M	43	MARKS OF DISEASED VISCERA, TENSE ABDOMEN EMACIATED, PUBLICAN HARD DRINKER	+	-	LIVED 1 YEAR. NEEDED REPEATED TAPPING OF ABDOMEN
142	F	47	ASTHMA 18 MONTHS ORTHOPNOIEC, VERY THIN NO APPETITE, CONFINED TO HER ROOM 4 MONTHS	+	?	MUCH RELIEVED WITHIN 1 WEEK. AFTER ABOUT 2 WEEKS COULD COME DOWNSTAIRS. 6 MONTHS LATER, SLIGHT RECURRENCE, SOME RELIEF BUT NAUSEATED
143	M	?	KIDNEY STONES, DYSURIA POOR APPETITE SENSE OF WEIGHT IN THE LOINS	+	+	"FELT NO MORE OF HER COMPLAINTS"
144	F	67	ASTHMA, VERY THICK HARD LEGS. MORE SHORT OF BREATH FOR 1-2 MONTHS, SWOLLEN BELLY, ANASARCA OF THIGHS, LITTLE URINE PASSED	+	+	BREATHING EASIER
145	F	22	ABDOMINAL DISTENSION EMACIATION, COUGH HECTIC FEVER	?	?	DIED OF TB
146	M	40	KIDNEY STONES, LOIN PAINS	?	?	IMPROVED, BUT THIS COULD HAVE BEEN DUE TO THE OTHER MEDICINES CONCURRENTLY ADMINISTERED
147	M	60	GOUT, DROPSY	?	?	SOME RELIEF

CASE	SEX	AGE	PRESENTATION	N/V	D	OUTCOME
148	M	35	PHTHISIS PULMONALIS DIFFICULT BREATHING AND PAIN	?	?	CONSIDERABLE RELIEF
149	F	68	A RARE CASE IN WHICH NO URINE WAS SECRETED	+	-	SOME URINE FORMED
150	F	28	PULMONARY CONSUMPTION DROPSY	?	?	NO BENEFIT
151	M	7	HYDROCEPHALUS	?	?	NO BENEFIT
152	F	65	PERIPNEUMONY DIFFICULT BREATHING COUGH, ORTHOPNOEA SWOLLEN LEGS, SMALL QUANTITY OF URINE	?	?	DIURESIS BY 5th DAY SYMPTOMS CLEARED IN 14 DAYS EXCEPT COUGH
153	M	42	HISTORY OF KIDNEY STONES, NUMBNESS OF LOWER BACK, WEIGHT ACROSS HIS LOINS	+	+	IMPROVED
154	M	55	HYDROTHORAX	?	?	"PRODUCED THE HAPPIEST EFFECTS"
155	F	50	OVARIAN DROPSY	?	?	NO BENEFIT
156	M	?	NO URINE PASSED FOR SEVERAL DAYS, HICCUPS, VOMITING TRANSIENT DELIRIUM	-	-	CHECKED THE VOMITING BUT NO URINE SECRETED

WILLIAM WITHERING'S DESCRIPTION
OF HOSPITALISED CASES TREATED BY HIM

CASES 157-163

He requested Mr. Cha. Hinchley, late apothecary to the Birmingham Hospital to supply him with the details. Hinchley provided details of cases 157 to 160.

157   John Butler, age 30. Asthma and swelled legs. Cured after 23 days having received three spoonfuls of Digitalis infusion every night.

158   Henry Warren, age 60. General anasarca and ascites, very asthmatic, unable to sit or lie, had to remain standing. Infusion of Digitalis, two spoonfuls every four hours. Diuresis occurred after thirty six hours. Breathing improved, and swellings disappeared in a few days.

159   Mary Crockett, age 40. Ascites and universal anasarca. One and a half drams of Digitalis to half a pint, one ounce every four hours. Copious output of urine, medicine then stopped as WW ordered.

160   Mary Bird, aged 61. Abdominal fullness, diseased liver and anasarca of legs and thighs. Digitalis presently removed all the swelling.

The following cases were communicated to WW by the apothecary who succeeded Hinchley. He wrote thus:

"Shiffnal, April 26th, 1785

DEAR SIR,

During my residence in the Birmingham General Hospital, I had frequent opportunities of seeing the great effects of the Digitalis in dropsy. As the exhibition of it was in the following instances immediately under your own direction, I have drawn them up for your inspection, previous to your publishing upon that excellent diuretic. Of its efficacy in dropsy I have considerable evidence in my possession, but consider myself not at liberty to send you any other cases except those you had yourself the conduct of. The Digitalis is a very valuable acquisition to medicine; and, I trust, it will cease to be dreaded when it is well understood.

I am, Sir, your obedient,
And very humble servant,
W. BAYLEY"

161   Mary Hollis, age 62, hydrothorax, fear of suffocation at night, so slept upright in a chair. Two grains of Digitalis night and morning, but after eight days developed sickness. Digitalis stopped for six days, then resumed. Some nausea ensued, gradual improvement due to diuresis.

162   Edward James, age 21. Difficulty breathing, headache, tightness of the stomach, with a small amount of swelling of the legs. Small volume, rapid pulse, blueness of mouth and eyes. Infusion of Digitalis prescribed, eight hourly, from the third to the seventh day. Became worse, with progressive increase in swelling, more short of breath, unable to lie down, very little urine passed. On the fifty fourth day, his legs and thighs were "one continued blubber.....his penis and scrotum were astonishingly swelled....Ordered to take a pill with two grains of powdered Fox-glove night and morning." Six days later, on the sixtieth day, his diuresis commenced, and his symptoms eased. By the sixty sixth day, he was producing "three chamber pots full in a day and a night, each pot containing two quarts and four ounces, moderately full." He was discharged about eleven weeks after admission, perfectly cured.

The apothecary went on to lament the fact that he had not been able to measure the prodigious amount of swelling of Edward James's belly, "having unfortunately mislaid the tape." (How often nowadays in hospital practice, as then, one fails to find the tape measure, patella hammer or ophthalmoscope on the ward- the author has taken to carrying his own around with him at all times!).

163   Sarah Ford, age 42, admitted with chest pain, difficulty breathing, swelling of the face, and anasarca of the thighs and legs. Produced little urine, and that she did with painful efforts. This had been the situation for six weeks. Once in hospital she was prescribed the powdered digitalis leaf. On the eighth day her breathing was much relieved, her legs and thighs became less swollen, and she produced five pints of urine in the course of a day and a night. The chest pain disappeared, and she was discharged symptom free about three weeks after admission.

In addition to these histories, there were several communications to WW from other doctors, chiefly those practising in the Midlands. Correspondents included the following:

Robert Cawley: London, Norfolk Street, May 31st 1785 (described his brother's response to the treatment - his brother being 'the late Dr. Cawley').
Mr. Daniel Boden, Surgeon at Broseley, in Shropshire, 25th May 1785 (2 cases).
Mr. Causer, Surgeon, Stourbridge, Worcester, date not stated (3 cases).
Dr. Fowler, Physician at Stafford, date not stated (1 case).
Dr. J. Freer, junior Surgeon, in Birmingham, date not stated (2 cases).
Dr. Jones, Physician in Lichfield, date not stated (24 cases).
Mr. W. Jones, Surgeon, in Birmingham, May 17th, 1785 (1 case).
Dr. E. Johnstone, Physician in Birmingham, May 26th, 1785 (2 cases).
Mr. Lyon, Surgeon at Tamworth, date not stated (1 case).
Dr. Stokes, Physician in Stourbridge, May 17th, 1785 (3 cases).

Mr. Shaw, Surgeon at Stourbridge, communicated by Dr. Stokes, date not stated (1 case).
Mr. Vaux, Surgeon in Birmingham, 8th May, 1785 (2 cases).
Mr. Wainwright, Surgeon in Dudley, April 26th, 1785 (recounts his experience of the digitalis generally, but gives no actual case descriptions).
Mr. Ward, Surgeon in Birmingham, 1st July, 1785 (1 case, himself).
Mr. Yonge, Surgeon in Shiffnal, Shropshire, May 1st, 1785 (8 cases).

THE CASE DESCRIPTIONS WHERE MENTION IS MADE OF THE PULSE

I feel it may be of interest to enquire into mention of the pulse and its characteristics, particularly in view of current thoughts regarding the circumstances in which digoxin (the form in which digitalis is nowadays given), is likely to be beneficial. Therefore, the reference cases will be mentioned, together with the verbatim comment, and, as far as can be deduced, the eventual outcome.

WW's cases.

Case 3 '—**his pulse quick and feeble,**—' Outcome:
'It operated as a diuretic, never made him sick, and he got on well without any other medicine.'

Case 4 '—**her pulse extremely weak and irregular**—' Outcome:
'It is now almost nine years since the Digitalis was first prescribed for this lady, and notwithstanding I have tried every preventive method I could devise, the dropsy still continues to recur at times; but is never allowed to increase so as to cause much distress, for she occasionally takes the infusion and relieves herself whenever she chooses. Since the first exhibition of that medicine, very small doses have always found sufficient to promote the flow of urine.
I have been more particular in the narrative of this case, partly because Dr. Darwin has related it rather imperfectly, trusting, I imagine, to memory, and partly because it was a case which gave rise to a very general use of the medicine in that part of Shropshire.'

Case 15 '**Pulse very small**;——' Outcome:
'His complaints still increasing, decoction of Digitalis was then directed, which relieved him in a few days; but his complaints returned, and he died in the month of June.'

Case 20 '**pulse intermitting**;—' Outcome:
'He is now active and well; but, whenever he takes cold, finds some return of difficult breathing, which he soon removes by a dose or two of the infusion.'

Case 28 '**pulse quick and very feeble**——' Outcome:

'A few doses occasioned a copious flow of urine without sickness or any other disturbance. The medicine was discontinued; and the next day the urine continuing to be excreted very plentifully, he lost his most distressing complaints,was in great spirits, and ate a pretty good dinner.—'

Case 31 '**her pulse very small and low**——' Outcome:
'I was desired to visit Mrs. H__, a very delicate woman, who after a severe lying-in, had her legs and thighs swollen to a very great degree; pale and semi-transparent. I found her extremely faint, her pulse very small and low; vomiting violently, and frequently purging. She was attended by a gentleman who had seen me give the Digitalis in a similar case of swelled legs after a lying in about six months before (see Case 26). He had not considered that this patient was delicate, the other robust; nor had he attended to stop the exhibition of the medicine when its effects began to take place. The great distress of her situation was evidently owing to the imprudent and unlimited use of the Digitalis. ....she recovered perfectly.' (WW having discontinued the Digitalis).

Case 52 '**quick and feeble pulse**——' Outcome:
'Pulv. fol. Digital. made into pills, with gum ammoniac and aromatic species, soon relieved his breathing.'

Case 72 'Infusion of Digitalis produced nausea, and **lowered the frequency of the pulse**;—' Outcome:
'—but had no other sensible effects. His disorder continued to increase and killed him about two months afterwards.'

Case 77 'The Digitalis was now directed; it **lowered his pulse**, but did not prove diuretic—' Outcome:
'He returned home, and soon after was tapped again, but survived the operation only a few hours.'

Case 88 '—her **pulse feeble**—' Outcome:
'Several medicines having been given in vain, the Digitalis was tried, but with no better effect; and in about a month she died.'

Case 106 '—**his pulse so feeble**—' Outcome:
'Finding himself relieved by this, he continued to take it, contrary to the directions given, and after the diuretic effects had appeared. The sickness which followed was truly alarming; it continued at intervals for many days, his pulse sunk down to forty in a minute, every object appeared green to his eyes...At length, however, he did begin to emerge out of the extreme danger into which his folly had plunged him......in about two months he came to enjoy a perfect state of health.'

Case 121 '..**pulse 132**——I mention this case——to point out the great effect the Digitalis has upon the action of the heart;—' Outcome:

'**for the pulse came down to 96**——the **pulse never became quicker**—, nor did the swelling return.'

Case 129 'The **intermitting pulse**——' Outcome:

'The effect of this plan was perfectly to our wishes, and in a short time he recovered his usual health.—'

Case 132 '—July 16th——**pulse 160 tremulous beats in a minute**, but the pulsation in the carotid arteries was such as to be visible to the eye, and to shake his head so that he could not hold it still—' Outcome:

'The next day he began to make water freely, and could allow of being put into bed, but was raised high with pillows. Omit the infusion. ——On the 25th. the diuretic effects of the Digitalis having nearly ceased, he was ordered to take three grains of the pulv. Digital. night and morning, for five days—August 15th. —the Digitalis infusion was repeated—About a month after this, he returned home perfectly well.'

Hospital case   Case 162

'Edward James. Aet 21. Admitted March 20th, 1784. Complained of great difficulty of breathing—**his pulse very small and quick**—54th day. To this period there was not the least probability of his existing; his legs and thighs were one continued blubber, his thorax quite flat, and his belly so large——. He made about three ounces of water in twenty-four hours: his penis and scrotum were astonishingly swelled——. Ordered to take a pill with two grains of powdered Fox-glove night and morning' Outcome:

'—about the 60th day—he now made much more water, and dared to sleep. ——66th day. Breathing very much relieved, the quantity of water he made was three chamber pots full in a day and a night, each pot containing two quarts and four ounces, moderately full.——69th day.—still made a prodigious quantity of water——and on the 12th—' (June)—'was discharged from this Hospital perfectly cured.'

CASES COMMUNICATED BY OTHER PHYSICIANS OR SURGEONS

From **Mr. Boden**   '—the **pulse very weak**—' Outcome:

'—the symptoms were mostly removed, making water freely—'

From **Mr. Causer**   Patient Mr. P.   'His breathing very bad, an **irregular pulse**, and unable to lie down.' Outcome:

'—he had taken the medicine regularly——and continued well till the evening of the following day, when a little sickness took place——but a surprising discharge of urine. —these discharges continued, with a continual sickness till the swelling was totally gone, which happened in three or four days.'

Patient Mrs. S   '—a **very irregular intermittent pulse**,—' Outcome:
'She took about three parts of the medicine before any effect took place. The first was sickness, succeeded by a considerable discharge of urine—I saw her again on the 12th. The quantity of urine was much increased, and the swelling diminished. Pulse and breathing better.—March 15th she was delivered——well until the 18th when she was seized with very violent pains——19th. Breathing short, unable to lie down, very **irregular low pulse** scarcely to be felt——20th. Much the same; makes very little water, and the legs begin to swell——28th The swelling considerably increased——30th. Breathing very bad, with cough and pain across the sternum, unable to lie down, legs, thighs, and body very much swelled, urine not more than four or five ounces in the twenty-four hours;—3rd. Breathing much improved by the blister, which runs profusely—12th. The cough very bad, pulse irregular, urine in very small quantity—' (Digitalis administered) '—17th. Considerable increase of urine—21st. Swelling a good deal diminished; urine near four pints in twenty-four hours——The Digitalis pills and opiate at bed-time continued. ——25th. swelling much diminished, makes plenty of water——May; the dropsical symptoms and cough are entirely gone, —'

From **Mr. Jones**   'alternate swelling of the legs and abdomen, a little cough, shortness of breath in a morning, thirst, **weak pulse**, and her urine, which was so small in quantity as to amount to half a pint in twenty-four hours, deposited a clay coloured sediment.—' Outcome:
'—the quantity of urine was increased to about a pint in the twenty four hours— On the 24th the legs were much swelled again——her **pulse was low**—' Outcome:
'On the 26th she was thirsty and languid. The swelling was removed; the quantity of urine discharged in the last twenty four hours was about a pint. She continued to mend from this time, and is now in good health.'

From **Dr. Johnstone**   Case 1 '—affected with great difficulty of respiration, and cough particularly troublesome on attempting to lie down, oedematous swellings of the legs and thighs, **pulse natural**—' Outcome:
'He took four doses of the mixture (Digitalis) without being in the least sick, and made, during the night upwards of two quarts of natural coloured water.——'

Case 2   '—He complained of difficulty of breathing, attended with cough, particularly troublesome on lying down——oedematous swelling of the legs——**pulse weak and irregular**— Outcome:
'Made near two quarts of water in the night, without being in the least sick. He continued the use of the mixture (Digitalis) three times a day——and made about three pints of water daily, by which means the swellings were entirely taken away——'

From **Mr. Lyon** '——dropsy of the abdomen, attended with anasarcous swellings of the limbs' Outcome:

'——he began the Digitalis on the 10th July——after which a considerable flow of urine ensued——but he remained excessive weak, a **fluttering pulse at the rate of 150 or frequently 160 in a minute**; he kept pretty free from water for upwards of twelve months——'

From **Dr. Stokes**, case 1 'Orthopnoea, pain, and excessive oppression at the bottom of the sternum. **Pulse irregular with frequent intermissions**.——Legs anasarcous.' Outcome:
'A third dose I found had been given, which was followed by vomitings. All her complaints gradually abated, but in about a fortnight recurred. Three months afterwards, a severe attack of gout in her legs and arms, removing to her head, she died.

Dr. Stokes had an opportunity of examining the dead body——there did not appear to have been any return of the dropsy.—'
Case 3. '——Orthopnoea. Sense of oppression at the praecordia. **Pulse intermitting**. Legs anasarcous. Urine scanty——' Outcome:
'Took six doses when nausea was excited. Urine a quart during the course of the night. The flow of urine continued——'

From **Mr. Yonge**. Case 1. '——awaked with a sense of suffocation, which obliged him to rise up suddenly in bed. I found him complaining of difficult respiration, particularly on lying down; the countenance pale, and the **pulse smaller and quicker than usual**. ——the urine which had hitherto been of——sufficient quantity, now became diminished——and the ankles oedematous.
—from some symptoms of relapse, the oxymel was used as before——The urine was made in the quantity of four or five pints each day——. But now the sickness being exceedingly depressing, the strength failing, and the diuretic effects beginning to cease, the following prescription was directed.
R. Fol. Digitalis purpur. pulv.'— Outcome:
'In three days the effect of this medicine became visible, and when the dose of the digitalis had been increased to six grains per day, the flow of urine generally amounted to seven pints every twenty four hours——at which time the dyspnoea was removed——'

Case 2. '—the **pulse varying between 94 and 100, and feeble**——' Outcome:
'—the flow of urine began to increase——'

(This case studied in full is suggestive of obstructive jaundice, and may have been due to a gall stone in a 48yr old female).

Case 3. '—slight difficulty in respiration, upon taking exercise or lying down in bed——symptoms increased gradually—. The urine was small in quantity——his pulse **feeble**, and intermitting; he breathed with difficulty when in bed—' Outcome:

'——nausea occurred, and the following day he began to make water in great quantity, which he continued to do for three of four days. The **pulse** in a few hours became regular, slower, and stronger, and, in the course of a week, all the symptoms entirely vanished——'

Case 5. '—slight cough and expectoration of purulent matter——skin became universally of a pale yellow colour. The abdomen was swelled and hard——**violent and constant palpitation of the heart**, which prevented him from sleeping. The urine pale and in small quantity. The **pulse exceedingly strong, and rebounding; beating 114 to 120 strokes every minute**. He suffered violent pain of his head.' Outcome:
'—without any sensible effect. Other diuretics were tried to as little purpose. Repeated bleeding had no effect in diminishing the violent action of the heart. He died—under complicated symptoms of phthisis and ascites.'

Case 6. '—became affected with oedematous swelling of his legs, for which he was advised to drink Fox Glove Tea.' Outcome:
'—suddenly seized with faintness and cold sweatings. I found him with a pale countenance complaining of weakness, and of pain—. The swelling of the legs was entirely gone, he having evacuated urine in very large quantities for the two preceding days. He was affected with frequent diarrhoea. The **pulse was very quick and small**, and his extremities cold. ——he recovered perfectly in the space of three weeks; except a relapse of the anasarca, for which the Digitalis was afterwards successfully employed, in small doses, without any disagreeable consequence.'

Case 8. '——a swelling of the lower extremities—and gradually increased for two or three months. The legs and thighs were greatly enlarged and oedematous. His belly was swelled——He made small quantities of high coloured water. —and **pulse feeble**—' Outcome:
'Upon the exhibition of the sixth dose, nausea supervened, and continued to oppress him at intervals for two or three days, during which he passed large quantities of pale urine. The swelling—rapidly diminished—returned to his labour perfectly recovered.'

Case 4, as recorded is of particular interest not only in illustrating his careful attention to detail, but also in perhaps causing antipathy with a colleague, Dr. Erasmus Darwin, as follows.
"July 25th. Mrs. H...of A....near N....between 40 and 50 years of age. ..I was desired to meet Dr. Darwin at the lady's house. I found her nearly in a state of suffocation; her **pulse weak and irregular**, her breath very short and laborious...She could not lie down in bed...Her stomach, legs, and thighs, were greatly swollen.....In this situation I knew of nothing likely to avail us, except Digitalis: but this I hesitated to propose, from an apprehension that little could be expected from anything, that an unfavourable termination would tend to discredit a medicine which promised to be of great benefit to mankind....Dr. Darwin very politely acceded immediately to my proposition, and, as he

had never seen it given, left the preparation and the dose to my direction......... The patient took five of these draughts, which made her very sick, and acted powerfully upon the kidneys, for within the first twenty four hours she made upwards of eight quarts of water. The sense of fullness and oppression across her stomach was greatly diminished, her breath eased, her **pulse became more full and more regular,** and the swellings of her legs subsided..... "

Interestingly, details of this particular case were recorded as an appendix to the posthumous thesis of Charles Darwin, the other son of Erasmus. He was the brother of Robert with whom WW had been involved in the Houlston case. Charles died tragically whilst still a medical student at Edinburgh. This was published in 1780, five years before WW's definitive work, but was clearly based on the case described. In fact, the thesis was published by Erasmus Darwin, and it was intended to appear as if the late Charles had used the drug. Possibly the actions of an ambitious but grief stricken father. (See p.116, for WW's comment regarding Dr. Darwin).

Appendix (iii) (b)

LETTSOM'S DESCRIPTION OF 8 CASES

Taken from "Memoirs of the Medical Society of London, Initiated in the year 1773. Vol II. London: Printed by Henry Fry. For Charles Dilly, in the Poultry, MDCCLXXXIX (1789) Of the Digitalis Purpurea, in hydropic diseases, by J.C. Lettsom, M.D.
Read February 4, 1788.

"——But in order to ascertain the virtues, which a medicine may really possess, in an equal or superior degree, to any other previously known, in the treatment of dropsies, trial should be made in such cases, as experience may have deemed remediable.
The following instances which a priori appeared not to be incurable, are related in the order and succession in which they occurred in practice, and copied verbatim from the notes which I committed to writing at the periods of attendance."

Case I. R. Gill, aged 30 years, male.

"———incipient ascites——no great degree of cough or dyspnoea." Digitalis was prescribed. "No effect (was apparent) until dose tripled, which resulted in nausea and vomiting (with)——confused vision, objects appearing as if enveloped in a red blaze of fire———fullness of the abdomen subsided, and the dropsy seemed totally removed—— The confusion of the head, and perverted vision, nevertheless continued, with the restlessness and jactitations, which evinced great uneasiness in the system, though the patient did not appear sensible of any particular pain. The prostration of strength could not be surmounted by the use of cordials, and the whole train of unpleasant symptoms only subsided with his death, which happened a week after the digitalis purpurea was relinquished."

Case II. Edward Wycherley, 48 years. "1st November——legs moderately swelled— —fullness about the region of the liver——ordered a decoction of the digitalis purpurea three times a day, gradually increasing the dose till a nausea ensued; and then diminishing it, so as just to admit of retention on the stomach.

On the 21st of November I saw him again, his urine had not been sensibly increased, though his legs appeared less swelled———he observed, however, that since he took it he found a dimness, and diminution of his sight. ——continued about fourteen days after leaving off this vegetable."

Case III. James Ogden, aged about 54 years. Ascites. treated with digitalis. Became weaker. No benefit.

Case IV. Mary Guest, about 40 years, gradual "swelling of lower extremities, with a diminution of urine."

He treated her with squills, resulting in an increase in the volume of urine, and reduction of the swelling. He then added digitalis which led to nausea, but no increase in urine output. She felt weaker and was only improved when squills and bark were administered.

Case V. W. Webb, aged 60 years, male. Dyspnoea, slight swelling of legs. Pulse not irregular, but weak, short of breath on exertion. Squills gave no benefit. Digitalis was given, which resulted in nausea and weakness. The drug was stopped. The swelling increased. He then received Peruvian bark and squills. However there was no increase in the amount of urine produced, but there was less leg swelling, and his breathing was improved.

Case VI. J. Poyner, 46 years, Male. Generalised anasarca, orthopnoea. Reduced urine formation, cough. No ascites. Squill was prescribed, but without benefit. Likewise with tobacco infusions, followed by a decoction of foxglove in reduced dosage.

"For the first week he certainly passed much more water, and gradually diminished in the anasarcous swelling. ——————I was extremely happy at the prospect I now had on seeing one successful case from the use of this vegetable——though he complained of great vertigo, and almost a total loss of vision——"

Case VII. Tho. Wright, aged 46 years. Poor appetite, abdominal fullness, diminished urine output, slight generalised swelling, jaundice. Able to lie flat at night. Treated with digitalis.

This resulted in a considerable increase in urine, but could not be ascribed necessarily to the digitalis, since it had occurred on several occasions previously. He lost two inches from his waist. he was able to walk better. There was no nausea or vomiting. However he subsequently relapsed.

Case VIII. EG aged 45 years. Female. Fullness of the abdomen. No response to digitalis therapy. Eventually fluid was drained from the abdomen. She died one month later.

"As I gave it in the manner prescribed by Dr. Withering, I am at a loss to explain the different results of our experiments. ——Some eminent practitioners, however, have confirmed the favourable relations of Dr. Darwin and Dr. Withering, and assured me of their having experienced the most salutary effects in hydropic affections, particularly in the hydrops pectoris and generalised anasarca."

Lettsom went on to give a good description of the effect of digitalis on the pulse rate, and of its side effects. He suggested that patients from different localities may respond differently, to account for the results he obtained compared to those of Darwin and Withering.

Appendix (iv)

WITHERING'S PUBLICATIONS

1766 Dissertatio medica inauguralis de angina gangraenosa, Edinburgh, Auld & Smellie.

1773 Experiments upon the different kinds of marle found in Staffordshire. Phil Trans 63: 161-2

1776 A botanical arrangement of all the vegetables growing in Great Britain. With descriptions of the genera and species, according to the celebrated Linnaeus...With an easy introduction to the study of botany. Shewing the method of investigating plants, and directions how to dry and preserve specimens. The whole illustrated by copper plates and a copious glossary. Two volumes. Printed by M. Swinney for T. Cadell and P. Elmsley and G. Robinson. London 1776.

1779 An account of the scarlet fever and sore throat, or scarlatina anginosa; particularly as it appeared at Birmingham in the year 1778. London: Printed for T. Cadell, B. White, and G. Robinson. 1779

1782 An analysis of two mineral substances, vz. the Rowley rag-stone and the toad stone. Phil Trans 72: 327-36

1783 Outlines of mineralogy. T. Cadell, G. Robinson, J. Balfour, and C. Elliott, London (Translation of Torbern Bergman's "Sciagraphia regni mineralis")

1784 Experiments and observations on the terra ponderosa. Phil Trans 74: 293-311

1785 An account of the foxglove and some of its medical uses; with practical remarks on the dropsy, and some other diseases. Birmingham. Printed by M.Swinney for GGJ and J Robinson, Paternoster Row, London

1787-1792 A botanical arrangement of British plants; including the uses of each species, in medicine, diet, rural economy and the arts, with an easy introduction to the study of botany. Including a new set of references to figures, by Jonathan Stokes. 2nd ed.; illustrated by copper plates. Birmingham. Printed by M. Swinney (& Walker) for G.G.J. & J. Robinson, London, 1787-1792.

1788 A letter to Joseph Priestley. LLD, on the principle of acidity, the decomposition of water. Phil Trans 78: 319-330

1790 An account of some extraordinary effects of lightning. Phil Trans 80: 293-5

1793 An account of the scarlet fever and sore throat, or scarlatina anginosa; particularly as it appeared at birmingham in the year 1778, 2nd edition, to which are now prefixed, some remarks on the nature and cure of the ulcerated sore throat. GG and J Robinson, London

1793 A chemical analysis of the waters at Caldas. Extract from Actas da Academica real das Sciencias.

1794 A new method for preserving fungi, ascertained by chymical experiments. Trans Linnean soc. 2: 263-6

1794 A letter on pulmonary consumption and other letters. In Letters from Dr. Withering, Dr Ewart, Dr Thornton, and Dr Briggs together with some other papers supplementary to two publications on asthma, consumption, fever, and other diseases (ed T Beddoes) Bristol
1795 Analyse chimica da aqua das Caldas da Rainha. A chemical analysis of the water of Caldas da Rainha. Lisbon (Portuguese and English)
1796 Observations on the pneumatic medicine. Ann Med 1: 392-3
1796 An arrangement of British plants, according to the latest improvements of the Linnean system, to which is prefixed an easy introduction to the study of botany. 3rd ed. Birmingham: Printed for the Author, by M. Swinney; London: Sold by G.G. & Robinson. 1796.
1799 An account of a convenient method of inhaling the vapour of volatile substances. Ann Med 3: 447-51

Part Two

THE TIMES OF WILLIAM WITHERING (WW)

Chapter 6

BRITAIN AND THE WORLD IN THE 18th CENTURY

When WW was aged 4 years, in 1744 Britain and France were at war in the struggle for Caribbean trade and for Silesia. This was part of a single global conflict that extended from North America to India and from the West Indies to Russia. The capture of Madras by Joseph Dupleix (Governor-General of the French establishment in India) in 1746 began the struggle for India. He was checked by our sea power at Trichinopoly in 1752 and after the capture of Bengal in 1757 the British could reinforce the Carnatic (the South East coastal region of India) at will. The capture of Pondicherry in 1761 destroyed French power.

The **Treaty of Utrecht in 1713** had sought to stabilize a state system in Europe based on the balance of power. Instead it resulted in colonial conflicts with serious clashes between Spain and Great Britain in Georgia, and Great Britain and France in North America. British efforts to suppress illegal trade by its American colonists provoked resistance and finally open revolt. In 1739-1740, Britain went to war with Spain in defence of trading rights, as Frederick the Great invaded Silesia. The **Treaty of Aix-la-Chapelle in 1748** settled none of the outstanding questions and fighting began again in North America in 1754. The key to colonial victory was control of the lines of communication, i.e. sea power. The outbreak of the **Seven Years War** transformed the local struggle. The war was a complex struggle between Prussia, supported by Britain against a coalition formed by Austria, Russia and France. It arose from attempts by Austria to regain Silesia which it had lost to Prussia in the **War of the Austrian Succession**, in 1748. In the wider conflict of 1756-1763, while France was handicapped by its continental commitments, Great Britain took control of the Atlantic and isolated the French forces in North America. Cut off from reinforcements, Louisbourg fell in 1758, Quebec in 1759. The capture of Montreal in 1760 completed the fall of French Canada. In the West Indies, by 1763 the British were in control of Spanish Havana and all the French islands except St. Domingue. These were restored at the **Treaty of Paris (1763)**, but Great Britain retained the North American mainland east of the Mississippi, including Florida which was ceded by Spain. (Incidentally, **1763 was also the year when the use of willow bark in treatment of ague** was described by the **Reverend Edward Stone of Chipping Norton**, Oxfordshire, in a letter to The Earl of Mansfield, President of the Royal Society. The active ingredient is a precursor of **aspirin**).

Thus, descriptions for the use of aspirin and digitalis appeared within 25 years of each other. From a strictly commercial point of view, aspirin was, and is, the clear winner.

The British triumph was short lived. Between 1763 and the **American War of Independence (1776-1783)**, France rebuilt both its navy and its alliances in pursuit of revenge. By 1781, confronted by a hostile coalition of France, Spain and the Dutch Republic, threatened by the 'armed neutrality' of the Baltic powers, and overstrained by the need to defend an empire stretching from Canada to India, Great Britain was forced to surrender control of North American waters. The French blockade of Yorktown forced **Cornwallis** to surrender, and although **Rodney's** victory off the group of islands known as The Saints in 1782 saved British possessions in the West Indies, Great Britain was obliged to recognize American independence at the **Treaty of Versailles (1783)**. The United States' triumph of 1763 allowed it to develop as an English speaking nation. Trade contacts revived and despite occasional differences, the cultural link between the two countries exercised a profound influence on subsequent history.

During these same years the British founded a new empire in India. The real foundation of the British Empire in India followed **Clive's** victory at Plassey (1757) which, assisted by the victory of the Afghans over the Marathas at Panipat (1761), gave the British control of the province of Bengal. During the Seven Years War reinforcements from Bengal enabled the British to eliminate French influence in the Carnatic.

In the main Britain fought its wars abroad. Exceptions to this statement were the two **Jacobite revolts**, in 1715 and 1745. The Jacobites were adherents, consequent upon the revolution of 1688, first of the exiled English king James II,(James = Jacobus), then of his descendants, and subsequent to their extinction, of the descendants of Charles I, i.e. the exiled house of Stuart. King James II of England reigned from 1685-1688. He was an ardent Catholic who was determined to secure ascendancy for his church. He bestowed preferment on Catholics out of proportion to their number. He purged the borough corporations of Anglicans and Tories. He placed Catholics in office in the universities. This led to general discontent, and seven eminent men including Lord Danby invited **William, Prince of Orange**, the king's son in law and the recognized head of the Protestant interest in Europe, to come to England with an armed force in order to effect the redress of grievances. He disembarked his forces at Torbay, and marched to London. Meanwhile, Danby and other disaffected Lords raised insurrections in the north. James, after the desertion of some of his supposedly close allies, sensed defeat and fled to France, leaving the way for William (III) and Mary to share the sovereignty. In Ireland, James influenced the Earl of Tyrconnel to fill the army with Catholic officers and everywhere placed Catholics in power. Many Protestants fled to England. Tyrconnel invited James to come and take control of the Irish. He came and received French assistance, but was defeated by William at the **Battle of the Boyne**, July 1st, 1690.

The history of the Jacobites, culminating in the uprisings of 1715, and 1745, is part of the history of England and Scotland. It is unlikely that WW was very aware of the 1745 uprising, as he would have been four years old at the time. However, it happened during his lifetime, and there is little doubt that he would have been told all about these events in the course of his early tuition by **Henry Wood of Ercall**.

There were also many Jacobites in Ireland. They were recruited largely from among the Roman Catholics. By 1745, the Jacobite movement in Scotland was moribund, but was galvanized into activity by **Prince Charles Edward**, (**'Bonny Prince Charlie'**) who wanted to regain the throne which his grandfather James II had lost. Hostile relations with Spain and France afforded an opportunity for which the Jacobite exiles had been waiting. The French troops were assembled for an invasion of Scotland in 1744, but a storm destroyed their transports. In July 1745, Prince Charles Edward decided to try without French aid, and despite little support in Scotland, except from Jacobite exiles. He had difficulty persuading some of the Highland chiefs to join him. However, the fact that many Government troops were at this time on the Continent, allowed him to make his play. His forces marched on Edinburgh, and on September 17th 1745, Charles as Prince Regent of the three kingdoms, took up his quarters at Holyrood. The commander-in-chief in Scotland, Sir John Cope, having gathered his forces after marching to Inverness and then Aberdeen, took ship to Dunbar, and met Charles' forces at Prestonpans, where Cope was immediately defeated. Flushed with success, but not by any large measure of recruits, Charles set out for London. He must have been bitterly disappointed because not even the Lancashire Jacobites joined his forces. By December 4th, he reached Derby. (This was only about 60 miles away from Wellington where Withering aged 4 years would no doubt have heard his parents discussing these events with great anxiety). By this time, his enemies, the Duke of Cumberland and Marshall Wade had assembled with troops recalled from the Continent, at Lichfield and the north of England respectively. Charles desperately wanted to continue, but was persuaded by his officers that to do so would be hopeless, so he commenced his retreat. The Jacobites marched back via Carlisle and Dumfries to Glasgow, and then on to Stirling where they besieged the castle. On January 17th 1746, the prince fought and won his last battle at Falkirk against a relieving force. Charles took Inverness and Fort Augustus, then waited for help from France. But none came. On April 17th Cumberland destroyed the Jacobite army on **Culloden Moor**. The prince escaped and reached France in September. 80 Jacobites were executed, and the Highlanders were forbidden to wear their distinctive dress, or play the bagpipes. The banning of the wearing of the kilt lasted until 1782.

Thus one may surmise that WW's time of study at Edinburgh was deprived of some of the essence of the Scottish way of life. No doubt the students at the time would have found other ways of spending their leisure time. There was for instance, a concert-giving society formed in 1728 which in 1762, the year WW matriculated, moved to the music room in the Niddry-Wynd in Edinburgh, and remained there until 1801.

In 1771, the liberty of the press was promoted by the Mayoralty of London, and opposed by the House of Commons. Parliament held that to report its proceedings was a breach of privilege. In March of that year, the hitherto custom of reporting names, dates and places fictitiously was abandoned by the press. The printer of the **Evening Post** was arrested by way of a speaker's warrant. This was opposed by the Lord Mayor and his alderman who protested to the House itself. Having been heard they were arrested and imprisoned in the Tower of London. They were set free after 6 weeks at the prorogation of Parliament. Thereafter the ban upon reporting was tacitly withdrawn.

In June 1780, following an act of parliament relieving Catholics of certain of their disadvantages, (e.g. the Test Acts which limited the holding of public office to communicant Anglicans, subsequent to the ever present Jacobite threat), there was rioting and much destruction in the city of London. The riots were led by **Lord George Gordon (1751-1793)**, who strongly opposed parliamentary moves towards Catholic emancipation. Prisons were broken open and property damaged. These became known as the **Gordon riots**. The disorder was put down by the military on the orders of George III (there being no police force yet), and the result was 285 people killed by musket fire, and casualties in the hundreds. Gordon was acquitted of high treason, but was later convicted of libel and died in Newgate Prison.

The **French Revolution of 1789** shattered the French navy, which ruined Napoleon's plans for the invasion of Great Britain. Here the greatest threat posed by the French Revolution was felt in Ireland, where three attempts at invasion by the French were made between 1796 and 1798. The first was at Bantry Bay, 43 ships and 15,000 soldiers having set sail from Brest, under the command of Hoche (Bonaparte's rival). Bad seamanship, bad discipline, and bad weather helped make this attempt unsuccessful. In 1798, a smaller force landed at Killala Bay, and eventually a rebel force of 15,000 made battle with the Loyalists and the regular troops at Wexford, where the rebels were defeated. A third force landed further north, and crossed the Shannon before they too were forced to surrender.

THE GLOBAL ECONOMY

Early in the 18th century, the Caribbean and the Brazilian coastal strip were providing Europe with most of its sugar, coffee, cacao, and cotton. The large (Red) Indian population had almost been exterminated by conquest and disease, leading to the massive importation of African slaves to build up the plantations. The North American mainland was settled by Europeans- English, Scots, Irish, Germans, Dutch. Many went into farming, producing grain, meat and butter. Unable to sell their surpluses in Europe, they sold them to the West Indies. The bills of exchange they received were then used to purchase Scots linen, Birmingham hardware and other imported manufactured goods.

The first three quarters of the eighteenth century saw enormous developments both in the absolute size and the geographical distribution of world trade even before there were any signs of the Industrial Revolution.

A few ports prospered mightily on international trade. London was the biggest sugar handler. Liverpool dominated the slave business and much general North American commerce. Glasgow became the largest tobacco importer.

For a century or more, the merchant class was dominant, its relative importance declining with the onset of the Industrial Revolution.

THE INDUSTRIAL REVOLUTION

This was the transition from a predominantly agrarian to an industrial economy. The methods of farming which had survived from feudal days would never have been able to feed the burgeoning populations of the new industrial towns. The **Enclosure Acts** of the late 18th and early 19th centuries transferred common land to landowners who were expected to make efficient use of it. One result was that **crop rotation** was practised, in place of the custom of letting land lie fallow. Consequently there was winter fodder for cattle which previously were nearly all slaughtered in the autumn. Drainage of land was improved, fertiliser imported, and breeding was improved. About 2 million acres of land was added to the total farmed within England and Wales. Thus cash crops became economically viable, as a consequence of which the great landowners had money available for investment in the Industrial Revolution.

There was a demand for improvement in farm tools and machinery. There was a transition from wooden to iron ploughs, seeds were sown by seed drills instead of by hand.

Naturally, many of the agriculture workers and their families, having been dispossessed of their common land as a result of the Enclosure Acts, were none too pleased. They were thus forced to migrate into the towns and factories, there to work in unhealthy and often dangerous conditions for meagre wages. In England, after 1750 the completion of enclosure of old common land by Act of Parliament and scientific farming increased the output of food for a growing population, and of raw materials for expanding industries. Increased prosperity enabled the agricultural community to buy more manufactured goods and to invest in new industries and public works. Essentially this took place during the reign of George III (1760-1820), when the structure of the British economy and of British society underwent fundamental changes in a very short period. There was an unprecedented rise in the output of coal, pig iron, engineering products and textiles.

But what was the reason for the Industrial Revolution starting in Britain and not in Europe? It may have been because continental Europe was embroiled in a series of military campaigns on its own Mother land, whereas Britain fought its wars abroad. We had many valuable resources including coal, iron, tin, copper, stone and salt. Our farmers supplied raw materials for cloth manufacture, leather work, corn millers and brewers. We had a transport system second to none (contrast with today!), including navigable rivers, (Clyde, Thames, Severn, Trent, Ouse, Humber), harbours (London, Bristol, Liverpool, Newcastle-upon-Tyne), as well as networks of new canals, toll roads and colliery railways. It was far cheaper then to send bulky goods by water than by land, and England's economic growth in the second half of the 18th century was stimulated by the heavy traffic on her inland waterways and along her coasts. A striking example was the movement of large quantities of coal from Tyne and Wear to London. Lancashire was blessed with a climate ideal for manufacturing cotton which was the major growth industry at the onset of the Industrial revolution.

It is interesting to speculate on the possible benefits that would nowadays accrue to the nation's economy if some enlightened government were to bring about a transformation of our existing dilapidated transport system - be it road, rail or waterways, as we enter the 21st century. (This comment was written in 2000 before the Hatfield rail crash, and all that has followed. We are now being promised improvement in essential services including transport. Time will tell if anything has changed).

MONARCHS, PRIME MINISTERS & MAJOR EVENTS

WILLIAM III (1650-1702), married his cousin **Mary II** in November 1677. William was never popular in England whereas Mary was popular among the Dutch people. She was the first daughter of **James II** who treated her badly financially, and she was faced with a conflict of loyalty to father and husband. She was next in line to the throne, so her choice of husband was somewhat fraught. William and Mary were proclaimed king and queen together, being crowned on 11th April 1689. She was a woman of modest and retiring disposition and unswervingly loyal to William. In his absence, she governed with the assistance of a committee of the Privy Council. She died childless, from smallpox (nearly 100 years before Jenner's discovery). William's unpopularity was not aided by his signing, in 1692, of an order for the extinction of the Macdonalds, a small clan living in the vale of Glencoe. The 'Glencoe massacre' was particularly barbaric. His greatness lay not in his domestic policies, but in his European policies, through his ability to grasp the central problems of his time. William and Mary reigned from 1689-1702. He was prince of the house of Orange and became king of England, Ireland and Scotland. A Protestant, he **defeated James II at the battle of the Boyne in 1690**, a major defeat for the house of Stuart.

ANNE (1665-1714), Queen of England, Scotland and Ireland from 1702-1707, and of Great Britain and Ireland from 1707-1714. She was the last Stuart sovereign, the younger daughter of James II. She was the sister of Mary II, and was brought up as a strict Protestant. She married George, prince of Denmark in 1683. Her father sought to settle the crown on her (although she was his second daughter after Mary), on condition that she embrace Roman Catholicism – which she refused to do. He did not press her, since by this time a son and potential heir had been born (but would not survive to succeed). She was forbidden by James II to visit her sister in 1688, but they nevertheless corresponded with each other. A Declaration of Rights would settle the succession of the crown upon her after William and Mary and their children. In the event they had no children. Anne would in her lifetime miscarry ten times, bear two children who died during infancy, and one son, born in 1689 who lived to the age of eleven years. Upon the death of William II, she succeeded to the throne in 1702. She detested Roman Catholics and dissenters alike. Through her influence fifty new churches were built in London. Though of no great ability she is generally regarded as having served the State well.

During the Glorious Revolution, she abandoned her father's cause, and supported her brother in law, William III. Her last surviving child died in 1700, and this led to the Act of Settlement, which was intended to prevent the Roman Catholic Stuarts from regaining the throne. It stipulated that the crown should go to James I's granddaughter, the Electress Sophia of Hanover, or her surviving Protestant heirs.

GEORGE I (1660-1727), king of Great Britain and Ireland from 1714 till 1727. He was the son of Sophia. He disliked England, spending most of his time in Hanover. His support for Walpole helped consolidate the supremacy of the Whigs. He divorced his wife Sophia in 1694, an heir George having been born in 1683.

GEORGE II (1683-1760), king of Great Britain and Ireland from 1727 till 1760, and Elector of Hanover. He was the monarch for the first 19 years of Withering's life. A son Frederick Louis was born in 1707, with whom he quarrelled. The opposition leaders who helped bring down Sir Robert Walpole frequently gathered at his home, Leicester House. Frederick died without succeeding to the throne, which passed to his son George.

GEORGE III (1738-1820), king of Great Britain and Ireland, and of overseas dependencies, king of Hanover, 1760-1820. He was a devoted family man, and patron of the arts. He was against the domination of government by a few powerful Whig families, and preferred to remain above politics. He was against conceding to the desires of the American colonists, and against their independence. It is generally accepted that he suffered from porphyria, a metabolic disease responsible for bouts of mental disturbance. He was the reigning monarch for the remainder of Withering's life.

PRIME MINISTERS IN THE 18th CENTURY

1721	Sir Robert Walpole
1742	Earl of Wilmington
1743	Henry Pelham
1754	Duke of Newcastle
1756	Duke of Devonshire
1757	Duke of Newcastle
	(W. Pitt and the Duke of Newcastle's administration)
1762	Earl of Bute
1763	George Grenville
1765	Marquis of Rockingham
1766-1768	Duke of Grafton
	(W. Pitt, Earl of Chatham, Prime Minister until 1768).
1770-1782	Lord Frederick North
1783	Fox-North coalition
1783-1801	Pitt the Younger

CONTEMPORARY EVENTS

Pre-Withering
1739-1740   Anglo-Spanish War

During Withering's lifetime:

Withering's age (approx.)
1744	3	Anglo-French War
1745	4	Battle of Fontenoy (11th May) during the War of the Austrian Succession
1745-1746	4	Jacobite uprising (Bonny Prince Charlie) The Battle of Culloden
1756-1763	15	The Seven Years War
1773	32	The Boston Tea Party
1776-1783	35	American War of Independence
1779-1783	38	The siege of Gibraltar
1780	39	The Gordon Riots
1789	48	French Revolution

Post-Withering
| 1805 | | Battle of Trafalgar |
| 1815 | | Battle of Waterloo |

UNIVERSITY EDUCATION IN 18th CENTURY BRITAIN

THE TEST ACTS

In 1567 no one was to be appointed to a public office or to be a notary who did not profess the Reformed religion. The Scottish Test act was rescinded by 1690. By 1700 renunciation of popery was to be made by persons employed in education. By 1707, all professors, principals, regents, masters, or others bearing office in any university, college or school in Scotland were bound to profess and subscribe to the Confession of Faith, and all persons had to be free of any oath of allegiance to any religion or church government other than the Protestant religion or the Presbyterian Church. Soon after the Reformation the principle that eligibility for public office should be withheld from all persons not professing the established religion was adopted by the Scottish and English legislatures. In England the acts of Supremacy and Uniformity and severe penalties against recusants (people, usually Roman Catholics, refusing to attend Anglican church services), whether Roman Catholic or Nonconformist, were the embodiment of the principle. Under Charles II, this meant receiving of holy communion within three months after admittance to office. The act did not apply to peers initially, nor the Duke of York. The provisions of the Test act were violated by Charles II and James II on the grounds of the dispensing powers of the Stuart kings. After a considerable number of amendments and partial repeals, the acts were all repealed during the 19th century. In Scotland a religious test was imposed immediately after the Reformation.

The Puritan revolt (which included the beheading of Charles I), was followed by the appearance of reformers like **John Milton** and **Samuel Hartlib**, who liberalized procedure and practice in schools and universities in England. I. Parker (1914), in 'Dissenting Academies in England' wrote;

'...during the Commonwealth and the Protectorate the door leading into the world of knowledge, of increased capacity, and of fuller life, was slowly opening to admit men who stood expectant without. But just as they were on the threshold, the door was shut - shut by the Restoration, and the way barred by the Clarendon Code.' The conformist legislation of Clarendon, referred to as the Test Acts, was made law in 1662. **Strict adherence to the Prayer Book and the Thirty-nine Articles was demanded of all who held public office or taught in the universities. This denial of freedom of thought spawned the foundation of the first dissenting churches and academies in Britain. Despite persecution they flourished in Manchester, Liverpool, Warrington, and later in Birmingham.** The resultant atmosphere of intellectual vigour contrasted successfully with the spiritual anaesthesia of the Clarendon Code, and as a result the world of arts and letters and science was uplifted into the next century. **Edinburgh during the second half of the eighteenth century was to become the strongest university centre in Britain, whereas Oxford and Cambridge under the influence of the Test Acts had degenerated into 'palsy-stricken shadows of their former selves.' They had become 'schools chiefly for the use of the clergy who had an almost exclusive part in their management.'** However the age of enlightenment was dawning in Holland and on the Continent, and many canny Scotsmen ventured there. Subsequently it focussed on Edinburgh. Those intent upon Medicine chose **Leyden**, where **Boerhaave**, a firm believer in the necessity of the basic sciences, from 1700 offered a new course in the area we know as physiology. **Andrew Sinclair,** in Leyden in the 1720's, was greatly influenced by a course of lectures on 'the institutes of medicine', given by Boerhaave. Subsequently, Sinclair became the first incumbent of the new Chair of the Institutes of Medicine, in Edinburgh in 1726. He was followed by **Robert Whytt**, an eminent neurologist and neurophysiologist, whose 'Essay on the vital and Involuntary Motions of Animals' introduced the concept of reflex action. He was still occupying the Chair when WW matriculated in Edinburgh in 1762, and by his lectures and writings was to be a profound influence.

The influence of Boerhaave cannot be overestimated, those who had been privileged to come under his mantle being proud to be known as 'Boerhaave's alumnus.' Mostly they returned to London, Edinburgh and Dublin. Boerhaave was a teacher at Leyden for thirty seven years, and over seven hundred English speaking students passed through his hands during this time.

Towards the end of the seventeenth century, England possessed but two universities, Oxford and Cambridge. For many years both had been granting medical degrees. This was a long drawn out process, and required close attention to the statutes of these institutions. Oxford required an initial degree in the Arts, a minimum of four years. After this, the student proceeded towards a Bachelor of Medicine degree, and then on to the Doctorate. In total, this was a thirteen year marathon! Interestingly, it was possible after a short period of medical study to obtain a 'licence to practise,' without technically possessing a medical degree. Not that the students were treated to a surfeit of wisdom from the Regius Professors. Far from it - many professors gave no lectures at all! Students were thus dependent on young lecturers, whilst themselves gaining clinical experience. To some extent the tutorial system helped in their instruction.

Meanwhile, over in Cambridge the situation was very similar, except that there was no need to have an arts degree as a preliminary. The Regius Chairs were Royal appointments, and were used for political purposes. This did not exactly stimulate the incumbents to give of their best in the cause of medical teaching.

Amazingly, prior to 1719, neither university had a hospital. Addenbrookes opened in 1766, and the Radcliffe at Oxford in 1770. In the main, students resorted to St. Bartholomew's and St. Thomas' hospitals in London, where many received instruction from **Richard Mead**, who had been taught by Boerhaave at Leyden. The other major influence on the development, or lack of it in England at the time was the requirement that students had to be members of the Church of England. As a consequence, many bright Nonconformists sought their education abroad (as indeed did many Oxford and Cambridge men who recognized the quality of the experience to be had there).

The most popular were the universities of Italy (Padua), Holland (Leyden and Utrecht), and France (Montpellier, Paris, and later, Rheims). The European universities conferred degrees after a considerably shorter period of study than did Oxford or Cambridge, so it could reasonably be enquired as to what was the advantage of sticking with these ancient English institutions. The answer was that **only graduates of Oxford or Cambridge were eligible for election to the Fellowship of the Royal College of Physicians of London.** Scotland at this time did not yet possess any facilities for the training of physicians. The Royal College of Physicians of London was situated in Warwick Lane, and is shown in the accompanying figure.

William the Silent, Prince of Orange, in 1574, offered the Burghers of Leyden a choice of either ten years freedom from taxation, or the foundation of a university. They chose the latter (one wonders whether the same choice would be made today!), and on 8th February 1575, the university was inaugurated. Leyden received students of any religious faith, and the university attracted even students with degrees obtained at other universities. Presumably, this was a consequence of the reputation for good instruction, and the influence further afield of the instructors. Of these, undoubtedly the greatest was **Boerhaave**.

He was born on 31st December 1668 at Voorhout, near Leyden, the son of a minister of the local Dutch Reform Church. He entered the university of Leyden in 1684, reading classics, philosophy and divinity. After six years he obtained his PhD. He then decided he wanted to study medicine. His method of so doing was most unorthodox, and perhaps excuses those students who make a habit of not turning up for lectures. It would appear

The Royal College of Physicians, Warwick Lane, London
(Copyright Royal College of Physicians of London. Reproduced with permission).

that Boerhaave never attended a formal medical lecture during this time! How then did he achieve this remarkable feat culminating in his graduating with the MD of the university of Harderwyck in July 1693? He first obtained a post in the university library, and whilst there he read the works of all the great medical writers, and attended dissections by Anton Nuck. He read from Hippocrates to Sydenham. He then practised as a physician in Leyden, and also taught mathematics privately. With the death of the then 'Professor of Medicine and the Institutes,' Charles De'rlincourt in 1697, Boerhaave was given the title 'lector' (Reader) and was appointed on May 1st 1701. His lectures were very successful, and under the term 'Institutes' he covered physiology, general pathology, symptomatology, and therapeutics. As with all great people, his professional life was not without controversy, as will now be briefly described.

For an example of the changes in medical thought and teaching at the time, let us consider the circulation of the blood as then known. **William Harvey's** description in his famous work **"de Motu Cordis"** (1628) was one of the greatest discoveries of the 17th century. However, his theory was not immediately accepted, with many preferring to believe the ideas propounded by **Galen** dating back to the 2nd century A.D. Harvey postulated the passage of blood from small arteries (arterioles) to veins, but it remained for **Malpighi** (1628-94) to observe this in reality using the lungs of a frog. It was description such as this which was required to understand body processes, and by its application, improve the practice of Medicine. Boerhaave gave chemistry a permanent place in his view of the essentials of medical education. He also greatly favoured a knowledge of mathematics and a mechanistic view of disease. Prior to him, medical practice had relied on a precarious degree of empiricism. Good bedside teaching and medical textbooks were very rare. A considerable contribution to this approach was made by **Descartes** (1596-1650), who had sought to distinguish material facts ("res externa") from thoughts and ideas ("res cogitans"). It was an attempt to separate mind from body, ending with the challenge to Medicine to concentrate its study of the body purely from the point of material facts, and apply this principle to studying pathology, and medical treatment. It is of interest therefore that Boerhaave was critical of Descartes, and was publicly challenged about it. Yet he sought to lead Medicine in the direction of a material science, using observation and experience, casting aside mere speculation and deduction that was not based upon scientific observation. Yet here is a paradox, which perhaps lies at the source of the greatness of the man. Whilst his success as a clinician has largely been ascribed to his knowledge of human nature, to his psychological insight and bedside manner, he considered it possible that emotions might cause disease, yet he kept this idea apart from his concept of scientific medical thought. It was the latter attribute which placed him to the fore in the promotion of the materialistic approach in Medicine. This was the direction of medical thought at the time, this was to be his road to greatness – yet his true intentions, and perception of human nature taken together with his scientific materialism – would undoubtedly today have marked him as one who could successfully integrate evidence based medicine with the healing as well as the teaching art.

It is of interest in passing, that during the 19th century, the pendulum of adulation swung the other way. Boerhaave's veneration was diminished in view of his paucity of "medical" research. The fact that he researched and published on the subject of chemistry held no sway, as chemistry was not at that time regarded as sufficiently related to Medicine. This attitude to research in general is currently undergoing great change, with much medical research relying on a good grounding in chemistry, biology, and physics. Historically, Boerhaave remains the great teacher, and among his pupils were **Albrecht von Haller**, a master scientist and founder of the University of Gottingen, **Gerard van Swieten**, founder of the old Vienna school, **Anton de Haen**, a great clinician and friend of van Swieten, and **Carl Linne (Linnaeus)** of Uppsala. E. Ashworth Underwood's book, 'Boerhaave's Men' includes a list of English speaking students promoted by Boerhaave, between 1709 and 1736. Included among them is the name Thomas Percival, Anglo-Britannus, who graduated on 30th August 1724. His nephew, also **Thomas Percival** q.v. was the author of a seminal work on medical ethics.

MEDICINE IN THE 18th CENTURY

The centre of anatomic teaching in the 17th century was Leyden, and at the start of the 18th, Paris. Next was the turn of Edinburgh, as a consequence of the foresight of **John Monro**, a surgeon in the Scottish army. He knew of the current superiority of teaching in Europe, and decided that, having settled in Edinburgh, he would start a medical school. Additionally, he intended his son **Alexander**, already educated at London, Paris and Leyden, to be instrumental in the events that were to follow. In 1720, Alexander was elected to the chair. His lecturing feats and teaching ability were renowned, and the chair was subsequently occupied by two further generations of Alexander Monros, in all Alexander primus, secundus and tertius. It was largely due to their teaching that Edinburgh received the reputation of a great medical teaching centre. Anatomy in London was boosted by the teaching of **John** and **William Hunter**. The latter was also involved in the advancement of obstetrics, as was his mentor, **William Smellie** (1697-1763).

In the field of surgery, **William Cheselden** (1688-1752) stands out. His particular expertise was in cutting for stone, being able to perform a lithotomy in 54 seconds, which was as well, since there was no anaesthetic. He became surgeon at St. Thomas's hospital in 1718. **Percival Pott** (1714-1788) was surgeon at St. Bartholomew's hospital from 1744-1787, and received acclaim not least for his publication on palsy from spinal deformity (tuberculous caries), in 1779. Towards the end of the century, he had the largest surgical practice in London.

Prior to **John Hunter**, surgeons operated in ignorance of the pathology of the condition. It was merely a technique. Subsequently, with the addition of physiology and pathology, it took its place as a branch of scientific medicine.

Clinical medicine advanced towards a greater degree of precision as a consequence of knowledge of pathology, gained from autopsies, and from the clinical discovery of the value of **percussion**. This was thanks to **Leopold Auenbrugger** (1722-1809), physician in chief in Vienna in 1751. In 1761, he revealed his new invention, namely the art of percussing the chest. He was the son of an innkeeper. In order to determine how much beer was left in barrels, the custom was to observe the sound that emanated after the barrel was thumped. Little fluid resulted in a hollow sound, whereas a full barrel gave an altogether different solid sound. He was able to compare the sounds obtained by gently thumping the chest of a patient (percussion), with the subsequent autopsy findings. He used cadavers to demonstrate the effect of the injection of fluid into the chest, and used this newly discovered adjunct to diagnosis to perform thoracentesis, which is the removal of fluid from the pleural cavity of patients with an accumulation of fluid (pleural effusion). This can afford great relief to patients in whom the presence of excess fluid around the lungs causes severe shortness of breath. As is not uncommon in Medicine, he received many slights and snubs, but ultimately, recognition.

Modern pathological anatomy owes much to the descriptions by **Giovanni Morgagni** (1682-1771), a pupil of Valsalva, and later, professor at Padua.

He gave the first descriptions of cerebral gummas (areas of brain destroyed by inflammation, due to syphilis) and of disease of the mitral valve. He also described syphilitic aneurysm, acute yellow atrophy of the liver, renal tuberculosis, and the first recorded case of complete heart block (Stokes Adams disease). He also proved, what Valsalva had claimed, namely, that the cerebral lesion in stroke is on the opposite side of the brain to the paralysed side.

Consultation fees in the 18th century are a subject of some interest. The guinea came into use in Restoration England in 1660. A well known physician, **Richard Mead (1673-1754)** used to charge a guinea as an office fee, two for a visit, and half a guinea for apothecaries, who sought his prescriptions whilst he was relaxing in a coffee-house, never seeing the patient for whom the prescription was intended. He earned £5,000-£6,000 per annum. **Fothergill** earned the same, **Lettsom** £12,000. However, the greatest fee of the time was earned by **Thomas Dimsdale** (qv) for inoculating Catherine of Russia and her son, namely $50,000, with $10,000 for travelling expenses, a pension of $2,500 for life, and the rank of Baron of the Russian Empire. At that time university professors were well paid, e.g. Morgagni earning $4,500 per year in Padua.

During the 18th century, the **London Pharmacopoiea** saw many changes. It appeared in 1721, 1746, and 1788. The first of these dropped many syrups and waters. The 1746 version condemned many old astrologic and folk remedies, though it still retained some. It was due to **Heberden's** writings that many were ridiculed and dropped from the 1788 version. **Unfortunately, despite Withering's publication on digitalis in 1785, it was not included until 1809, 10 years after his death**.

Surgery, except in France, enjoyed very little status during the 18th century. It owed its status in France to the good fortune (for surgery) of Louis XIV developing a fistula, successfully treated by **Felix**. Felix and his successor **Mareschal** obtained from Louis the facility to open five chairs in surgical instruction at St. Come. This was too much for the physicians, who, headed by the Dean of the medical faculty, and accompanied by the beadle and an usher, resplendent in their finest robes despite the snow and sleet, strode out in anger to protest at the door of St. Come. All in vain, as they were jeered and dispersed by the students within. On December 18th, 1731, the Academy of Surgery was founded. In 1743, Louis XV decreed that barbers and wig-makers were forbidden to practise, and that no-one in surgery could be a master without being a master of the arts. Thus did the surgeon in France achieve independence. Instrumental in the King's decision, was the influence of **La Peyronie**, surgeon in Montpellier, who founded the Academy of Surgery together with Mareschal. Montpellier had four chairs in surgery, each surgeon being required to lecture also to midwives. Through La Peyronie, Paris became the surgical centre of the world during the 18th century. Yet, unbelievably, as a consequence of the French revolution, 18 medical faculties and 15 medical colleges of France were abolished by vote, together with the Académie de Chirugie and the Societé Royale de Médecine. Instead, by 1794, there were created Écoles de Santé, and henceforward, doctors were to be replaced by 'health officers' (officiers de santé). Physicians and surgeons could no longer be distinguished; anyone who paid a fee for a license was eligible to practise. The Écoles de Santé (situated in Paris, Strasbourg and Montpellier), were in effect schools of military medicine, designed to supply military surgeons for the armies of the Republic. It was not until 1803-4 that medical and surgical faculties were restored, with the revival of examinations and diplomas.

In England, the future of surgery lay in the capable hands of Pott, Cheselden, Hunter and Abernethy. **In 1745, surgeons were formally separated from barbers**, and named themselves "Masters, Governors, and Commonality of the Art and Science of Surgeons of London," with the power to examine and grant license to practice within seven miles of London. In 1800, George II rechartered the Corporation of Surgeons into what became the Royal College of Surgeons.

Many new hospitals were built during the 18th century. Their dates of opening are shown in the table.

NEW HOSPITALS COMPLETED IN THE 18TH CENTURY

In London:

THE WESTMINSTER	1719	THE LONDON	1740
GUY'S	1725	THE MIDDLESEX	1745
ST.GEORGE'S	1733	THE SMALL POX	1746

Provincial Hospitals:

YORK	1710	STAFFORD	1769
SALISBURY	1716	OXFORD	1770
CAMBRIDGE	1719	LEICESTER	1771
BRISTOL	1735	NORWICH	1771
WINDSOR	1736	BIRMINGHAM	1778
NORTHAMPTON	1743	NOTTINGHAM	1782
EXETER	1745	CANTERBURY	1793
WORCESTER	1745	NEWCASTLE	1751
MANCHESTER	1753		
CHESTER	1755		
LEEDS	1767		

Scotland:

EDINBURGH	1729	MONTROSE	1780
ABERDEEN	1739	GLASGOW	1794
DUMFRIES	1775	DUNDEE	1795

Ireland (North and South):

CORK	1720-22	LIMERICK	1759
DUBLIN	1726	BELFAST	1797

MEDICAL SCHOOLS IN NORTH AMERICA

Prior to 1800, there were five good medical schools:

University of Pennsylvania (1765)

King's College (New York) (1767) later (1792), to become Columbia College

Harvard University (1782)

College of Philadelphia (1790)

Dartmouth College (1798)

Subsequently, many more medical schools were founded. Standards were very variable, and in 1910, Abraham Flexner's report to the Carnegie Foundation for the Advancement of Teaching, titled "Medical Education in the United States and Canada" was published. This was a sort of QAA (Quality Assurance Agency) report. In the case of the University of Pennsylvania for instance, it stated that its laboratory facilities were new and admirably suited to their purpose, whereas other places received comments such as "hardly more than nominal" (clinical facilities), "Neither of these schools has either resources or ideals; there is no justification for their existence—the (——) school is an utterly hopeless affair, for which no word can be said——"

MUSIC IN WITHERING'S TIME

Edinburgh was the great social centre of Scotland in the eighteenth century, and was also active in the field of music. Many foreign musicians settled in the city at this time, and orchestral activity was considerable. One notable musical family was the **Gow** family. **Niel Gow (1727-1807)**, was a famous violinist, who performed at balls and assemblies. He only played traditional Scottish music, and composed many reels and strathspeys. Folk songs were plentiful, of which the **Highland Vocal Airs** of **Patrick Macdonald (1781),** were amongst the foremost.

With Purcell's death in 1695, a period of decline set in. Whereas the continent of Europe was to spawn works by such as Haydyn, Mozart, Beethoven, Wagner and others, England could only claim Handel (who anyway was naturalised). A notable exception however, was **The Beggar's Opera** (1728), the song lyrics and dialogue of which were by **John Gay** (1685-1732), and the music by **John Pepusch** (1667-1752), the producer was **John Rich** (1692-1761). The work was said to have made Rich gay (within the contemporary meaning of the word), and Gay rich. This piece of political satire hit at the Prime Minister Sir Robert Walpole, and alluded to the political corruption that was rife at the time. The sequel, or second part of the opera, titled **Polly**, was banned by the Lord Chamberlain of the time, and only reached the stage in 1777. Its popularity, and that of several imitators which followed, temporarily drove Italian opera off the English stage, which did not please Handel overmuch. The origin of the opera was a chance remark to Gay by Pope, "A Newgate Pastoral might make an odd pretty sort of thing." Some of the scenes are set in Newgate prison. The age was one of callous indifference to poverty and suffering, with capital punishment enforced for minor theft, which in turn was the consequence of poverty. The conditions within the prisons caused **Lettsom** (q.v.) to lobby for improvements to be made, and for basic hygiene standards to be established, and to be illustrated by **Hogarth** (q.v.). The Beggar's Opera reached Paris in 1750 ("L'Opera des gueux") and New York. The possible effect of this opera on morals was much discussed. It was bitterly condemned by Burke, (who also condemned the French Revolution), but Dr. Johnson said:

"I am of opinion that more influence has been ascribed to The Beggar's Opera than it in reality ever had; for I do not believe that any man was ever made a rogue by being present at its representation," though on another occasion he remarked:

——(there was in the work) "such a labefactation of all principles as might be injurious to morality."

The leading English composer of this period was **Thomas Arne** (1710-1778), who received several commissions from theatre managers. He wrote incidental music and operas, and a masque called "Alfred" for the Prince of Wales, from which came "Rule, Britannia."

The **Glee** was very popular. It was designed for male solo voices, and consisted of a number of short movements, set to a poem. The high period for glee composition was 1750-1830. Several Glee Clubs were formed, the first so called being formed in London in 1783. George IV both as Prince of Wales and king, was a keen participant.

Generally however, in England in the eighteenth century, there was a serious decline in the domestic cultivation of music, which was mainly left to the females of the more affluent sector of society. It was regarded as an accomplishment, or cultural adornment, rather than as a source of serious pursuit and mastery. By contrast, the stars of the time were Italian operatic virtuosos. England's desire to import talent and to ignore its own was already in evidence.

The spinet and harpsichord existed side by side throughout the later 17th and 18th centuries, but a new player in the field was the pianoforte. At the end of the 18th century it was seriously competitive, and by the 19th century, it reigned supreme. The last public performance on the harpsichord in the 18th century was at St.James's Palace in 1795, whereas it remained in common use in France for a further twenty years.

Chapter 7

CONTEMPORARIES OF WITHERING, BOTH FROM MEDICINE AND OTHER FIELDS

TABLE SHOWING CONTEMPORARIES OF WITHERING

NAME	DATES	STATUS
EDMUND BURKE	1729-1797	STATESMAN & POLITICAL THEORIST
THOMAS CHIPPENDALE	c.1718-1779	CABINET MAKER
ROBERT CLIVE	1725-1774	STATESMAN
DAVID GARRICK	1719-1779	ACTOR
JAMES GILLRAY	1757-1815	CARICATURIST
THOMAS GAINSBOROUGH	1727-1788	PAINTER
EDWARD GIBBON	1737-1744	HISTORIAN
OLIVER GOLDSMITH	1728-1774	PLAYWRIGHT & POET
WILLIAM HEBERDEN	1710-1801	PHYSICIAN, LONDON
WILLIAM HOGARTH	1697-1764	SATIRICAL PAINTER
JOHN HUNTER	1728-1793	ANATOMIST
HALL JACKSON	1739-1797	PHYSICIAN, USA
EDWARD JENNER	1749-1823	PHYSICIAN, GLOUCESTER
JOHN LETTSOM	1744-1815	PHYSICIAN, LONDON
JAMES LIND	1744-1794	NAVAL PHYSICIAN, HASLAR
THOMAS PERCIVAL	1740-1804	PHYSICIAN, MANCHESTER,
JOSHUA REYNOLDS	1723-1792	PAINTER
BENJAMIN RUSH	1745-1813	PHYSICIAN, USA
THOMAS SHERATON	c.1751-1806	CABINET MAKER
RICHARD SHERIDAN	1751-1816	PLAYWRIGHT & POLITICIAN
VOLTAIRE	1694-1778	AUTHOR
JOHN WESLEY	1703-1791	FOUNDER OF METHODISM
WILLIAM WORDSWORTH	1770-1850	POET
JOHANN ZOFFANY	1733-1810	PAINTER

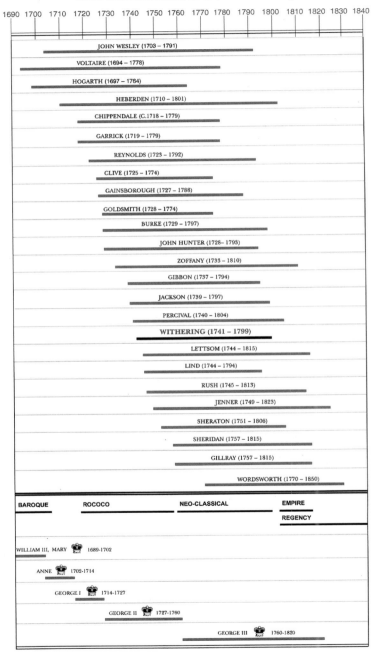

Exits and Entrances in the 18th Century

The 18th century was a time of accelerated change. The Industrial Revolution undoubtedly played its part in altering the lives of everybody. Other political events, alluded to in chapter 1 were of equal importance. It would perhaps be of interest to chronicle the lives of some contemporaries, not necessarily known by WW, to weave a little colour into the tapestry of the time. Liberty is taken to include not only the lives of physicians, but also politicians, writers, painters, artisans and others, as shown in the foregoing table

WILLIAM HOGARTH (1697 - 1764)

The great English painter and pictorial satirist, died when WW was only 23yr, but would undoubtedly have been heard of by WW as a consequence of his famous works.

Hogarth painting the Comic Muse is seen above, self-portrait.
(Reproduced by permission of the National Portrait Gallery, London).

Hogarth's works depicted aspects of life ranging from everyday scenes such as **Beer Street** (1751), to those of utter depravity, **The Rakes progress**, and **Gin Lane**. **The Company of Undertakers** (1737) was an expression of his venom towards physicians. A contemporary writer stated that the physicians depicted by Hogarth were not caricatures: "The full dress with the sword and great tye-wig, and the hat under the arm, and the doctors in consultation, each smelling to a gold-headed cane...are pictures of real life in his time."

Above is shown the first of the "Four stages of cruelty." Here Tom Nero, with the badge of the Parish of St. Giles below his right shoulder, is shown holding the hind legs of the unfortunate canine which one suspects is not the subject of a genuine sigmoidoscopic examination.

"The Reward of Cruelty" seen over the page, depicts an anatomy lesson given by the President of the Royal College of Physicians, who is seen beneath the logo of the College, a hand feeling a pulse. The Royal Arms are also shown. The skeletons belong to James Field a pugilist on the left, and a highwayman, Macleane, whose arm is seen on the right. Tom Nero, lately hanged, (he had murdered his girl friend after she had stolen her mistress' possessions and given them to him, - the source of another picture), is here shown as the subject of the anatomy lesson. He is having his entrails removed and placed in a bucket, whilst his heart is providing sustenance to a dog. This carries with it a certain poetic justice, bearing in mind his previous misdemeanour to a canine. The noose is still tied around Nero's neck. His skull has been transfixed by an iron hook connected to a block and pulley for rapid transport, probably for storage above the dissecting room. The fact that his heart is about to be eaten lessens the credence of the seriousness of this anatomy lesson. The skull and its contents would be somewhat affected by the aforementioned apparatus.

The Reward of Cruelty.

Bones are seen cooking in a cauldron, possibly to remove the soft parts so that the skeletal remains could be used to teach anatomy. Three skulls and three femurs (thigh bones) are seen.

ROBERT CLIVE (1725 - 1774)

Was born in 1725 in Moreton Say, in the parish of Market Drayton, Shropshire, at Styche the family estate, within 15 miles from Wellington, WW's birthplace. The Clives were one of Shropshire's oldest families, having held the manor of that name in the reign of Henry II. Robert's father for many years represented Montgomeryshire in parliament. He was educated at the Merchant Taylor's school where he forfeited education for adventure, to the despair of his teachers. At the age of 18, (when Withering was a toddler of 2), he was sent out to Madras as a writer for the civil service of the East India company. In 1746 he obtained an ensign's commission. He was one of the 'soldier-politicals' to whom Britain owed the conquest and consolidation of India. He became famous for his defence of the citadel of Arcot, under siege in 1751. Following this and the repulse of the Chandar Sahib with his French supporters, Clive established a European reputation. Pitt pronounced him a 'heaven-born general' (he was 27). He married Margaret Maskelyne in 1753, and returned to England. He went back to India as Governor of Fort St. David in 1756, and as

A statue to Clive is situated in Shrewsbury, as seen above.
Also shown is a portrait of Clive by Nathaniel Dance
(the latter reproduced by permission of the National Portrait Gallery, London).

Lieutenant-colonel in the king's army. In 1760, aged 35 he returned after many achievements together with a fortune of £300,000 and the quit-rent of £27,000 a year. The money had been honourably and publicly acquired with the approval of the East India company. He was well received at court, and was made Baron Clive of Plassey, in the peerage of Ireland. He then set himself to reform the home system of the East India company and began a bitter war with Sulivan, chairman of the court of directors, whom in the end he defeated.

Things were going badly wrong in Bengal, 150 English were butchered at Patna, the civil and military components of the company were the victims of bribery and corruption, with plundering of the company's revenues. Thus, Lord Clive was sent to Bengal as governor and commander-in-chief. Within two years, he had taken control of the situation, and founded the empire of British India. On his return to England he found himself attacked by many enemies claiming that he himself had corruptly received large amounts of monies. Every civilian whose illicit gains he had cut off, every officer whose conspiracy he had foiled, every proprietor or director, like Sulivan, whose selfish schemes he had thwarted, now sought his opportunity. General John Burgoyne, of Saratoga memory, did his best to induce the House of Commons, in which Lord Clive was member for Shrewsbury, to impeach the man who gave his country an empire, and the people of that empire peace and justice. The result was a compromise, in which the House divided 155 to 95, carried the motion that Clive 'did obtain and possess himself' of £234,000 during his first administration of Bengal, but refusing to express an opinion on the fact, it passed unanimously at five in the morning the second motion 'that Robert, Lord Clive, did at the same time render great and meritorious services to his country.' The effects on Clive were profound. In his greatest speech, replying to Lord North he said, 'My situation, sir, has not been an easy one for these 12 months past, and though my conscience could never accuse me, yet I felt for my friends who were involved in the same censure as myself.....I have been examined by the select committee more like a sheep stealer than a member of this house.' He also suffered physically, and attempted to assuage his pain with opium. On November 22nd 1774, at the age of 50, he took his own life.

Though there is no record of direct contact with Withering, these dramatic goings on would doubtless have been endlessly discussed (along with matters of a scientific nature), over port and pipe at the meetings of the **Lunar Society**, of which Withering became a member in 1775.

DAVID GARRICK (1719-1779)

Born in Hereford, he was descended from a French family named Garric or Garrique. His father was a sea captain, who married Arabella Clough the daughter of the vicar of Lichfield cathedral choir. He was educated at Lichfield Grammar school, before being sent to one of Samuel Johnson's academies at the age of 19 years, Johnson being 26 years old. Within six months it had closed and both men went to seek their fortune in London. Shortly afterwards his father and uncle died, the latter leaving him £1000, with which he and his brother set up wine businesses in Lichfield and London. It did not prosper however, and in any case Garrick was by now totally engrossed in the stage. His first play

Portrait of Garrick by Thomas Gainsborough.
(Reproduced by permission of the National Portrait Gallery, London).

was called Lethe or Aesop in the Shades, and was performed at Drury Lane on April 15th 1740. His first stage appearance was a year later at Goodman's Fields Theatre. His performance as Richard III in 1741 brought him acclaim. From 1742 to 1745 he played at Drury Lane. He was a fervent admirer of a Margaret (Peg) Woffington who was reputedly reckless and beautiful. However, he was to marry Eva Maria Veigel, a German dancer. In 1764 whilst in Italy Garrick became seriously ill, and by 1766 had practically ceased acting. He organised the Shakespeare celebrations at Stratford-upon-Avon in 1769 which Withering, currently practising in Stafford, attended.

JAMES GILLRAY (1756-1815)

He was born in Chelsea, and the only one of five children to survive childhood. He was educated at the Moravian academy for boys in Bedford. The essential faith of the Brethren of that establishment was the essential depravity of man. The total worthlessness of life was drummed into the children. Death would be a glorious release from a life of bondage. Fortunately the Moravian Brethren had to disband their schools in 1764 for financial reasons (one anticipates their schools were never really popular). Gillray's caricatures are divided into the political, royalty, and the social series. The former are a record of the latter part of George III's reign. The cast included George III, the Queen, the Prince of Wales, Fox, Pitt, Burke and Napoleon.

His portrait is shown below, artist unknown.

Portrait of James Gillray
(Reproduced with permission of the National Portrait Gallery, London).

The Cow-Pock — or — the Wonderful Effects of the New Inoculation!

He also captured the public's imagination with his portrayal of Dr. Edward Jenner testing his new vaccine with some dramatic bovinesque results, as portrayed above.

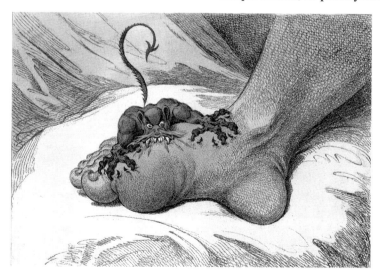

The Gout

From a medical point of view, perhaps his best known illustration is "The Gout", shown above which was published on 14th May 1799, just four months before Withering's death. No doubt Withering would have appreciated Gillray's humour.

EDWARD JENNER (1749-1823)

Was born about eight years after Withering, in Chauntry Cottage, Berkeley, Gloucestershire. He was the eighth child of Stephen Jenner, Deacon of Berkeley and his wife Sarah, née Head. Two male siblings died, Henry at two and a half years of age, and Edward at five. Two weeks after the death of the first Edward, our subject was born. In 1754, when Edward was 5, his mother gave birth to a sixth son, who died within days, and his mother died next day, aged forty six. His father died two months later, aged fifty two. Thus orphaned, Edward was looked after by his sisters. In 1757, he attended Wooton-under-Edge Grammar school, boarding with the headmaster. Jenner was not an enthusiastic pupil, changing schools twice. At age thirteen, he became apprenticed to Mr. John Ludlow, a surgeon-teacher of Chipping Sodbury. He was the first of his family to have embarked upon a career in medicine, and he remained apprenticed for the next six years. At that time it was common knowledge to those working in dairies, that cows often carried an infection in their teats, called Cow Pox, and that this could also infect the hands of the milkers. Furthermore, people thus infected seemed less likely to contract the smallpox. In 1770, Jenner enrolled as a boarding pupil at St. George's Hospital, when

Edward Jenner, portrait by James Northcote.
(Reproduced by permission of the National Portrait Gallery, London)

John Hunter was chief surgeon, and communicated these facts to him. John Hunter's elder brother William, ran a private medical school in Great Windmill Street, in which Jenner also studied until May 1772. It is likely that his medical education by this route was far superior to that available at Oxbridge during that era.

Whilst at school, Edward was treated by the procedure termed 'variolation' to prevent him getting smallpox. Variolation involved injecting serum obtained from a smallpox papule into the body of a healthy person. The logic was that people who were known to have had smallpox and recovered did not succumb to it again. Therefore, since the likelihood of being smitten was great, better to have it when fit and strong than when debilitated and vulnerable. **Avicenna** (979-1037), a great Arab physician was originally credited with this technique, but there is no hard evidence. In India and China, a similar practise was carried out, which differed in that the dried out smallpox scabs were sniffed instead of any injection being given. Today, this would be regarded as utilizing the mucosal immune system, much as the giving of oral polio vaccine. Variolation was introduced to England by **Lady Mary Wortley Montagu** (1689-1762). In a letter from Constantinople to a friend, on April 1st 1717, she said:

"Apropos of distempers, I am going to tell you a thing that will make you wish yourself here. The small-pox, so fatal, and so general amongst us, is here entirely harmless, by the invention of **ingrafting**, which is the term they give it. There is a set of old women, who make it their business to perform the operation, every autumn in the month of September, when the great heat is abated.

People send to one another to know if any of their family has a mind to have the small-pox: they make parties for this purpose, and when they are met (commonly fifteen or sixteen together) the old woman comes with a nut-shell full of the matter of the best sort of small-pox, and asks what vein you please to have opened.

She immediately rips open that you offer her, with a large needle (which gives you no more pain than a common scratch) and puts into the vein, as much matter as can lie upon the head of her needle, and after that binds up the little wound with a hollow bit of shell; and in this manner opens four or five veins.

The Grecians have commonly the superstition of opening one in the middle of the forehead, one in each arm, and one on the breast, to mark the sign of the cross; but this has a very ill effect, all these wounds leaving little scars, and is not done by those that are not superstitious, who chose to have them in the legs, or that part of the arm that is concealed.

The children or young patients play together all the rest of the day, and are in perfect health to the eighth. Then the fever begins to seize them, and they keep their beds two days, very seldom three. They have very rarely above twenty or thirty on their faces, which never mark, and in eight days they are as well as before their illness. Where they are wounded, there remain running sores during the distemper, which I don't doubt is a great relief to it.

Every year thousands undergo this operation; and the French Ambassador says pleasantly, that they take the small-pox here by way of diversion, as they take the waters in other countries. There is no example of anyone that has died in it; and you may believe I am well satisfied of the safety of this experiment, since I intend to try it on my dear little son.

I am patriot enough to take pains to bring this useful invention into fashion in England, and I should not fail to write to some of our doctors very particularly about it, if I knew any one of them that I thought had virtue enough to destroy such a considerable branch of their revenue, for the good of mankind. But that distemper is too beneficial to them, not to expose all their resentment, the hardy weight that should undertake to put an end to it. Perhaps, if live to return, I may, have courage to war with them. Upon this occasion, admire the heroism in the heart of your friend." ("Letters of the Right Honourable Lady M-y W-y M-e, written during her travels in Europe, Asia and Africa." London, 1777, pp. 108-109).

(Lady Montagu clearly did not hold the medical profession of the time in high esteem. Smallpox would seem to have been, in her view, the profession's bread and butter).

Subsequently, she had her two children variolated, without undue problem. Since she went public, it was no surprise that it caused considerable controversy. The clergy were against it for interfering with the ways of Providence. More examples were now needed in order to demonstrate the safety of the procedure. Luckily, Lady Montagu had a friend in a high place, Princess Caroline, who persuaded the monarch, George I to promise a free pardon to any criminal resident in Newgate prison who agreed to undergo variolation. Six volunteers were safely treated on August 9th, 1721. But the procedure was doomed after the variolation of Mary Batt, daughter of a Quaker in Hertford in October 1721. She recovered, but six of the family's domestics developed smallpox after contact, and subsequently an outbreak occurred in Hertford. Doomed, but not yet. The disease was still such a scourge, and the successes previously achieved so compelling, that variolation still had its race to run. **Robert Sutton**, a surgeon-apothecary of Framlingham, Norfolk, and later Ipswich, practised variolation from 1757, and claimed to have inoculated 2,500 patients over an eleven year period without a death. His son Daniel settled in Ingatestone, Essex, which was convenient for the London clientele, yet outside the jurisdiction of the Corporation of Surgeons. He established his house of inoculation, as well as several other houses in which his patients lodged during the course of the treatment (the local inns would not take them in order to dispel fears of contagion). He treated the poor free, and this meant the place was teeming with eager patients. The locals were most displeased and took him to court in 1765 at Chelmsford Assizes, where he was found not guilty of spreading abroad the contagion of smallpox.

But what was his secret? Why was he able (like his father) to inoculate thousands without a single recorded death? The answer lay in the so-called Suttonian technique, which he published in 1796. This involved the use of the serum from a four day papule as the inoculum. Use of later papules was fraught with danger, since they had by then become super-infected with bacteria - and were in fact pustules. It was the overwhelming superadded bacterial infection which so often proved fatal in unskilled inoculation, as in the naturally occurring disease itself.

Many imitators followed, the most successful of whom was **Thomas** (later **Baron) Dimsdale** (1712-1800), of Theydon Gernon, in Essex. He came from a family of Quakers long associated with the medical profession. He had studied at St. Thomas's, but failed to get on the staff, and settled as a surgeon at Hertford. In 1761 he took the Aberdeen MD. He studied the Sutton technique and adopted it. Whereas Sutton's appeal was populist, Dimsdale's was to a somewhat more up-market clientele. Joseph Cockfield, in a letter dated March 26th 1766, wrote:

"The terms (of Sutton) are so moderate that men in mean circumstances, men of low education and dissolute life, repair to his house, which is so confused and disorderly a place that one would admire one-tenth part of his patients do not perish by their irregularities." Dimsdale's fame arose out of the consequence of his acceptance of the invitation of Empress Catherine II of Russia to introduce inoculation over there (Sutton having been asked first and declined). He returned a Baron, in receipt of a fee of £10,000, the rank of Major-General, and a pension of £500 per year. He subsequently eclipsed the Suttons and became the talk of London. The discerning reader will deduce, by reference to page 141, that the rate of exchange then was approximately $5 to the pound.

A great controversy over inoculation arose out of the opposing views of the Suttonites (mass inoculation for the poor, at greater risk of contagion), and the more costly technique of Dimsdale, requiring several weeks of preparation, followed by a similar period of recovery and relative avoidance of close contact. A group of philanthropists wished to start an Inoculation Dispensary, and sought support. Dimsdale not unexpectedly refused, whilst another physician, **J. Coakley Lettsom** (qv) got dragged into the dispute, and supported the idea. This led to a clash between Dimsdale and Lettsom, with to and fro correspondence. Whilst the technique saved lives, it was unreliable, and **very expensive**. This was because the procedure commenced by two to four weeks of preparing the patient, up to two weeks for the disease to run its course, plus a month's convalescence. From 1754, the technique was modified and involved inoculating the serum as apart from the pus, from a vesicle. Thus, there was a much reduced risk of bacterial infection. This method was approved by the Royal College of Physicians. Variolation was on the increase, and in London, the Smallpox and Inoculation Hospitals cared for the poor during the natural disease and after variolation. In Gloucester, a smallpox hospital opened in 1768, and by 1771, had inoculated 4,829 people. But if a procedure were to be developed which meant that patients did not require hospitalisation, and which was at least equally efficacious, its success would be guaranteed. (Recognition of the advantage of day-case procedures!).

To return to the Cow Pox. Hunter mentioned Jenner's communication regarding the immunity to smallpox of dairy maids previously infected by cowpox, to Dr. **Thomas Beddoes** of Bristol. Beddoes subsequently published his own book, containing these facts, but acknowledging Hunter's communication. Contrast this with Robert Darwin's clumsy attempt to append the clinical information about the use of digitalis for the dropsy, given him in good faith by Withering, to his ill-fated son's thesis.

Meanwhile in 1771, **Captain Cook** returned to England aboard the **Endeavour** having circumnavigated the globe. On board were the botanist Joseph Banks, with his

Portrait of Sir Joseph Banks, by Sir Joshua Reynolds.
(Reproduced with permission of the National Portrait Gallery, London).

assistant Daniel Solander from the British Museum. They brought back many specimens previously unclassified. John Hunter recommended Jenner to Banks, as a suitable person to assist in the classification. (This pre-dated Withering's publication of his classification 'The Botanical Arrangement of all the Vegetables naturally growing in Great Britain' by 5 years, otherwise it would seem that Withering would have been the obvious person to have approached for this task). According to John Coakley Lettsom, Jenner was invited to accompany Cook on his second voyage, but refused 'partly guided by the deep and grateful affection.....for his eldest brother....and partly by an attachment to the rural scenes and habits of his early youth.' This speaks volumes of Jenner's lack of sense of adventure, and 'placidity' as described by Richard B. Fisher in his book. Jenner was to refuse two other offers: Hunter's offer of a partnership, and an offer of a medical appointment in India with an annuity of £30,001.

In the course of Jenner's medical practice, which extended over an area calculated by R.B.Fisher to extend over about four hundred square miles, he sought the advice of **William Heberden** (qv) in regard to treating a patient probably suffering from angina. This is an indication of his willingness to refer for advice, the sign of a mature approach to a medical problem. Jenner also attracted attention as a chemist, botanist and ornithologist. In 1783, he published 'Cursory Observations on Emetic Tartar' (antimony potassium tartrate). The act of emesis (vomiting) at that time was thought to combat fever by releasing matter from the gut. Jenner's contribution was to elaborate a technique for its purification. Hunter's reply (quoted from R.B.Fisher) is interesting:

'I have a great deal to say about it. First, do you mean to take out a Patint? Do you mean to advertise it? or do you mean to let it take its chance. I approve of it much, and will do all in my power to promote the sale, but I would advise you to give it a new name expressive either of the composition or of its virtues in the body viz sal antim: or sal sudorif: or sal antim:sudorif: I would also desire you to burn your Book for you will have all the world making it.'

However much we may admire these men, the call of money was never far distant, certainly as far as Hunter was concerned. In the event, Jenner dithered, despite the cajoling of Hunter, and it was a decade later that he published his method. He made no attempt to keep the method secret - his intention was to be made a Fellow of the Royal Society.

Between 1780 and 1782 he undertook several experiments on the horticultural properties of human blood. This work was carried out at the behest of Joseph Banks, President of the Royal Society.

However it was Jenner's 'Observations on the Natural History of the Cuckoo' which was to attain for him the prize he craved.

The question at issue, nowadays taken for granted, was by which means was the ejection of the host bird's young from the nest brought about? Was it by act of the parent, ejecting its own in favour of its fosterling? Thus did Jenner report in an earlier paper titled 'Observations on the Cuckoo.' The essential observations which led to this conclusion were based on the data provided by his nephew Henry, whose job it was to tour various nests in the locality, and report his findings. John Baron, in his biography on Jenner has implied that perhaps Henry was not as diligent as he might have been, and therefore the observations were not entirely correct. But Jenner was not really convinced, and decided to carry out further observations.

He used hedge sparrows' nests which had a cuckoo's egg naturally deposited there. After the usual sequence of events i.e. the gradual expulsion of the host chicks, he decided to experiment further. If the parents were turfing out their own young (which would take a bit of explaining), then by placing two cuckoos in the same nest, they would presumably both be cared for. On the other hand, if the cuckoo chick was to blame, then one might expect some action between the chicks. This in fact was what he observed. In another experiment, he tied some lead weights around the legs of a cuckoo chick, which as a consequence was unable to eject its nest-mates. Jenner went further,and by careful dissection, was able to demonstrate a small dip in the back of cuckoo chicks up to the age of 12 days. This dip was used as a kind of ladle to gather up the host chicks, transport them to the edge of the nest, and then eject them to oblivion. These claims were very controversial, and only received cinematographic proof in 1921. However, it was sufficient to gain him his Fellowship of the Royal Society, being elected in February 1789.

The mystery as to why a creature should adapt to its environment by adopting such peculiar behaviour was also explained ingeniously by Jenner. An earlier theory had it that cuckoos could not hatch their own because their large stomachs were unusually susceptible to rupture by sitting. Jenner did not believe this. Instead, from an understanding of the migratory habits of these birds, (they stay in our land for not more than 11 weeks, but the time needed from laying the egg to eventual independence of the chick, can be as long as 15 weeks), it seems the cuckoo thought it all out very carefully and hit upon the idea of enforced fostering. How this pattern of behaviour became a genetic trait, together with the anatomical modifications required is fascinating, and not a little puzzling (to the author at least).

Jenner's greatest contribution, as is universally known, was the prevention of smallpox, as a consequence of the technique of vaccination, using fluid from a cowpox pustule. But before this, it was necessary to obtain the vaccinial fluid, and cowpox was not all that common. If the cowpox could be transmitted from human to human, than we would have a readily available source of this fluid, and not have to await the natural event in a cow.

Sarah Nelmes, the daughter of a farmer, having scratched her hand on a thorn, was milking cows. She subsequently developed cowpox. On 14th May 1796, Jenner inoculated some cowpox fluid taken from a pustule on Sarah's hand into each of two incisions about an inch long, on the arm of an eight year old boy, **James Phipps**, the son of a labourer who worked for the Jenner family. On day 4, some redness was apparent in the vicinity of the inoculations, and on days 8 and 9, two pustules appeared which resembled those seen after variolation. James did not become ill, suffering only a mild lassitude with fever for a couple of days. 6 weeks after the vaccination, he was variolated (i.e. inoculated with smallpox material, which under normal circumstances would have resulted in the typical sequence of events described previously under variolation, and typical of this procedure). This would have included an illness of about two week's duration. Amazingly, there was no reaction. A state of immunity had been achieved! (Of course, it is very unlikely all this would have been ethically approved nowadays, and additionally, positive and negative controls would be considered necessary before jumping to any conclusions). What is of considerable interest, is the fact that Jenner did not himself variolate James Phipps, leaving this to another (possibly Henry Jenner, his nephew). Strange indeed that so momentous an experiment was delegated.

Now Jenner was faced with the challenge of publication of his work. But before doing so, he needed more data. Subsequently, Jenner and others were to use both cowpox vesicle fluid from cows with cowpox, and humans, in order to vaccinate. Problems with superinfection, leading to pustular eruptions occurred, and caused controversies, as this seemed to occur with differing frequency depending on the source of the material and who was administering it. One must remember that the germ theory of disease at this time had not been proved, and bacteria (let alone viruses) had not been visualised. Jenner, describing what might be involved in the storage and transportation of variolous lymph (fluid from a smallpox vesicle - though the same argument would apply in the case of cowpox) observed that the fluid would be placed on a piece of cotton or lint which was then put inside a corked vial, which in turn was placed inside a warm pocket. "Putrefaction" frequently followed, and yet this same material was subsequently used for inoculation. Small wonder that inflammation and swollen glands followed. Worse still, such material was likely to have lost its protective properties against the smallpox - and the unfortunate patient would not know this, assuming in their lay ignorance, that the inflammation and suffering were part of the price to pay for protection against the dreaded disease. This led to controversy, that the vaccination was not protective. Jenner dismissed this by talking about "spurious cowpox" which just muddied the waters. Considering the following:

1. The germ theory of disease was not at that time proved.
2. Bacteria (the cause of putrefaction) had never been visualised.
3. There were several diseases that affected cows' udders, not just vaccinia, also producing pocks.
4. There was no concept of sterility, or availability of sterile lancets for inoculating.
5. There were no antibiotics to combat secondary (bacterial) infection.
6. Serum hepatitis had not been discovered, blood transfusions were not yet in use, but it would seem likely that the virus existed, and that it would readily be propagated as a consequence of vaccination using human cowpox fluid.
7. Cowpox cases on farms were not particularly common, just when there was a great need for them, in order to further the work, and to answer several important questions.
8. Sound experimental methods including appropriate statistical analyses were not yet described.
9. To the intelligent experimenter, there was the fear that others would jump on the band-waggon, and without the application of any measure of scientific rigour, obtain results that would give a bad name to whatever the genuine seeker after truth was painstakingly seeking to prove. (This was what prompted Withering to write his account of the foxglove and its medical uses).

It therefore seems incredible that there were no deaths from septicaemia, or hepatitis as a consequence of these practises. It may be that they did occur, but were ascribed to any of several other endemic diseases, including typhoid and typhus. It is even more amazing that a monumental scientific truth and the basis of the greatest scientific thrust in the field of preventive medicine was revealed despite all these disadvantages. Without Jenner's historic observations, it is unlikely that immunology, the jewel of the latter half of 20th century medicine, would have advanced as it did.

Jenner's recognition of the typical cowpox pustule, and the optimum time to take the lymph, bear testament to great powers of observation, together with the experimental design of non-reaction to subsequent variolation. He also recognised the requirement for a reasonable time period to elapse after vaccination before the beneficial effects could be assessed. These are all in accord with what we now know about immune responses. And all this despite the difficulties under which he laboured. One thing is certain - anyone nowadays possessed of the same knowledge that he had, and attempting to experiment as he did, would be doomed to failure. No ethical committee in its right mind would agree to such practises, and no-one would indemnify the investigator. Yet this is the only disease thus far eliminated from this planet as a consequence of immunisation, though polio may soon follow.

Perhaps one thing was in his favour, as it still is. Observation of the beneficial effects of drugs or procedures depends on the demonstration of an end-point. Death is irrefutable and plainly obvious, even (especially) to the lay public. Procedures such as Jenner's, would therefore be tolerated if the results justified them. Many anecdotal instances of individuals vaccinated and avoiding smallpox whilst those all around not having been so protected caught the disease, served to spread the reputation of this procedure far and wide.

Despite his success, there were the inevitable jealousies of a professional nature that arose. One such was the attempt by **Dr. George Pearson**, physician to St. George's hospital, to establish the first institution for the promotion of vaccination, by vaccinating the poor free of charge, and supplying materials for vaccination to others who wished to carry out the practise elsewhere in the land. Patrons included the Duke of York, and Lord Egremont. Pearson established himself as head of the Institute for the Inoculation of the Vaccine-Pock at a formal meeting on 2nd December 1799. A week later he wrote offering Jenner to become some sort of affiliate. This not unnaturally displeased Jenner greatly, as he felt that he should have been consulted and included from the outset. He remained adamant in his refusal to join the Institution, and succeeded in getting Lord Egremont and the Duke of York to withdraw their support.

Jenner died of a stroke which had affected his right side, on 26th January 1823.

HALL JACKSON (1739 - 1797)

Hall Jackson, the man responsible for the systematic introduction of digitalis into America, was well known in the New England colonies and states as both physician and patriot. He was a man of many talents and interests. At the time Withering's book on the use of digitalis appeared (1785), he was a prominent New Hampshire physician. He studied medicine under his father, Dr. Clement Jackson, in Portsmouth New Hampshire. He also reputedly attended lectures at the Middlesex Hospital in London for three years. Most colonial American doctors received no academic training at all, and few could afford to attend British or European medical schools. The numbers of Americans who received their MD at the university of Edinburgh is shown in the table.

YEAR	MD GRADUATES
1740-1750	1
1751-1760	5
1761-1770	25
1771-1780	22
1781-1790	23
1791-1800	42
1801-1810	30
1811-1820	11
TOTAL	**159**

This list is taken from Samuel Lewis's "List of the American Graduates in Medicine in the University of Edinburgh from 1705 to 1866, with Their Theses" New England Historical and Genealogical Register, 42, (1888), 159-165.

The quality of instruction for medical apprentices varied widely because there was no standardization of the medical curriculum. However formal curricula were appearing at Pennsylvania and King's College (later renamed Columbia). By the end of the century, sufficient numbers of medical graduates were emerging with the addition of Harvard, Philadelphia and Portsmouth. Of the approximately 3,500 practitioners of medicine at the outbreak of the Revolution (1776), only 5% had university degrees in medicine.

Hall Jackson had a special interest in dropsy even before Withering's publication in 1785. He was familiar with the technique of paracentesis. On the 9th February, 1786, he wrote to Withering from Portsmouth, New Hampshire:

"Sir,

Your inestimable treatise or account of the Foxglove and its medical uses, with practical remarks on dropsy, and other diseases, has found its way to this remote part of the globe. It must greatly add to the satisfaction that daily arises in your mind, on seeing so many distressed fellow-mortals relieved by your personal advice and administrations, to reflect that thousands at the most distant ends of the earth are wishing to offer their tribute of gratitude for your indefatigable endeavours for the good of mankind.

The Gentlemen of the Society of medical observations, and enquiries, in London, the ingenious and worthy Doctors, **Percival**,(qv) and White, of Manchester, with many others, of this day in England, will never know how much the world is indebted to them for their publications; not only the present age, but generations unborn will bless their memory.

There is no disorder more prevalent in this country than dropsy, our summers are extremely hot, our winters intensely cold; only two of the spring and fall months may be called temperate; our days in the winter are short; consequently our labouring people work but a few hours, the remainder of the time is spent in a sedentary, idle manner, and too often in an immoderate use of spirituous liquors. Our lumber trade to the West Indica Islands returns us large quantities of rum, and Molasses; of the latter is distilled amongst us an inferior, cheap kind of rum, which is evidently unwholesome, it is generally used immediately from the still, it has an empyrheumatic taste, and is wholly destitute of the mildness of rum that has undergone agitation at sea, and a few months age; a common labourer may receive five quarts of this new, strong, and fiery spirit, for a short day's work from this plenty and cheapness. The use is too general and immoderate, and it is a just observation that those who indulge too freely in the use of spirit are least anxious for substantial food, their appetites are palled, the solids weakened, the fluids vitiated, and increased obstructions formed, and dropsies become frequent. As yet no specific has been found, but in most cases after a longer, or shorter time, the disease has proved mortal. Life in many cases has been prolonged to a considerable length of time by repeated tappings, but this has generally been with female subjects, where the disorder was of the encysted kind. Our remedies in general have been such as are used in Europe, in like cases; the squills have been considered as the most powerful diuretic, and mostly depended upon, and some few have been relieved by their use, where resolution has been strong enough to persevere against the nauseating effects thereof.

I have taken your treatise in my pocket for six weeks. I have shown it with the incomparable, accurate, and elegant drawing, to all my acquaintance within twenty miles, but no one can recollect of ever seeing any of its kind in America. I am persuaded, however, that it would arrive in sufficient maturity in this country, by attentive cultivation as our natural productions in general are much the same as those of England, with this difference, the wood of our large trees is not so compact and hard, our fruit trees, nor the fruits, so large, smooth, and succulent, as those of the same kind in Great Britain, our plants and herbage in general are a degree, or two, inferior as those of the same kind in England, planted in equal good soil, and cultivated with equal attention. Chamomile will not flower in this country, tho I have seen, in a very favourable season, a few single scattered flowers in a large bed. These remarks are from my own observations, having spent the year 1762 in England for the advantage of medical improvements.

I have the honor of being acquainted with John Lane Esq., Mercht, in London. To him I have sent for a small invoice of medicines; I have directed a small quantity of Fol. Digitalis purp; siccat., also some of the powder, and seeds, but I greatly fear they have not as yet become articles of the shops in London. Could I be so fortunate as to obtain (to the care of Mr. Lane), thr' your influence, and direction, a small quantity of the genuine seed, the plant should be most attentively cultivated, most carefully prepared; and as opportunities will not be wanting to administer it, the most accurate observations and remarks on its operation, and effects, shall be noted, and if you will permit me the honor, shall be communicated to you, for any further satisfaction, or remarks, you may wish to make on this truly valuable discovery.

And now, Sir, I should be most painfully embarrassed for an apology in troubling a Gentleman of your character with so lengthy, and uninteresting a letter, without the least personal knowledge, or the remotest introduction, was I not assured that where so much merit, and goodness obtains, an indulgent candour will not be wanting towards one who is sincerely desirous of doing all the possible good, in the narrow sphere in which providence has placed him, and hopes not altogether from those motives that too often actuate the generality of mankind.

I am, Sir (tho' unknown)
with the utmost veneration
and respect, your most
obliged most obedient
humb: serv:
Hall Jackson

P.S. I have directed to be sent me two or three sets of your account of the Foxglove for the purpose of dispersing them. Also your Scarlatina Anginosa, outlines of Mineralogy;

and anticipate with great pleasure your promised Botanical Arrangement. I hope it will be published before my directions are compleated and sent out from London.

The extreme heat and cold in this country may be judged from the following:

The Thermometer, Fahrenheit's scale, stood as followeth:

Portsmouth	1785	July 1st	83 degrees
		July 15th	75 degrees
		July 30th	80 degrees
		August from the 15th to 30th	80 degrees
	1786	January 15th to 19th	8 degrees below zero

N.B. The Thermometer was placed in the open air, and the observations made at noon.

Withering's reply came eight months later.

"Birmingham 27th October 1786

Sir,

Your letter of Febr: 9th arrived here in due time, and the Seed of the Digitalis purpurea which accompanies this, will shew that I have not been inattentive to your request. I send much more than will be necessary for your own use, in the hope that you will distribute it into other provinces, and... to transmit some to my friend Dr. Jones in Virginia for the same purpose. Mr. Cutler, in the memoirs of the American Academy of Arts and Sciences, printed in Boston 1785 and now before me, gives in his account of indigenous American vegetables page 465, the Linnaean character of Digitalis purpurea and supposes it a native of that part of America; but I have reason to believe that his species is not the purpurea. Perhaps you may have the opportunity of sending him a few of these seeds; and please to mention my suspicion to him.

It has been remarked that in cold countries the sedentary and the intemperate are particularly the victims to disease, and the diseases which attack them are I think mostly such as arise from debility. If the kind of rum you mention be really more unwholesome than that we have from the West Indies, it must be from some combination with the ardent spirit, though I am inclined to suspect that the intemperate use of Spirits, as such, will occasion the disorders you mention. If however the new rum distilled from the Molasses be as you believe more deleterious than such as we use, and that deleterious quality abates by keeping, we must suppose its amelioration is caused by separation of the hurtful impregnation. The noxious part I believe to be sometimes Lead, and sometimes an essential Oil. The oil escapes in time, and I know the Lead will be precipitated by the astringent extract the Spirit gets from the Casks; but I never have been satisfied whether the Lead is held in solution by an Oil or an Acid; probably by the latter, for we find the corks of rum bottles soon become rotten. If you suppose with me that dropsies, either with or without glandular disease in the abdomen, may be caused by want of action in the absorbent vesicles and too great laxity in the exhalants, you will readily conceive that this inaction must follow the repeated use of strong stimulants, such as ardent Spirits, Essential oils, or both combined, nor will you be at a loss to judge why a cold climate and an inactive Life should aid the formation of the disease. I should attempt in your dropsies to evacuate the Water by the Digitalis, and to prevent its repeated aggregations by frictions, exercise, flannel Shirts and other warm clothing, and I should also call in the aid of Aromatics, Steel, & sometimes Mercury.

I am more & more convinced that the Digitalis, under a judicious management, is one of the mildest & safest medicines we have, as well as one of the most efficacious. It is I believe **never** necessary to create nausea or any other disturbance in the system. I never now use more than 1 drachm fol: sicc: to one pound of infusion, and in substance rarely 3 grains in 24 hours. An Account of your tryals with this medicine will be highly grateful to me, and fully recompense any trouble you have given me.

The Exp^{t}s on the freezing of Quicksilver were extremely well conducted, & correspond sufficiently with the most accurate we have had from any other quarters. I read them to a Society of Philosophic friends in this place, and they met the approbation of all. Reason and Philosophy are making rapid strides in every quarter of the globe to emancipate and to enlighten Mankind.

We cure our intermittents"—(intermittent fevers, most of which were caused by malaria), —"of every kind by a solution of white Arsenic in Water, 1 grain to 1 ounce - Dose 25 to 30 drops, 3 times a day in 6 or 8 ounces of Gruel or Barley Water. In or out of the paroxysms we go on, until the disease is stopped. The cure is then to be finished with the usual tonics. Under proper management it produces no sensible effects.

I must beg you to accept my grateful thanks for the opinion you are pleased to entertain of me, and I believe that no one is more happy to promote the spread of Science than your obliged and very obd^t. serv^t.
W. Withering

The new Botan^l. Arrangement will not be out sooner than the beginning of next summer.

Digitalis has cured 2 other cases of insanity in this neighbourhood and 3 cases of Haemoptoe. The latter were of the kind attended with a quick bounding pulse, and I directed the Medicine from (the) quality I knew it possessed of abating the action of the heart."

The mention of treatment for intermittent fevers was probably by way of dissemination of what at the time was regarded as a significant addition to the armamentarium by **Thomas Fowler (1736-1801)**, in the form of arsenic solution. Fowler was well known to Withering, having succeeded him at Stafford, and published his work in 1786. The postscript regarding digitalis' effectiveness in cases of haemoptysis associated with (presumed) atrial fibrillation - "quick bounding pulse"- is of interest bearing in mind that Withering did not know by what means it exerted its beneficial effects. Although he concluded that -"it has a power over the motions of the heart—"— together with his observation of pulse rate change in 14 of his own 162 cases- nevertheless he still was of the opinion that its chief effect, namely diuresis, occurred as a consequence of a direct action on the kidney. However, it is clear that this did not blind him from making observations that were puzzling, and at first sight at variance with the ongoing hypothesis. This is a sign of a good scientist.

Hall Jackson sought to communicate the news concerning digitalis to other regions, and doctors, amongst whom was Dr. Edward Holyoake, of Salem, Massachusetts. In 1787 Hall Jackson wrote to Holyoake:

"..from several trials made here, I am fully convinced that neither Doctor Withering or his numerous correspondents have exaggerated its salutary effects: It is perhaps the greatest diuretic in nature, and possesses in a remarkable manner, a power of abating the action of the Heart, and retarding the circulation of the blood. In the last Ship from London and last post from Boston, I was honoured with a very polite, obliging, and interesting letter from Doctor Withering, together with some of the Seeds of the Foxglove...It is with much pleasure that I inclose you some of the Seeds. I am perswaded you will have equal pleasure in cultivating the Plant, which besides its utility in medicine, bears a beautiful flower, with a place in any garden...." He also sent seeds on to various other medically interested men, including ? (William) Jones of Virginia, Edward Holyoake of Salem who in turn supplied Nathaniel Appleton of Boston, all in 1787.

It remains a mystery as to when the foxglove was first recognized in North America, but it would appear likely that its therapeutic introduction is owed to the correspondence between Hall Jackson and Withering of 1786. Botanical catalogues as late as 1739 (John Clayton) contain no mention of it.

The results of digitalis therapy from Withering (1785), through Jackson (1790), to Beller (1971) have been collated, as shown below (taken from Hall Jackson and the Purple Foxglove, by J. Worth Estes, University Press of New England, Hanover, New Hampshire, 1979).

AUTHOR	PREPARATION	PATIENT NUMBERS	SUCCESS RATE	SIDE EFFECTS
Withering (1785)	Decoction	15	80%	55%
	Dried leaf	35	77%	14%
	Infusion	78	69%	19%
Jackson (1790)	Infusion	11	73%	9%
Quin (1790)	Infusion	11	46%	18%
Maclean (1810)	Infusion	94	83%	16%
Ferriar (1816)	Not specified	29	45%	21%
Blackall (1818)	Infusion & Tincture	35	71%	17%
Beller (1971)	Leaf& pure glycosides	135	100%	23-29%

The question that beckons is whether the various protagonists of this form of therapy had any ideas as to its mode of action. The concept of the role of the heart was elusive, and it seems that even Withering was off target in this respect. It must be remembered that at that time, dropsy was regarded as a form of fever which could be affected by purging. The effects on the pulse were thought to reflect intrinsic pulsatory changes of the vessels themselves, as it does not appear that the transmission of the impulse from heart to vessel was appreciated.

Subsequently in the nineteenth century, after Withering's death (1799), there was a vogue for using digitalis in tuberculosis. This may have been, at least in part, due to the treatise of Dr. William Hamilton of Bury St. Edmunds, 'Observations on the Preparation, utility, and Administration of the Digitalis Purpurea, or Foxglove' (London, Longman, Hurst, Rees, and Orme, 1807). Hamilton thought that it was effective because either it promoted absorption of matter from tuberculous ulcers, or, that by slowing the pulse it would reduce the blood supply to the pathologically affected area and by this means permit resolution.

In 1808 digitalis gained its place in the pharmacopoiea of the Massachusetts Medical Society, being based largely on the British pharmacopoeias. By 1816 it was listed in the New York hospital pharmacopoiea, and in 1820, in the United States Pharmacopoiea. The popularity of digitalis followed the customary pattern of discovery (1775), enthusiasm 1800-1820, and disappointment (1830-1910) followed by subsequent establishment of its true role (1910 onwards). In Osler's "The Principles and Practice of Medicine" (1892), its use is described in the chapter on chronic valvular disease, under the heading "The use of Remedies which stimulate the Heart's Action."

"Of these, by far the most important is digitalis, which was introduced into practice by Withering. The indication for its use is dilatation: the contra-indication is a perfectly balanced compensatory hypertrophy, such as we see in all forms of valvular disease...... It acts upon the heart, slowing and at the same time increasing the force of the pulsations....."

Its loss of popularity stemmed both from its side effects when incorrectly prescribed, mostly due to overdosing, but also because it was found wanting in treatment of tuberculosis. It must be remembered that at this time the organism responsible for tuberculosis had not been identified (**Robert Koch - 1882**), there were no stains to visualize the tubercle bacillus (**Ziehl-Neelsen**, published by Ehrlich in 1882**)**, there were no stethoscopes to hear mitral murmurs (**Laennec 1819**), (the mitral valve is interposed between the two chambers of the left side of the heart, and is especially prone to narrowing —"stenosis"- as a consequence of rheumatic fever incurred many years previously), yet both tuberculosis and mitral stenosis could lead to weight loss, haemoptysis (the coughing up of blood), and dyspnoea (difficulty in breathing). Atrial fibrillation (a quivering motion of the smaller chambers of the heart, instead of the normal contraction, often a feature of rheumatic heart disease, and nowadays recognised as being particularly susceptible to the beneficial effects of the administration of digitalis) had not yet been recognized. Chronic constrictive pericarditis (inflammation of the membranous sheath which is wrapped around the heart) in patients over the age of 40 is also associated with atrial fibrillation in 70% of cases, and most cases, at least earlier this century, and more than likely in the preceding two centuries, were tuberculous in origin. Yet even Hall Jackson felt that digitalis should be effective for the treatment of consumption.

George B. Wood, (1797-1879), a distinguished Philadelphian physician, wrote:

"At one time digitalis had a high reputation in phthisis," (tuberculosis) " and great success was apparently met with, in the cure of the disease, by its use. The journals teemed with favourable reports of its efficiency. It is needless to say that, with the imperfect means then existing of diagnosing thoracic disease, chronic catarrh and other affections of the chest were not unfrequently confounded with genuine tuberculous consumption, and that the cases cured belonged in all probability to the former category. No one now expects to cure phthisis with digitalis...although there are occasions, in the course of phthisis, in which the remedy may be advantageously resorted to as a palliative...."

In 1835, a compilation of all the cases in which digitalis had been administered (excepting Withering's data), was published by A.L.J. Bayle of Paris. This table is shown over the page:

DIAGNOSIS	NUMBERS	CURED/HELPED	NOT CURED
Dropsy, other forms of edema	144	91%	9%
Other heart disease	18	61%	39%
Phthisis (consumption)	151	78%	22%
Scrofula	11	100%	0%
Other pulmonary disease	16	50%	50%
Central nervous system disease	13	53%	46%
Miscellaneous	96	7%	33%
(all non dropsical diseases)	218	74%	26%

Surprisingly the percentage success rate for consumption and scrophula was nearly as great as for dropsy. The possible reasons have been discussed.

JOHN HUNTER (1728-1793)

John Hunter (JH) was the youngest of ten children, born at Long Calderwood, East Kilbride, Lanarkshire.

His elder brother by five years, **William Hunter** (WH), studied medicine as an apprentice under William Cullen, newly established in medical practice five miles away, in Hamilton. In 1739, he entered Edinburgh university and attended lectures on anatomy given by Alexander Monro. In 1740, WH left for London, having agreed with Cullen to continue his studies there with a view to returning to set up a partnership. However, he was tempted to assist James Douglas, a well-respected 'midwife' for the purpose of assisting in dissections to further Douglas's work on osteology.

John Hunter, portrait by John Jackson.
(Reproduced with permission of the National Portrait Gallery, London).

In 1745, the barbers and surgeons went their separate ways. The surgeons were temporarily without a hall, and WH realised that here was an opportunity to open his **private school of anatomy and surgery**. This he did in **Covent Garden**. His course included lectures on anatomy, and operative surgery plus bandage application. It was a very successful undertaking. In 1748, he visited Leyden, and learned the technique of injecting organ preparations so as to demonstrate their finer details. In September 1748, he was joined by his brother, JH.

The task of an anatomist was hindered by difficulties in obtaining and preserving bodies. Therefore there sprung up the art of making models in various materials including metal, wood, wax or glass. WH's practice was expanding and flourishing at the same time as his anatomy school. He needed and obtained the assistance of his brother who proved within a very short time to be very able indeed. In 1749, JH was permitted by **William Cheselden**, one of London's foremost surgeons, to attend at Chelsea hospital, in order to observe operations, and learn the rudiments of surgical technique. In 1751, JH attended St. Bartholomew's hospital, where **Percival Pott** was a senior surgeon. In 1756, JH was appointed house-surgeon at St. George's hospital. In 1762, he served his country on the Portugese frontier, where he obtained invaluable experience in dealing with gunshot wounds.

He was imbued with an intense curiosity of the workings of living creatures, including man. He collected, and was donated, thousands of specimens of all sorts of animals, and he also conducted living experiments. He collaborated with Jenner, in particular in studies on hibernating animals, including hedgehogs.

Following a rupture of his own Achilles tendon, in 1767, he experimentally severed this tendon in dogs, in order to study the healing process. From his work, the practise of tenotomy (tendon severing) was adopted to minimise limb contractures accompanied by shortened tendons. In 1768, he was appointed surgeon to St. George's hospital, and shortly thereafter, membership of the Corporation of Surgeons. Amongst his subsequent house pupils were **Edward Jenner**, and **Astley Cooper**.

JH's approach to further understanding, was by observation and experimentation. In 1772, he gave a course of lectures (eventually 86), delivered on alternative evenings, between seven and eight. Surprisingly, unlike WH, he was a very poor lecturer, who read his notes, scarcely ever looking up.

He was appointed surgeon-extraordinary to the king in 1776, and the same year commenced his series of Croonian lectures, which he delivered annually (except 1777), until 1782.

In 1780, he read a paper to the Royal Society, in which he claimed to be the first to have described the utero-placental circulation. This was to be followed by a protracted period of professional jealousy with his brother, who claimed to have himself been the first to describe it. This led to an almost permanent estrangement between them, which was to last until WH's last illness. In 1785, his portrait was painted by **Sir Joshua Reynolds** (qv).

One of JH's claims to fame was his operation for popliteal aneurysm (an aneurysm is a ballooning of an artery which, like a car tyre, makes it susceptible to a blowout (rupture), or a stripping –"dissection"- along its layers). Conventional wisdom by surgeons was either to tie a ligature above and below the aneurysm, and then cut into it, in order to evacuate the blood. This usually proved fatal. Percival Pott's method was to amputate the limb and have done with it. JH's answer, (based on his prior experimental observations that tying off a blood vessel did not necessarily lead to the death of the area it had hitherto supplied, at least using deer's antlers), was simply to tie a ligature above the aneurysm. The result was that the patient and the limb survived. The place in the thigh where he tied the ligature was henceforward called 'Hunter's canal.'

He died, attending a board meeting at St. George's hospital in 1793.

His collection, the Hunterian collection, was purchased for the nation by decision of parliament, in 1799, for the sum of £15,000. Custodianship was refused by the Royal College of Physicians, but snapped up by the Corporation of Surgeons (from 1800, the Royal College of Surgeons)!

THOMAS PERCIVAL (1740-1804)

Thomas Percival was born in Warrington, Lancashire in 1740, a year before Withering. Orphaned at the age of three, he inherited from his uncle, an extensive library, at the age of ten. This seems to have imbued him with his interest in Medicine. Percival considered going to Oxford or Cambridge to study, but decided not because he would have had to agree to the Thirty Nine Articles of Faith, required by statute for matriculation. Therefore he went to Edinburgh in 1761, a year before Withering. During his course, he spent a year in London, where he formed a close acquaintanceship with Lord Willoughby de Parham, who became his friend and patron and recommended him for election to the Fellowship of the Royal Society. This was duly bestowed in 1765. It seems odd that this nowadays great honour could be bestowed at such an early stage in those days. The example of Robert Darwin has been quoted. At least Withering earned this honour the hard way! In any event, Percival then went on to Leyden, where he obtained his doctorate with a dissertation 'De Frigore.' He then returned to Warrington, married Elizabeth Bassnett, and moved to Manchester to start his medical practice in 1767. It will be interesting to compare and contrast the subsequent lives of Withering and Percival, both born within a year of each other, both at Edinburgh together though a year apart, and both working in major industrial cities (Manchester and Birmingham) during the Industrial Revolution. Both suffered ill health, Withering had pulmonary tuberculosis, Percival had severe incapacitating headaches and weak eyesight, eventually requiring his early retirement. It has been suggested this was due to astigmatism. He imbibed the spirit of Enlightenment medicine in both Edinburgh and Leyden. As with Withering, many of his teachers had been pupils of Boerhaave whose careful bedside observations and experimental verification of medical theory were ever stressed. This knowledge, attitude and skill clearly played its part in the subsequent careers of both these men. It is interesting to speculate why one chose to visit Leyden, the other to go straight into practice. Maybe Percival did so in gratitude to his uncle who had studied there before him, and may on numerous occasions have mentioned Boerhaave. We do not know why Withering chose not to go, as he so easily could have done. By this time it will be realised, the pressing need to visit Leyden was less, because the age of Enlightenment had been permitted access to Edinburgh, in contrast to Oxbridge. Both were writers. Percival published a volume of 'Essays, Medical and Experimental,' and in 1773, a second volume, titled 'Essays, Medical, Philosophical, and Experimental.' In 1775 the first three parts of 'A Father's Instructions' appeared, consisting of letters and advice to young people, the last part appeared in 1803. He also wrote 'Moral Tales, Fables and Reflections' which was generally popular for thirty years, and was translated into French and German.

Perhaps the defining circumstance that influenced his path was illness, as a consequence of which he resigned from Manchester Infirmary a mere two years after his appointment, which had taken place in 1778. He remained closely attached to its affairs however, as Physician extraordinary from 1782. He engaged a series of young medical apprentices as secretaries, to read aloud to him (his eyesight was obviously very bad), and to take down his dictated thoughts. In 1789, the Manchester Infirmary experienced a heavy influx of cases of typhus and typhoid which naturally imposed a heavy burden on the staff. The trustees of the hospital decided therefore to double the staff in order better to cope with the emergency (imagine that nowadays!). Instead of displaying gratitude, the medical staff resigned en masse as they felt their professional competence to deal with the situation was being called into question. (I suppose nowadays there would be more medical input into the decision making process - in that sense we have made progress). An acrimonious dispute ensued, with opinions sharply divided. Thomas Percival, towards the end of 1791 or early in 1792, was asked to draw up a scheme of professional conduct that might prove some guidance for resolving the dispute.

By spring 1792, the first chapter of 'Medical Ethics' was written. He was further induced by an earnest desire to promote the honour and advancement of his profession, to enlarge the plan of his understanding, and to frame a general system of medical ethics; "that the official conduct and mutual intercourse of the faculty might be regulated by precise and acknowledged principles of urbanity and rectitude." This work was privately printed under the heading 'Medical Jurisprudence,' and circulated to many prominent people including Drs. John Aitkin, George Baker, Erasmus Darwin, William Falconer, John Ferriar the Elder, William Heberden, and William Withering. The message was surely crystal clear to both Erasmus Darwin whose son Robert had been involved in the Houlston case, and William Withering, the other physician involved in 1788. In particular I would like to quote from 'Medical Ethics' chapter II, part Part VIII. Special consultation.-Conduct of the physician called in.

"As circumstances sometimes occur to render a **special consultation** desirable, when the continued attendance of another physician or surgeon might be objectionable to the patient, the gentleman of the faculty, whose assistance is required, in such cases, should pay only two or three visits; and sedulously guard against all future unsolicited interference. For this consultation a double gratuity may reasonably be expected from the patient, as it will be found to require an extraordinary portion both of time and attention.

In medical practice, it is not an infrequent occurrence, that a physician is hastily summoned, through the anxiety of the family, or the solicitation of friends, to visit a patient, who is under the regular direction of another physician, to whom notice of this call has not been given. Under such circumstances, **no change in the treatment of the sick person should be made, till a previous consultation with the stated physician has taken place, unless the lateness of the hour precludes meeting, or the symptoms of the case are too pressing to admit of delay**."

Had this been possible in the Houlston case, then maybe the acrimony could have been avoided.

By 1794, a printed copy was circulated privately, under the title 'Medical Ethics; or, a Code of Institutes and Precepts, Adapted to the Professional Conduct of Physicians and Surgeons.'

Like Withering, Percival was interested in chemistry, and collaborated with Priestley. He pioneered the establishing of a board of health in association with Manchester Infirmary, and persuaded the city of Manchester to keep accurate statistics. He fought to promote health, working and living conditions of the poor, as well as the design of prisons and care of their inmates. He was thus a pioneer in environmental, occupational and preventive medicine, as well as medical ethics. He petitioned for the abolition of the slave trade. He worked hard for the repeal of the Corporation Tests Act.

BENJAMIN RUSH (1745-1813)

Benjamin Rush was born near Philadelphia, and received his education at the College of New Jersey, later to be known as Princeton University. After this he was apprenticed to Dr. John Redman, the leading medical practitioner in the city. This was followed by a period of study at Edinburgh, where he received his MD in 1768. Next, he stayed in London, receiving further training from William Hunter, then on to Paris, where he visited the Hôtel de la Charité and the Hôtel Dieu. He returned to Philadelphia in 1769, establishing his own medical practice, and was made professor of chemistry at the University of Pennsylvania Medical College. In 1789 he was awarded professorship in the practice of medicine, and in 1791, in physiology. About Rush it has been said:

"Rush's theory of illness appears idiosyncratic and antiquated to modern readers. Devoutly religious, he saw God's unifying hand in everything earthly and consequently viewed all disease as having a unitary character. In the human body, he made this a question of excitability, stimulus, and the production of excitement. In his thinking, he followed Albrecht von Haller's proposals for the basic responsive capacities of the body (irritability and sensibility) and William Cullen's and John Grown's development of a simplified medical theory of energetic response. Rush differed from Cullen, who had made the nervous system central to his responsive theory, by going back to the circulatory system. This arose from and simultaneously justified his great belief in the efficacy of bleeding in the treatment of a wide variety of illnesses."

He is best known for his book 'An account of the bilious remitting yellow fever, as it appeared in the city of Philadelphia, in the year 1793.' It was printed by Thomas Dobson, at the Stone-House, No. 41 South Second Street, Philadelphia, in 1794.

The book starts with an account of the diseases which preceded the yellow fever. There follows a blow by blow account, detailing the cases as they arose, the ambient weather conditions, and the results of Rush's administrations - chiefly bleeding and purging.

"........The weather was uniformly warm in July. The scarlatina continued during the beginning of this month, with symptoms of great violence. A son of James Sharswood, aged seven years, had with the common symptoms of this disorder, great pains and swellings in his limbs, accompanied with a tense pulse. I attempted in vain to relieve him with vomits and purges. ....The next day he was nearly well."

Rush builds up the tension as he chronicles the appearance of the epidemic.

"There was something in the heat and drought of the summer months, which was uncommon, in their influence upon the human body. Labourers everywhere gave out (to use the country phrase) in harvest, and frequently too when the mercury in Fahrenheit's thermometer was under 84°. It was ascribed by the country people to the calmness of the weather, which left the sweat produced by heat and labour, to dry slowly upon the body.

The crops of grain and grass were impaired by the drought. The summer fruits were as plentiful as usual, particularly the melons, which were of an excellent quality...."

I now enter upon a detail of some solitary cases of the epidemic, which soon afterwards spread distress through our city, and terror throughout the United States.

On the 5th of August, I was requested by Dr. Hodge to visit his child. I found it ill with a fever of the bilious kind, which terminated (with a yellow skin) in death on the 7th of the same month."

Rush went on to describe more cases.

A colleague, Dr. Hodge, told Rush that a malignant fever had carried off four or five people within sight of Le Maigre's house. From these facts, Rush was able to list several of the index cases and come to the conclusion that they had been in the vicinity of some putrid coffee in a dockside area, and that this was the likely source of the outbreak which he named the 'bilious remitting yellow fever.' He had previously witnessed an epidemic in Philadelphia in 1762, and had taken notes at the time:

"In the year 1762, in the months of August, September, October, November and December, the bilious yellow fever prevailed in Philadelphia, after a very hot summer, and spread like a plague, carrying off daily for some time, upwards of twenty persons." Rush let it be known that in his opinion, the city was in the grip of a 'malignant and contagious fever.' But there were many who expressed doubt, feeling that this was just the usual annual fever, albeit with a higher than expected mortality, and sought to discredit him. Nevertheless, the governor of the state directed Dr. Hutchinson, the inspector of sickly vessels, to inquire into events. He wrote to Rush:

"Dear Sir,

A considerable alarm has taken place, in consequence of the appearance of an infectious disorder in this city; from which the governor has been induced to direct me to make enquiries relative to the existence and nature of such disorder. In executing this duty, I must rely on the assistance of such of my medical brethren as may have been called to attend any of the persons supposed to have been infected: as I understand you have had several of them under your care, I would be much obliged to you to communicate to me (as speedily as can be done with convenience to yourself) such facts as you have been able to ascertain relative to the existence of such disorder; in what part of the city it prevails; when it was introduced; and what was the probable cause of it.

I am, Sir,

With the greatest respect,
Your obedient servant,
AUGUST 24th,
1793
J. HUTCHINSON"

Rush replied,

"Dear Sir,

A MALIGNANT fever has lately appeared in our city, originating I believe from some damaged coffee, which putrefied on a wharf near Arch-street. This fever was confined for a while to Water-street, between Race and Arch-streets; but I have lately met with it in Second-street, and in Kensington; but whether propagated by contagion, or by the original exhalation, I cannot tell. The disease puts on all the intermediate forms of a mild remittent, and a typhus gravior. I have not seen a fever of so much malignity, so general, since the year 1762.
From, dear sir,

Yours sincerely,
August 24th,
1793
BENJ. RUSH"

J. Hutchinson, the physician of the port, replied with his information, to Nathaniel Falconer, the health-officer of the port, to the effect that the current death toll was about 40, and that the disease originated from some damaged coffee, or other putrefied vegetable and animal matter. It was felt not to be an imported disease, as no foreigners or sailors had been affected. Clinically, it exhibited great variation, from mild remittent fever to the worst type of typhus.

On 25th of August, the local college of physicians met in order to plan their strategy for coping with this disease. Their recommendations based on fragmentary data, preconception of ideas, and a well motivated intention to avoid panic were as follows:

"1st. People should avoid mixing with those affected.
2nd. Houses containing sufferers should be marked.
3rd. Infected persons should be placed in the centre of large and airy rooms, abed, without curtains, with strict regard to hygiene etc.
4th. That a large and airy hospital be provided in the neighbourhood of the city" (one wonders if some people saw the disease as a heaven sent opportunity to acquire a hospital!) "5th. Stop tolling the bells.
6th. Burial to be kept as quiet and private as possible.
7th. Keep the streets and wharves clean.
8th. Avoid all fatigue of body and mind." (One wonders how this was to be achieved given the circumstances).
"9th. Avoid standing or sitting in the sun; also to have moving air, especially the evening air.
10th. Dress appropriately, and keep warm.
11th. Avoid inebriation, but to take wine, beer and cider in moderation.

The college conceives **fires** to be very ineffectual, if not dangerous means of checking the progress of this fever. They have reason to place more dependence upon the burning of **gun-powder**. The benefits of **vinegar and camphor**, are confined chiefly to infected rooms, and they cannot be used too frequently upon hankerchiefs, or in smelling bottles, by persons whose duty calls them to visit or attend the sick.

Signed by order of the college,
WILLIAM SHIPPEN, JUN.
Vice President
SAMUEL P. GRIFFITHS
Secretary"

However doubt was expressed in various quarters both in regard to the actual existence of an epidemic outwith the usual seasonal crop of fevers, and whether the present one which Rush was treating so enthusiastically by bleeding and purging had in fact originated from the putrefying coffee.

He made the interesting observation, revealing an understanding of human psychology in regard to the denial of the possibility of serious disease.

"The answers to the first question upon visiting a patient, were calculated to produce a belief in the mind of the physician, that the disease under which the patient laboured, was not the prevailing malignant epidemic——I was particularly struck with this self deception in many persons, who had nursed relations that had died with the yellow fever, or who had been exposed to its contagion in families—"

He noted the tendency to haemorrhage, but went on to remark how few signs there were of damage to the liver. He also stated that he wished to record that the yellow fever "like all other diseases" is influenced by climate and season. He believed the vomiting and constipation to be due to the morbid state of the brain in the first stage of the fever, but on day 4 or 5 he believed it to be the effect of inflammation. Under the heading "Secretions and excretions" he mentioned that on the 4th and 5th days there was "a discharge of matter from the stomach, resembling coffee impregnated with its grounds." He attributed this to "a modification of vitiated bile, but I was led afterwards by its resemblance to the urine——to suspect that it was produced by a morbid secretion in the liver, and effused from it into the stomach. Many recovered who discharged this coffee-coloured matter." (This as any medical student would know, was in fact the presence of blood that had been acted upon by acid in the stomach – commonly described as "coffee ground vomit").

"A total deficiency of the urine took place in many people for a day or two, without pain.——It generally accompanied or portended great danger. I suspected that it was connected in this disease, as in the hydrocephalus internus, with a morbid state of the brain."

Rush described many other symptoms of doubtful specificity including lymphadenopathy (swollen lymph glands). He went on to discuss the skin colouring— "The yellow colour from which the fever has derived its name, was not universal. It seldom appeared where purges had been given in sufficient doses. The yellowness rarely appeared before the third, and generally about the fifth or seventh day of the fever—The eyes seldom escaped a yellow tinge; and yet I saw a number of cases in which the disease appeared with uncommon malignity and danger, without the presence of this symptom. Two very different causes have been supposed to produce this colour of the skin. By some it has been attributed to the dissolution of the blood; but I shall say hereafter, that the blood was seldom dissolved in this fever. The yellow colour, moreover, occurred in those cases where the blood exhibited an inflammatory crust, and it continued in many persons for five or six weeks after their recovery. From these facts it is evident, that the yellowness was in all cases the effect of an absorption and mixture of bile with the blood."

"Many persons had eruptions which resembled moschetto bites. They were red and circumscribed. They appeared chiefly on the arms, but they sometimes extended to the breast. Like the yellow colour of the skin, they appeared and disappeared two or three times in the course of the disorders."

"Petechiae were common in the latter stages and in most cases were the harbingers of death."

With use of Rush's remedy - purging and bleeding - "putrefaction did not take place sooner after death than is common in any other febrile disease, under equal circumstances of heat and air."

His inability to discern a clear pattern in the majority of cases was explained thus:

"It was my misfortune to be deprived by the great number of my patients, of that command of time which was necessary to watch the exacerbations of this fever under all their various changes, as to time, force, and duration. From all the observations that were suggested by visits, at hours that were seldom left to my choice, I was led to conclude, that the fever exhibited in different people all that variety of forms which has been described by Dr. Cleghorn in his account of the tertian fever of Minorca.......I think I observed the fever to terminate on the third day more frequently in August, and during the first ten days of September, than it did after the weather became cool.....The danger seemed to be in proportion to the tendency of the disease to a speedy crisis, hence more died in August in proportion to the number who were affected than in September, or October, when the disease was left to itself. But, however strange after this mark it may appear, the disease yielded to the remedies which finally subdued it, more speedily and certainly upon its first appearance in the city, than it did two or three weeks afterwards."

Rush went on to describe three classes of patients:

1. Those in whom the disease produced symptoms of indirect debility e.g. coma, languor, sighing, syncope and a weak or slow pulse.

2. Those in whom the disease, acting with less force, resulted in headache, and pain elsewhere (unspecified), delirium, vomiting, heat, thirst, and a quick, tense or full pulse, with remittent or intermittent fever.

3. Mild manifestations of disease, insufficient to confine the patient to bed, or to remain housebound. This third class was very numerous, and many recovered without medical aid. Many were (allegedly) saved by "moderate bleeding and purging," whilst some died (these were patients who ascribed their symptoms to a common cold, and neglected to

take proper care (i.e. bleeding and purging). Rush went on to point out that this was an area of controversy, many authorities being of the opinion that the yellow fever was not the most likely cause of fevers at that time, whereas Rush was prepared to diagnose the condition in many more cases. He went on to state:

"I have before remarked, that the influenza, the scarlatina, and a mild bilious remittent, prevailed in the city, before the yellow fever made its appearance. In the course of a few weeks they all disappeared, or appeared with symptoms of the yellow fever; so that after the first week of September, it was the solitary epidemic of the city." Rush went on at length to cite others who had observed similar phenomena in other disorders: smallpox (Sydenham, and Huxham). He went on:

"I beg pardon for the length of this digression. I did not introduce it to expose the mistakes of those physicians who found as many diseases in our city, as the yellow fever had symptoms, but to vindicate myself from the charge of innovation, in having uniformly and unequivocally asserted, after the first week in September, that the yellow fever was the only febrile disease which prevailed in the city. I shall hereafter mention some facts upon the subject of the extent of the contagion, which will add such weight to the assertion, as to render the disbelief of it, as much a mark of a deficiency of reason, as it is of reading and observation.

Science has much to deplore from the multiplication of diseases. It is as repugnant to truth in medicine, as polytheism is to truth in religion. The physician who considers every different affection of the different systems in the body, or every affection of different parts of the same system, as distinct diseases, when they arise from one cause, resembles the Indian or African savage, who considers water, dew, ice, frost, and snow, as distinct essences: while the physician who considers the morbid affections of every part of the body, (however diversified as they may be in their form or degrees) as derived from one cause, resembles the philosopher, who considers dew, ice, frost, and snow, as different modifications of water, and as derived simply from the absence of heat....."

Rush here displayed a quaint naivety in attempting to make all-encompassing pigeon-hole diagnoses, whereas we now recognise multiple pathology as the norm, and the brilliant all-encompassing diagnosis as pretty unusual. Thus, a patient with diabetes, cirrhosis, and arthritis, is more likely to have type I or II diabetes, portal cirrhosis, and osteo- or rheumatoid arthritis, than haemochromatosis. On the other hand, it could be argued that to treat peripheral vascular disease, retinopathy, and obesity as separate when all may be linked by diabetes, would be wrong. By optimising the treatment of diabetes, one would improve the prognosis of the other complications, but in actual practice, one would treat each complication as well as the underlying disease. So when Rush stated;

"The sword will probably be sheathed for ever, as an instrument of death, before physicians will cease to add to the mortality of mankind, by prescribing for the names of diseases" he was probably right insofar as the prescribing habits of the profession are concerned, though incorrect in assuming that thereby mortality would be increased. This is a reflection of Rush's reductionist theory, whereby his critical faculties were not to the fore when confronted with the outbreak of yellow fever, which he almost certainly over-diagnosed. As a consequence, he could claim remarkable success in cure rates, as a result of his bleeding and purging regimen.

Rush described many (to him) possibly relevant associations, or lack of associations of the disease. Included in the former were servant maids, families living in wooden houses, people who frequented narrow streets and alleys; whereas the latter included those living on board ships moored in the bay, people confined to the House of Employment, the hospital, the jail (ascribed to the airiness and remoteness of these places).

He continued;

"A meteor was seen at two o'clock in the morning on or about the twelve of September. It fell between Third-street and the Hospital, nearly in a line with Pine-street. Moschetoes (the usual attendants of a sickly autumn) were uncommonly numerous...."

How ironic that he did not at any time consider the mosquito as in any way relevant, yet all manner of other things attracted his attention - mainly things that were obvious to the special senses - if not to a scientific sixth sense. He described the post-mortem findings, again without anything conclusive emerging. However, his best achievement was in counting the numbers of deaths on each day from August 1st to November 9th. He compared this data with the register of the weather. In all, there were four thousand and forty four deaths in this time.

The effect of wet and (relatively) cold weather was not lost to Rush, but as to why this was the case was not obviously addressed. When deaths per week was plotted against mean daytime temperature during the months of August, September and October, it was apparent that the number of deaths increased with falling temperature.

The remainder of Rush's book is devoted to detailed descriptions of his experiences with bleeding and purging. The mosquito is not subsequently given mention though we now know that yellow fever is a viral infection spread by the bite of the mosquito. The elucidation of the cause of this disease was to take many years, notwithstanding a period of time during which it was confused with leptospirosis (a bacterial infection spread by sewer rats).

JOHN COAKLEY LETTSOM (1744 - 1815) (JCL)

JCL was born 22nd November 1744 in Little Jost Van Dykes, near the main island of Tortola, West Indies, and died 1st November 1815, in Sambrook Court, London.

A contemporary of Withering, it will be of interest to compare the life of an eminently successful London physician with his Birmingham counterpart. He was an English Quaker on his father's side, his mother was Irish. There was a high mortality rate among the Tortola population, possibly due to its inclement weather. JCL was a twin, the last of a total of seven sets of twins born to his mother Mary Coakley and father Edward. The previous six all died. Therefore his parents decided that at the age of five years JCL should be sent to England for his health and education, to a Quaker family living in Lancaster. Here he met **Samuel Fothergill**, a renowned Quaker preacher, and brother of **John Fothergill**, a famous London physician. He attended a Quaker school at Penketh, which from his memoir he evidently enjoyed. At the age of 16, he was sent to Abraham Sutcliff, a surgeon and apothecary, in Settle, as an apprentice. Earlier in the year he had been informed of the death of his father and his mother's subsequent remarriage. In his memoir he wrote:

"I went to Settle, an apprentice, a fatherless lad. I rode (on a pack horse) from the house of Samuel Fothergill at Warrington alone; and my guardian when he parted with me, impressed upon my mind his last words: 'Please thy master, and above all please thy mistress. If thou turnest out well, I will recommend thee to my brother, the doctor. And never forget, that to be good is to be happy'." In the course of his apprenticeship, JCL learned how to conduct a practice on business lines, which was clearly going to stand him in good stead eventually when he amassed considerable wealth from his medical practice.

At this time, a favoured hobby of his was botany:

"My most favourite study indeed was Botany; to assist me in it, I borrowed Gerard's Herbal. In my excursions in the vicinity of Settle I collected many good specimens of rare plants, from which I made a Hortus siccus.

With other specimens I made impressions on paper, which resembled drawings, and may be done with very little trouble. For this purpose some printer's ink, and a pair of printer's bosses or cushions, such as are used for laying the ink on types are necessary. After rubbing them with a little of the ink, lay the plant between them, and press them so as to give the plant sufficient colour. Then remove it, and lay it on a sheet of paper, and give it a little pressure, in order to convey the impression of the plant to the paper, which may afterwards be coloured according to nature. A piece of paper should be placed between the plant and the hand, to prevent the latter from being dirtied by the ink." (Autobiography p.20). The above instructions appeared in the second edition of his book, "The Naturalist's and Traveller's Companion", 2nd Edit. 1774, p.26.

He was also interested in mineralogy, often visiting a copper smelting house and collected specimens of ores, variegated stones and pebbles.

JCL was known for his spontaneous gaiety, his frank pleasure in the company of the fair sex, and his great generosity. Through his master, Sutcliff, he attained a good knowledge of Latin, being able with ease to read a textbook. This was necessary as most lectures in English universities at the time were given in Latin, and theses were defended in this language.

At the age of twenty one, it was time to proceed from the apprenticeship to a place at university. JCL wished to go to London, although it would have been anticipated that both for academic as well as geographical reasons, he might have chosen Edinburgh. In the summer of 1766, (the year that WW graduated), clothed in a long flapped coat, a little bobbed wig, and over it the Quaker's flat brimmed hat, he came to London. (Pettigrew's "Lettsom" Vol. 1, Letters, p.96). A description of the scene in London is given "Lettsom his life, times, friends and descendants" by James Johnston Abraham; London. William Heinemann Medical Books Ltd 1933:

"....London was a city of 750,000 souls. What it was like we can still visualise from Hogarth's drawings. The lighting of the main streets was by oil lamps, which burnt from 6 to 11 p.m. in winter; and the side streets were not lighted at all, except by the candles placed by law in the shop windows. There was no lighting by gas in London before 1807.

.....At inns there was one candle at each table....The streets were paved with round cobbles, which inclined to a central kennel where water ran, and rubbish thrown out from the houses accumulated. Often there were great holes between the cobbles, where water collected, and from which passing vehicles and horses' hooves plentifully bespattered the unfortunate pedestrians who happened to be near enough.

For there were no footpaths in those days. Instead there was a sidewalk in main streets with posts at intervals, sometimes, but not generally connected by chains. These however were not as useful as they might have been, because the windows of the shops and houses were allowed to project into the street, and every house had its steps rising from the pathway. In addition, the cellar doors, frequently uplifted, were a constant trap for the unwary. Little wonder then, people often, particularly at night, preferred to walk in the kennel. There however one was in danger of being deluged by rain.

London in 1770 did not extend much beyond Old Street. Moorfields was still open country, and for east to west traffic, an arterial road was constructed from Old Street through Finsbury Fields to Islington, and so on to Paddington where it joined the Great West Road. These nowadays comprise City Road, Euston Road and Marylebone Road.

Into this scene came JCL, with letters of introduction to **Dr. John Fothergill** (1712-1780), one from his brother Samuel, the other from his master, Sutcliff. He became a surgeon's dresser at St. Thomas's Hospital, which at that time was situated in the Borough, where it remained until relocated in 1871. There were three surgeons at St. Thomas's and three at Guy's. One of the three at St. Thomas's was Benjamin Cowell, also a Quaker. He had volunteered in 1745, to go with the Duke of Cumberland to suppress the rebellion in Scotland. JCL resided in Gracechurch Street, and walked over London Bridge each day to get to work. The hospital then was situated on the site now occupied by London Bridge station, and was built in a series of squares. The front one was devoted to women, the second was administrative, the third reserved for men, and the fourth for "Foul wards" for the treatment of venereal disease. The salary of a physician was £40 per annum, and of a surgeon £40 6s. 8d. The three surgeons on the staff at St. Thomas's were men of no great distinction, whereas the physicians at the time were of a different calibre. Mark Akenside was also well known as a poet, Alexander Russell FRS, was an author of "The natural history of Aleppo," and James Grieve, the "Translator of Celsus." JCL was keen to study under Akenside, having read some of his poetry. He was therefore particularly disappointed to find him "....the most supercilious and unfeeling physician that I had then, or have ever since known. If the poor affrighted patients did not return a direct answer to his queries, he would often instantly discharge them from the hospital....." Despite Akenside's deficiencies in patient interaction, he was nevertheless a considerable figure in the literary world of his time. JCL studied under these physicians for one year, this being the limit to which his finances would permit. He would have liked to have gone up to Edinburgh, but could not afford to. He stated:

"I devoted my time incessantly to the Hospital, and the lectures which London afforded. As a small gratuity admitted me to see the books of the physicians, and to accompany them through the wards, I embraced as many opportunities as I possibly could to avail myself of these advantages. In the morning, early, before any attendance was given, I usually visited many select patients, wrote out the symptoms, and afterwards examined the prescriptions of the physicians on some particular cases. I compared the writing and practice of authors, and by degrees I acquired some precision in anticipating both the practice and the remarks of the faculty. If I thought myself much at a loss, I repeated my visits to the Hospital in the afternoon, and this not only confirmed the little knowledge I had acquired, but likewise gave me a frankness and ease of demeanour at the bedside. During all my attendance, however, no other pupil, I believe, adopted this system, which I found so highly interesting to my advancement. At the same time I continued to take notes of, and made reflections upon, what I saw, and thus acquired a method of investigation and decision, which ever afterwards proved of the highest use in determining my medical conduct and practice......." Patients were taken in on Thursdays, JCL went round on Fridays, and then on Saturdays the physicians and surgeons went round together.

Thus, by his own efforts, JCL was attending the equivalent of ward rounds, and reading up on the patient's notes. Furthermore, by returning to the wards in the afternoons, he was gaining in confidence and knowledge. He would appear to have been an exemplary student.

Once a week he breakfasted with Fothergill, and thus met many of his distinguished contemporaries. These included **Benjamin Franklin**, who at this time was agent for the Quaker colony of Pennsylvania, and thus came into contact with London's Quaker community, and David Barclay, a great city merchant. (As an aside, Benjamin Franklin at that time was living at 36 Craven Street, close to Trafalgar Square. Workmen have recently dug up the remains of ten bodies beneath this house in the course of restoration. Researchers believe there could be more bodies buried beneath the basement kitchens. Most of the bones show signs of having been subjected to dissection or possibly crime. The clue may be through a Dr. William Hewson - like Franklin a Fellow of the Royal Society - who at one time ran a school of anatomy with William Hunter. After an argument, Hewson left to live in Franklin's house, Franklin having (conveniently) moved up the street for a while to live with a Mrs. Stevenson. He did not necessarily know what was happening below stairs at number 36 during his absence. At the time of writing, the case is being considered by the Westminster Coroner, Dr. Paul Knapman, (as reported in The Times, of February 11th, 1998). Subsequently, in November 2000, in a lecture to the Leicester Medical Society titled 'Benjamin Franklin and the Craven Street bones,' Dr. Knapman revealed that Franklin introduced Hewson to Mrs. Stevenson's daughter Mary, to whom he was married in 1770. In 1772, the young couple moved to number 36. Whereas William Hunter, being Professor of Anatomy at the Royal Academy of Arts, had the right to the bodies of eight hanged men, other private anatomy schools had to rely on other (illegal) sources of provision. Grave robbing was the most likely source, a crime warranting the death penalty or deportation. Understandably therefore, the natural thing to do when the anatomy school was closed was to bury them, where they remained undisturbed for over two hundred years.

To return to JCL. He was impeded from further progress by lack of funds, his meagre share of his father's estate being insufficient for him to continue his career in London. He therefore decided to return to Tortola, in order to work as a doctor, make money, and then return to further his medical education. He sailed from Liverpool on the brig 'Alice' on October 8th 1767, via Cork for provisions, and then a seven weeks run to the West Indies.

On his return to the islands, he found many changes since he departed seventeen years previously. With the European market opened, following the ending of the war of the Austrian succession, there was a great demand for what the islands could cultivate. This required manual labour, which was largely provided by slaves. George III ascended the throne in 1760, Great Britain had won Canada from the French through the genius of Wolfe, and driven them from India by the strategies of Clive. The king was popular, London was becoming increasingly wealthy. All seemed well, but the American War of Independence was ahead. The West Indian planters were wealthy, and travelled, displaying their wealth extravagantly. Fothergill wrote:

"Were the possessors of lands in these hot countries obliged to labour for themselves, we should not see the many instances we do of idleness and extravagance; but the slave trade enables the inhabitants of these warmer regions to procure, not only the necessaries and conveniences of life, but vast wealth, at the expense of people, who, born under a hotter sun, are found able to bear labour equal almost to a native of the north in his own country, and compelled to work by sore and grievous stripes.......The conduct of these people" (the West Indians) "when they arrive in England, approaches nearer to show and extravagance than the northern inhabitants" (the Americans). "Bred for the most part at the breast of a negro slave, surrounded in infancy with a numerous retinue of dark attendants, they are habituated by precept and example to sensuality, selfishness and despotism....."

Upon arrival in Tortola, JCL found his mother living with his step-father Samuel Taine. The property due to him from his father's estate amounted to less than £50 and a few slaves. As a consequence of the teaching of Fothergill, he released his slaves soon after his arrival. Writing to Sir Mordaunt Martin, Bart., on April 4th 1791, he referred to these events:

"In giving my slaves their freedom I acted from an impulse I could not overcome.These negroes constituted a decent patrimony; I was injured by my executor, so that when I revisited my native Island, I found myself some hundreds in debt. Nevertheless I emancipated my slaves, and left myself penniless. I had youth and health, and I never feared the world, whilst I remained without a female to suffer with me."

JCL commenced medical practice on the island. His clientele included potentially 1,200 whites, and 10,000 blacks. He made £2,000 in the first six months. He apparently saw from fifty to a hundred people before breakfast. These were probably negro slaves sent by their masters, and paid by the head, hence the large throughput. Slaves, like horses were a valuable commodity, and it was advantageous to their masters to have them physically fit. JCL's business-like attributes first acquired during his apprenticeship to Sutcliff were, quite literally, beginning to pay off. He saw many cases of fever, of various types, and this early experience no doubt was useful later when he wrote his book on fever. In September 1768, he returned to Liverpool, with £1000 and his servant Sam. Dr. John Fothergill gave him a letter of introduction to Edinburgh, where he arrived the following month. (At this time, William Withering was in his second year at

Stafford). The renowned William Cullen was there at the time. He had had the temerity to question the teaching of Boerhaave. Additionally, in a break with tradition, he lectured in English instead of Latin. JCL's stay in Edinburgh was notably brief, for the next spring he left for London, prior to commencing the European grand tour. He would visit Paris, Spa, Aix-la-Chapelle and Leyden. Benjamin Franklin, Fothergill's friend, gave him a letter of introduction to a Dr. Dubourg. He obtained the Leyden MD on June 20th, 1769. The title of his thesis was "Observationes ad vires Theae pertinentes" - the medicinal properties of tea. He published an amended and extended version, in English, in 1772: "The Natural History of the Tea-Tree, with Observations on the Medical Qualities of Tea, and Effects of Tea-Drinking" by John Coakley Lettsom, MD, FSA, London: Edward and Charles Dilly, 1772.

It included a coloured folding plate of a tea tree, reproduced from a painting owned by John Fothergill. The tree used for the purpose was one that flowered at Sion House in 1771, owned by the Duke of Northumberland. Of interest is the fact that JCL was able from seeing the tree to correct the classification of the great Linnaeus, who stated it to be monogynous (working from dried specimens), when in fact it was trigynous. (Linnaeus had a tea plant in Uppsala, but it would not flower).

In his choice of subject for his thesis, Lettsom was choosing a very topical and high profile subject. It was very much in the public mind in 1770, regarded as either a delightful and safe social form of relaxation, or a pernicious habit, depending whether you were a Quaker, or like minded to John Wesley.

In order for JCL to practice in the City and for seven miles around, it was necessary to possess the Licentiate of the Royal College of Physicians of London, then based at

Portrait of John Coakley Lettsom and his family
at Grove Hill, Camberwell, by Johann Zoffany.
(Reproduced by kind permission of the Wellcome Trust, London.)

Warwick Lane. This he achieved on June 25th, 1770, having satisfied the examiners of his knowledge of medicine, and familiarity with the Latin classics.

JCL and his wife were blessed with eight children. He worked very hard, seldom retiring before midnight, though from a financial viewpoint, there was no pressing need as a consequence of his marriage. In 1772, he wrote three books. They were:

1. Reflections on the General Treatment and Cure of Fevers.
2. The Natural History of the Tea Tree.
3. The Naturalist's and Traveller's Companion.

The first book was dedicated to the Earl of Dartmouth. JCL's political astuteness is shown, since the Earl was President of the Aldersgate Dispensary. Based on his experiences in the West Indies, he described confidently his method of treating malaria and yellow fever:

"The situation of practitioners in the West Indies affords them frequent opportunities of seeing the sick, and prescribing remedies at the first attack of the disease. I had there many occasions of observing the success of the practice recommended in the succeeding sheets, when applied at the beginning of fevers, particularly of such as often prove fatal within the Tropics."

The role of the mosquito not at that time having been elucidated, he subscribed to the well-held view that:

"From this source chiefly, if not solely, all kinds of intermittent fevers at last are produced. These miasmata arise from marshy ground, lakes and woods, when acted upon by certain degrees of heat, particularly in warm climates, and in warm seasons, where the ground is liable to inundations, and is therefore left in a moistened state."

He argued that it was necessary to have heat and moisture, neither by itself being sufficient. The danger arose when areas of inundation began to dry off. Neither did he subscribe to the putrification theory, since:

"Many large cities are filled with animal matter, particularly Edinburgh and Madrid, but as they stand high on dry soil, these noxious effects do not take place."

He was also against the custom of bleeding, but not purgation. It is interesting to compare his attitudes with those of Benjamin Rush, in regard to the yellow fever, which Rush ascribed to putrefaction, and for the treatment of which he was a strong proponent of bleeding and purgation. In his book he quoted freely from accepted authorities of the time, but omitted the name of Cullen. This led Cullen to write, on September 3rd, 1773:

"I must own to you that I thought myself entitled to some acknowledgements in your former publication, but I am willing to accept your excuse........"

Several of Cullen's works at the time were being pirated, and inaccurately at that, despite having obtained an injunction against the pirates of his Materia Medica in 1771.

His third book, the "Naturalist's and Traveller's Companion" appeared in 1772, and went to three editions, the last appearing in 1799, and consisting of 202 pages. In common with others JCL carried out experiments into the composition of air, which was very much a source of scientific enquiry at that time. Whereas it appears Withering corresponded on the subject, but did not carry out any experiments, JCL did, and described his experiments in his second edition (1774), adding as a footnote that at the time, he was not aware of Joseph Priestley's discoveries. JCL also carried out analyses of medicinal waters, (as did Withering) and this too appeared in this work, which appears to be a collection of various works, ranging from collecting butterflies, preserving birds and animals, transporting seeds and plants from far away places, analysis of medicinal waters, analysis of air, collection of fossils, to making casts of coins and medals - altogether a bit of a hotch potch - but it sold well. JCL perhaps appealed to the less scientifically critical amongst the medical fraternity, but was evidently the author of very readable and popular work skirting on talked about issues of the time.

In 1773, aged 29 years, he founded the **Medical Society of London.** On November 18th, of the same year **JCL was elected a Fellow of the Royal Society.** (This honour did not befall Withering until the age of 44 years). The grounds for his election were:

(that he be) "recommended as a gentleman well qualified to make a useful member of the Society."

The signatories were Benjamin Franklin, William Watson, John Ellis, John Ives, Josiah Colebrooke, Daniel Solander, Marmaduke Tunstall and James Ferguson.

The obvious name to meet the eye is that of Benjamin Franklin. JCL had known him from his student days when they had met in Fothergill's house. Franklin was the agent for the Quaker colony of Pennsylvania. It is clear that JCL's proposal by Franklin was a political one.

Daniel Solander was a botanist, friend of Linnaeus, and was present on Captain Cook's 'Endeavour' which circumnavigated the world in 1768-1771.

The society suffered considerable internal dissent, and lack of papers to be read. The cause of the dissent was removed from the minutes book, so we shall probably never know the reason. On January 18th, 1775, Lettsom was elected President, Sims Treasurer, and Hulme Librarian.

JCL also joined the **Royal Humane Society** on April 25th, 1774. This society was formed with the express intention of concentrating on the "Recovery of Drowned Persons."

JCL made a major contribution to the problem of typhus, also known at the time as putrid fever, gaol fever, or spotted fever. The disease was rife in prisons and hospitals. The source (body lice) was not known at that time. JCL frequently contributed articles to the "Gentleman's Magazine" which was the great journal of the time. It reproduced one of his articles on "Putrid Fever." At that time it was customary to treat fevers by keeping the sufferers shut away in dark rooms, and to bleed and purge them (a la Benjamin Rush). JCL recommended nursing victims out of doors with consequent exposure to light. He made general recommendations regarding diet. At that time there was a Bill before Parliament (1774), "An Act for Preserving the Health of Prisoners in Gaol, and preventing the Gaol Distemper." It provided for whitewashing walls once a year, for routine washing out of rooms, for the supply of fresh air, for isolation rooms for both sexes should disease appear in the prison, for baths for the use of prisoners whilst in prison, and especially before being released from prison. JCL pointed out that though all this was admirable practice:

"Bathing the body will avail little, while that body is still to be covered with garments as poisonous as the shirt of Nessus, and peculiarly capable, not only of retaining, but also of communicating the infection."

All his life, JCL was a keen advocate of the medicinal value of baths and personal cleanliness. It seems that this was a Quaker fashion, not subscribed to by the general population, and not even the wealthy. It was due to immigrants from foreign countries where bathing constituted a part of normal hygiene, that the custom of taking a bath was introduced to this country.

One wonders what JCL would have suggested had he been transported to Philadelphia during one of its outbreaks of typhus. Whilst his ideas clearly could and would make a difference in typhus when the body louse was the vector, (even though no-one yet knew), what might his intuition have told him had he found himself in Philadelphia? Would the mosquito have attracted his attention? He had certainly seen plenty of malaria and yellow fever whilst in the West Indies, but that was at an earlier stage in his career, at a time when his analytical skills were not yet so well developed. In fact he did once meet Rush, at Fothergill's house. JCL wrote:

"On his return from Edinburgh I first met him at the house of Dr. John Fothergill, with whom I then resided: and from that period, to the time of his decease, our correspondence was maintained by an uninterrupted intercourse of literary communication: the first letter I received being dated from Phuladelphia, Nov. 29th, 1771, soon after his return to that city." (Recollection of Dr. Rush, 1815, p.5).

It is apparent that JCL did not agree with Benjamin Rush's ideas on management of cases of the yellow fever, for in Rush's reply to JCL's responses to his imputations that "The yellow fever is now acknowledged everywhere (Philadelphia excepted) to be of American origin" (writing in 1796); and again in 1803- "The doctrine of the importation of our fever has been relinquished by many of its former advocates," he complained, in 1804;

"I am sorry to perceive by your letter that we still differ in our opinion respecting the origin and means of preventing the yellow fever. It is always the offspring of putrid inhalations from dead animal and vegetable matter....It is not contagious and never spreads beyond the influence of the atmosphere in which it is generated. It dies when carried into the country, even in crowded rooms where the attendants upon the sick receive their breath for days and weeks. It even dies in our yellow fever hospitals in the vicinity of our cities." (Lettsom, by Pettigrew, Vol.III. p.197).

In JCL's time, and for many years after, clinical teaching in the London hospitals was practically non-existent. There was no systematic lecturing, and students would be lucky if pearls of wisdom were occasionally cast on their behalf. In the case of would be surgical students, they could secure instruction of a practical nature, but only after payment of considerable sums, in order to become apprentices. The impecunious mere student had to feed on the dregs of information he could scavenge for himself. As a consequence numerous private schools sprang up and flourished in the latter part of the eighteenth century. Best known was the Great Windmill School, (now part of the Lyric Theatre in Shaftesbury Avenue), where the Hunters gave complete courses in anatomy, physiology, surgery and midwifery. JCL realised there was a great need for better teaching, and came up with the idea of out-patient teaching. Many dispensaries were springing up. He suggested that students would find it advantageous to accompany physicians and surgeons when visiting cases in private practice, and also that lectures be given back at base (the dispensary).

JCL also opposed quackery, which was rampant at the time. Oddly, the Royal Colleges did nothing, lest by their actions they created any martyrs.

After 1773, when JCL was appointed Physician to the General Dispensary, he first became interested in prison reform. As a consequence of meeting with that section of the extreme poor whom he would be unlikely to have been asked to visit in their homes, he found to his surprise that **typhus** was endemic in the seething courtyards and cramped alleys and passages of the city. It was also known as the **Jail Fever**, and for good reason. One of his Dispensary patients late of Newgate Prison, whilst in a court off Long Lane, Aldersgate Street infected fourteen people attending the court, of whom one died, and eleven recovered under the care of JCL. Close by Aldersgate was a prison for debtors - the Wood Street Compter - in which eleven people had died early in 1773. Finding there was no doctor assigned to the prison, JCL volunteered to look after them. From what he experienced, he enthusiastically pursued the cause of improvement in prison conditions. He was able to persuade the Governors of his Dispensary to supply drugs and dressings free to the inmates. He also took food and drink from his own cellar (Pettigrew's Lettsom, Vol. I, p.64 (memoir). An even more dramatic example of the consequences of Jail Fever had been the so called **'Black Assize'** at the Old Bailey in 1750. At this sitting, the Lord Mayor, a justice of the Common Pleas, a Baron of the Exchequer, an alderman, a barrister, a number of attendants, several of the jury, and forty of the audience were infected by a prisoner, and all died! After this event, it became the custom to bring lavender into the Old Bailey - an example of soothing the senses whilst leaving the basic cause unaddressed.

In 1793, the authorities requested JCL to report on the state of health of the prisoners in Newgate. He duly carried out his visit on November 10th. He found typhus to be endemic in the women's side of the prison. This area was separated from the State prisoner's area by a narrow corridor, which led to the main entrance. Through this narrow thoroughfare, prisoners and visitors passed and in so doing inevitably came into close contact. Thus was the infection spread - the lice had no need to leap far! Following upon his inspection he made the following recommendations:

1. Clothing - Every prisoner should have two suits of clean clothing, one of which he should wear for three days, and then change. The first suit should meanwhile be washed.
2. Personal cleanliness - Prisoners should be compelled to bathe twice weekly.
3. Diet - Fresh meat and vegetables should be provided whenever they could be procured.
4. Air and exercise - Each prisoner should be obliged to spend at least an hour in walking in the area, or in some amusement.
5. Bedding and General Accommodation - In place of the wooden beds or hammocks, he recommended iron cots, since they could be fumigated or sprinkled with vinegar once weekly.

It is of interest to note that his recommendations were very sound, despite ignorance of the role of the body louse. This was a good example of the adage that 'prevention is better than cure.' For no cure was available - that was to take another two hundred years. In his quest for prison reform, he was accompanied by **James Neild** (1744-1814), known for his great work on surveying the prisons of England, accounts of which were published between 1801, and 1812.

Another significant landmark in the life of JCL was his founding of the **Sea Bathing Hospital at Margate** which was opened on August 1st 1796. His interest stemmed from the sudden craze for sea-bathing which struck in the middle of the eighteenth century, championed by Richard Russell M.D. F.R.S. (1687-1759), who published a book on the value of sea water for curing cases of enlarged glands. He had studied at Leyden possibly under Boerhaave. He moved to Brighton (then Brighthelmstone) in 1754, and quickly established its reputation. Visiting the seaside for health reasons became fashionable, as the public tired of their traditional inland watering holes such as Bath and Tunbridge Wells. Thus George III after recovering from his second attack of insanity (?porphyria) in 1789, convalesced at Weymouth, making the whole concept of visiting the sea-side as a healthy form of recreation most fashionable. JCL thought that what was good for the rich would be good for the poor, and thus hit upon the idea of a hospital by the sea. His concept gave rise to open-air sanatoria throughout the world, for the hospital he founded possessed these facilities at his insistence. The hospital was intended chiefly for the London poor suffering from scrofula (TB). Margate could be reached from London by ship in twelve to fourteen hours sailing from Wool-key, near the Custom House every Thursday at high water. The journey took about the same time as travelling by coach, but was far cheaper. The hospital was renamed the Royal Sea-Bathing Hospital in 1898, and its bed numbers eventually rose from 30 to 300.

JCL played an active role in the practise of variolation, and later, of vaccination, which is described in the section on Jenner.

In 1779, he built his famous country mansion, Grove Hill, in Camberwell, at which he entertained many distinguished foreign guests. He died in 1815, a highly respected physician and philanthropist.

OLIVER GOLDSMITH (1728-1774)

Oliver Goldsmith was a poet, playwright, and man of letters. He came of a Protestant and Saxon family, and was born in Ireland, probably at Roscommon.

He was ugly, small, and pock marked as a result of the smallpox. Aged 16yr, he went to Trinity College, Dublin, as a sizar, i.e. too poor to pay normal fees, therefore in receipt of free accommodation, free or cut price tuition, a small allowance for food, but required to perform certain duties such as waiting in hall. He obtained his Bachelor's degree in 1749. He was wont to dress in bright colours, play cards, sing Irish airs, play the flute, go fishing in summer, and tell ghost stories by the fireside in winter. He tried about half a dozen professions in succession, failing at all of them. He applied for the church, but his sartorial inclinations had him disqualified. He became a tutor to a well-to-do family,

Oliver Goldsmith. Portrait by Sir Joshua Reynolds.
(Reproduced with permission of the National Portrait Gallery, London).

but that was ended after a dispute regarding pay. Emigration to America was then the thing to do, and he succeeded in obtaining the sum of £30 from his relations, with a good horse to get him to Cork for his ship. 6 weeks later he returned home, having missed his ship which had had the temerity to sail earlier than (he) expected, whilst he was busy enjoying himself at a party. Next he fixed his ambitions upon the law, and with the backing of an uncle, went to Dublin. Unfortunately, this took him by way of a gaming house where he had the misfortune to lose all his money. Subsequently he considered the medical profession, and having obtained some money, went up to Edinburgh at the age of 24 years (1752). For the next 18 months, he attended the odd lecture, then did the fashionable thing, and went on to Leyden to study physic. After 3 years, he left without a degree though with a smattering of medical knowledge. Subsequently he wandered through Flanders, France and Switzerland, playing his flute to entertain and earn a crust and a bed. Aged 26 years he returned to England, and scraped around for a couple of years, until, aged 30 years, he started producing articles for reviews, magazines and newspapers. Gradually his name became known, and he was introduced to **Samuel Johnson**, considered at the time to be foremost among living English writers, to **Joshua Reynolds**, foremost among painters, **Burke**, the eloquent exponent of the art of conversation, though not yet in parliament. In 1763, he was one of the nine original members of the **Literary Club**. His literary works of note commenced in Christmas 1764, with his poem, **Traveller**, which drew great praise from the critics. In 1766 appeared the novel **The Vicar of Wakefield** which remained popular for over a century. His best known play, **She Stoops to Conquer**, appeared in 1773, a five act farce.

In order to acquire a little money (for his work hitherto did not bring him much, rather it helped to pay his accumulated debts), he turned to educational writing. He wrote a **History of Rome, History of England, History of Greece,** and **Natural History**. Notable amongst these lucrative works was the fact that they were somewhat lax on factual interpretation (since he had no in-depth knowledge of what he was writing about, basing the writing on the work of others), however he possessed a literary style that was very easy for the reader, and this made his work so popular.

An interesting facet of this man is the great divide between his art of writing, when compared to his skills (if one may flatter by use of this term) in conversation. When commencing to speak, he tended to be ridiculous, before eventually succeeding in expressing himself in a more focussed way.

He died, in poverty, in 1774. His poverty was the outcome of his inability to manage his not-inconsiderable income, and his weakness for gambling and giving money away to almost anyone whose pitiable plight struck him.

JAMES LIND (1716-1794)

A native of Scotland, he began his medical career as a registered apprentice to a surgeon. In 1748, he obtained his MD at Edinburgh. In 1758 he was appointed physician to the Royal Naval hospital at Haslar four years after its foundation. He is well known for his treatises on naval hygiene (1757), and tropical medicine (1768). From 1739-1748 he was a Surgeon in the Royal Navy. Whilst on a ten-weeks cruise he observed 80 sailors out of 350 laid low by scurvy. Other reports of fatal scurvy stimulated him to write his acclaimed **"Treatise on the Scurvy" (1754)** which he dedicated to Lord Anson. Scurvy had ravaged the sailors of Lord Anson's expedition of 1740. Despite this, in 1779 the Channel fleet had 2400 cases after a ten weeks cruise. In his treatise of 1754, Lind advocated the use of preserved orange and lemon juice. Eventually, in 1795 the admiralty issued an order enjoining the use of lemon juice, after which scurvy in the navy disappeared. Why did it take them 40 years to take this idea on board? (pun intended).

RICHARD BRINSLEY SHERIDAN (1751-1816)

Sheridan was the son of a playwright (Thomas Sheridan), one time manager of the Theatre Royal, Dublin. RBS was born in Dublin, and educated at Harrow. In 1770, the Sheridan family moved to Bath, where he met the beautiful Elizabeth Linley, the daughter of a composer. Her portrait was painted by Gainsborough, and she had many suitors, including our subject. He had the ingenuity to spirit her off to France with a secret marriage near Calais, then returning to fight two duels with Major Mathews, another suitor. As is well known, he became a playwright. His first comedy, **"The Rivals,"** was performed at Covent Garden on January 17th, 1775.

Its first performance was poorly received, but the second, eleven days later, was acclaimed. Together with several partners, he bought Drury Lane theatre. **"The School**

Richard Brinsley Sheridan. Portrait by John Russell. (Reproduced with permission of the National Portrait Gallery, London).

Warren Hastings. Portrait by Sir Joshua Reynolds. (Reproduced with permission of the National Portrait Gallery, London).

for Scandal" was produced on May 8th, 1777, and is universally regarded as Sheridan's masterpiece. In 1780, he entered parliament for Stafford, and his first speech was to defend himself against bribery. He was able to exhibit his powers of oratory in the **impeachment of Warren Hastings** (1732-1813), first Governor General of British India.

At last in 1795, the House of Lords gave a verdict of not guilty. It has been written: "If Clive's sword conquered the Indian Empire, it was the brain of Hastings that planned the system of civil administration, and his genius that saved the empire in its darkest hour." Sheridan's last years were characterised by debt and political disappointment, failing to secure the seat at Stafford in 1812. He died in 1816, and was buried in Westminster Abbey.

THOMAS CHIPPENDALE (c.1718-1779)

He was the most famous of English cabinet makers, the son of a joiner in Otley, Yorks. He came to London when he was twenty, and in his early thirties set up first in Long Acre, and then 60 St. Martin's Lane, where the adjoining three houses constituted his factory. In 1754, he published his folio called "The Gentleman and Cabinet Maker's Director." It had a large list of subscribers and went to three editions. His furniture has been described as solid, but not heavy.

Partner's library table, in the manner of Thomas Chippendale circa 1765.
(With acknowledgement to the Grosvenor House Hotel, London).

His work is seen at its best and most characteristic in the chair, and in settees, which always took the form of two or three conjoined chairs. He made many bookcases, cabinets and escritoires. He designed mirrors in Chinese or rococo style. He was buried in 1779 at the church of St. Martin-in-the-Fields.

THOMAS SHERATON (c.1751-1806)

He was born in Stockton-on-Tees in humble circumstances. After being apprenticed to a cabinet-maker, he learned geometry and technical drawing. Little was heard of him prior to 1790, when he was working on his first book on furniture, published the following year. It was titled 'The Cabinet-Maker and Upholsterer's Drawing Book,' and was issued in parts by T.Bensley, of Bolt Court, Fleet Street; a second edition appeared in 1793, and a third in 1802. He also gave drawing lessons. His designs ranged from perfectly proportioned pieces simple in form, to other works spoiled by an over-abundance of ornamentation. Chairback designs were influenced by Hepplewhite and Adam. He employed slender forms and sweeping curves, and made extensive use of satin-wood. His books were intended for the practical use of the trade, but served also as a catalogue, subsequent orders from which were placed with other cabinet makers.

Many charming little work-tables are attributed to his design, as are beautiful sideboards and bookcases. He devised the so-called combination or 'harlequin' furniture, examples of which were a library table with concealed step-ladder, a dressing table would double as washstand and escritoire; also looking-glasses with enclosed dressing cases, writing tables or work-tables. His most remarkable piece was an ottoman with heating urns beneath.

George III period serpentine-shaped commode, a similar design to one published in Sheraton's Drawing Book 1793. (With acknowledgement to the Grosvenor House Hotel, London).

Sheraton's style was less restrained than that of Chippendale, who always retained a certain 'Englishness' about his designs. Sheraton made lavish excursions into Chinese and Louis Quinze modes. He was ever ready to adopt foreign styles with a lightness of form and grace that were unsurpassed. He especially made use of highly polished grained woods and delicate inlays. Sadly, his later extravagant creations in the Empire style contributed to the perceived ruin of British furniture design of the period.

WILLIAM HEBERDEN (1710-1801). (WH)
(The majority of this potted history is taken from Ernest Heberden's excellent book on William's life, which contains far more detail).

WH was born in Southwark on 13th August 1710, the fourth of six children. His father was an innkeeper in the parish of St. Saviours. Together with three brothers, William attended the Free Grammar School, which stood in the precincts of St Saviours church, now Southwark Cathedral. At this time, life for most was harsh and brutal, **only 25% of children attaining their fifth birthday**. Life in the city meant being subjected to smoke from countless fires, people living in extremely cramped surroundings, and with the added hazard of almost complete lack of sanitation. The contrast in early education and environment enjoyed by Withering, the son of a well-to-do apothecary in rural Wellington, together with the personal tuition of a local curate, and that of Heberden is extreme.

196

Portrait of William Heberden.
(Copyright The Royal College of Physicians of London. Reproduced with permission).

Like Withering, we unfortunately have no record of his early life. Heberden's educational prospects would have been unremarkable had he not shown himself to be an extremely able pupil whose headmaster at Southwark, William Symes, wanted him to continue his education at university. This would have presented no problem had not Heberden's father died intestate, and with financial affairs that remained unsettled for four more years. This delay meant that William Heberden had insufficient funds to proceed. However, his school awarded him an exhibition, value £7 per annum, which he was to receive for seven years, and with this assistance he was able to matriculate at Cambridge. He attended St. John's College from December 1724, aged a mere 14 years. At this time, subsequent to the accession of William and Mary, all Fellows of the college were expected to swear allegiance to the House of Orange. Many who refused were ejected. Students were categorised as either:

1. **'Sizars'** (too poor to pay normal fees), therefore were in receipt of free accommodation, free or cut price tuition, a small allowance for food, but were required to perform certain duties such as waiting in hall.

2. **'Pensioners'** (the majority), who enjoyed no special privileges, but were required to pay modest fees for board, lodging and tuition.

3. **'Fellow-commoners,'** (sons of the wealthy and of the aristocracy), enabling them to take their meals at the Fellows' table in hall.

Unlike Withering who went up to Edinburgh to read Medicine from the start, Heberden studied for a Bachelor of Arts degree, comprising mainly classics, divinity and philosophy. He obtained his degree in 1728. In 1731, he was elected to a Fellowship at

St. John's which required him to take Holy Orders. In 1732 he obtained his MA, and in 1734, obtained a medical Fellowship, which meant he was no longer required to take Holy Orders. In the same year, he was made Linacre Lecturer in Physic, though apparently there were no specified duties. The medical faculty at this time was small, and commanded little respect, being stuck with pre-enlightenment doctrine. He obtained his MD in 1738, having at some stage also trained in a London hospital, probably St. Thomas's. He prepared a course consisting of no fewer than twenty six lectures on **Materia Medica,** the first lecture being delivered on 9th April, 1740. This series of lectures he gave annually until 1748. Included in his course was a description of Peruvian Bark, obtained from the South American cinchona tree, and which we know to be the source of quinine, which at the time was used extensively in the control of fevers. Included also was Heberden's view on how to ascertain whether or not a drug was of use: "....the first of these is Experience, with which Mankind, as we have seen, set out, but soon grew weary of this tedious but safest method of finding the true effect of medicines. Tho' this may justly be called the most unerring guide, yet even this may prove an useless or dangerous one unless followed with caution. Experience is either that of our own, or what we receive from the testimony of others. In original experience many have been misled by coming to a conclusion before they had a sufficient number of tryals to ground it upon. Almost everyone thinks himself able to pronounce what was the cause of a disease, & to what the recovery was owing. But those who are aware of the difficulties of coming at truth in this matter will agree that it may be very false reasoning to conclude that such a medicine cured a man because he took it and recovered. It is not therefore a single fact, but facts repeated in a variety of circumstances that can establish the just reputation of a remedy..." This clearly shows that Heberden was aware how misleading anecdotal experience can be, and how much more likely the truth will be revealed by proper clinical trial.

We are told Heberden never ventured overseas, but no reason is given. Given his poor origins this is understandable, but later in his career, it might have been extremely interesting to have done the 'Grand Tour.' Nevertheless, he did travel in England, collecting specimens of possible medical interest. During vacations, he was fond of visiting spas, particularly Scarborough, where he met many well-to-do patients, which no doubt contributed to his success.

Heberden was involved in the publication by the Royal College of Physicians of London, of the **London Pharmacopoiea.** Most of the remedies included were useless, many were dangerous, and nearly all consisted of mixtures of many things e.g. Theriaca Andromachi (Venice Treacle) comprised 65 ingredients including dried vipers, and Mithridatium had 50 components. In 1746 appeared the new edition of the **Pharmacopoiea,** in the introduction of which, appeared Heberden's writings taken from his Materia Medica lectures. His influence was quite clear.

"It would be a disgrace and a merited reproach to us if our Pharmacopoiea abounded any longer in discordant and random mixtures introduced by primitive ignorance or thrust into it by fear of poison and perpetual suspicion...."

In 1746, having satisfied the censors the previous year, Heberden was elected to Fellowship of the Royal College of Physicians, (FRCP).

He was very interested in the medicinal properties of vegetables, and attempted to establish a garden at Cambridge for the culture of plants of medicinal value, which would lend themselves to research. It took 15 years however before this was achieved. Heberden now sought further advancement, as well as marriage. Quaintly, fellows of his Cambridge college were by statute forbidden to enter into matrimony! Therefore, he decided to seek his fortune in London, aware that he would find much competition there, and that he would need considerable start up capital.

His first London house was a terraced property in Cecil Street, situated where the Savoy Hotel now stands. There he moved with his wife, Elizabeth Martin, daughter of a banker from Overbury in Worcestershire and MP for Tewkesbury. Before the marriage, Heberden applied for, and was granted a coat of arms, which included a row of lozenges (physic), two suns (health and light), between which was a ring of barrel-hoop shape referring to the Coopers' Company of London. His marriage unfortunately was to bring tragedy in good measure, first in the shape of the death of their first child John, and later, following the birth of another boy, Thomas, by the death of his wife about four weeks later, from puerperal fever. Ironically perhaps, Heberden wrote on the usefulness of a register of births, diseases and deaths. He collected the annual Bills of Mortality for London parishes from 1657 to 1758.

"It can only be from a long series of such registers, that we are enabled to make any near approaches to truth, in the calculations founded upon them; and the longer the series is, the nearer will our approaches be."

He was aware that inaccuracies could arise because records were only kept of baptisms and burials ceremonially performed according to Church of England rites. Many of the dead were taken into the country for burial, and therefore were not included in the register. Other deficiencies included carelessness on the part of parish clerks or their deputies in recording everything accurately and no account of people buried in other Church of England burial grounds.

When it comes to the actual cause of death, whereas today this duty would fall to a qualified medical practitioner, and in some cases require an autopsy, in those times the cause was determined by the 'searcher' who was appointed by the parish. He was an unqualified person, for whom no particular respect was held. He would form his opinion, in cases of natural death, by an inspection (necessarily cursory), of the body, and by enquiry from friends and family.

The many defects were widely recognised, by amongst others, Dr. Fothergill, (q.v.), but attempts to get a Bill through parliament whereby births and deaths were registered, as apart from baptisms and burials, failed. He clearly possessed a keen epidemiological interest, and from a perusal of Bills for the plague years, surmised that London had been free from this scourge for nearly 50 years on account of:

"——the greater freshness and purity of the air of London, since the rebuilding of it after the great fire; the streets being wider, and the inhabitants not crowded so closely together——"

During the first half of the eighteenth century, there was much needless loss of life, largely attributable to poverty, lack of sanitation, and drunkeness. Heberden drew attention to the importance of statistics upon which to base policies designed to improve matters. Many petitions were made to the House of Commons, and eventually the Government was forced to increase the duty on spirits in order to reduce their consumption. This led to a fall in gin consumption (Hogarth had depicted conditions in his picture 'Gin Lane'), better sanitation, and the founding of more hospitals. Also, at this time, the practise of inoculation against the smallpox was gaining ground. This involved inoculating material from a smallpox sufferer (variolation), not vaccination which was shortly to supersede it. Heberden was strongly in favour of variolation, despite the fact that he was aware that the smallpox itself could be induced by this means.

In January 1760, Heberden re-married. The lady in question was Mary Wollaston. She was to bear him seven children, three of whom died in infancy. His second child, William (future Royal Physician) was born in 1767. (The name William was clearly in vogue, this also being the name of William Withering's son). About 6 years earlier, Heberden had received an invitation to become physician to the Queen, but declined, no doubt on account of his many commitments; to his thriving practice, to the Royal Society, (where he had been elected a Fellow in 1750), and to the Royal College of Physicians. Among Heberden's many friends and colleagues in the Royal Society were Joseph Priestley, and Josiah Wedgwood. On 30th December 1784 Priestley wrote to Henry Cavendish on the subject they were both investigating - the properties and composition of air. He ended his letter:

"I will be obliged if you will show this letter to Dr. Heberden who is pleased to interest himself in my experiments and to whom I have not written lately, though he is already acquainted with many particulars of this letter." In 1788 Josiah Wedgwood wrote: "I shall be in London in about ten days and the copy intended for the Society may then pass through my hands, as you propose, to Dr. Heberden."

Though no reference is made to Withering, it is very likely they were friends, since Withering, having read his paper on the composition of the terra ponderosa the previous year, was elected a Fellow in 1785, when Heberden was 75 years old. It was also the year his account of the foxglove appeared.

Heberden was involved in the following major row at the College.

As a Fellow of the Royal College, Heberden had his share of administrative duties. In 1750, he was made a Censor, and among his duties was **to decide who could be elected to a Fellowship.** Those who could not, were still permitted to practise as Physicians in the London area provided they held a Licentiateship of the College. This diet of profound wisdom was based on the following principles:

1. The candidate had of necessity to be born on English soil, thus being assured of being part of our culture, and able to speak the language.

2. He must not be tainted by Roman Catholicism, which was synonymous with plotting and treason.

3. He must have enjoyed the 'advantages'(?) of an English university, the cream of which was Oxbridge, and which exclusively could spawn Fellows. The progeny of other universities (however enlightened) could grovel only for Licentiateships.

4. The nature of his practise would specifically exclude anything that smacked of the lesser art of surgery, or of the realm of the apothecary.

In 1765, the College revised its statutes, and circulated them to both Fellows and Licentiates. There was a great argument brewing. It centred on the desire of Licentiates to achieve Fellowship, (in effect to become members of the College). Twenty three Licentiates wrote to the College in order to seek admission as Fellows and thus enjoy voting rites and permission to attend College meetings. This was refused. In June 1768, ten Licentiates gate-crashed a meeting, and claimed the right to speak. The President told them to withdraw quietly or else he would send for constables to have them ejected.

William Hunter, the dissecter, (aptly named) announced that the first to attempt to remove him would be run through with a knife. The President (wisely), brought the meeting to a close.

The Licentiates withdrew to make further plans. In September 1768, they hired some thugs to break through the locked gates of the College, and to smash a few windows. Using sledge-hammers and crow-bars they broke down the Hall door, and thereby again gatecrashed a meeting that was taking place. The President was once again forced to close the meeting. There was to be no solution, at least not in the eighteenth century. Nowadays Licentiate candidates take an examination, usually as an alternative or adjunct to their basic medical degree (M.B.), then, later and after a suitable period of approved training, they are eligible to sit the examination for membership of the College (M.R.C.P.). Then after a period of years in medical practice, they become eligible for election to the Fellowship, (F.R.C.P.). It is highly unlikely that many current Fellows, the progeny of Redbrick, know anything about the struggles of the past which have enabled them to reach this point in their professional careers. The situation caused no end of amusement in the eyes of the public, and did little for the image of the profession. Indeed, the whole sorry affair was satirised in a play that was the hit of the 1768 season. It was called "The Devil upon Two Sticks" by Samuel Foote.

With the increased demand for doctors in London, many came who were not eligible for Fellowship. This included many who had graduated in Scotland, where, especially in Edinburgh, they had received a considerably better training than the unenlightened fare on offer at Oxbridge. London's Fellows naturally closed ranks, fearing for their professional pre-eminence.

In 1769, now the father of three children, Heberden acquired a larger property, in Pall Mall, a freehold once owned by Nell Gwynn. One of his neighbours was **Thomas Gainsborough**. In 1774, Heberden was one of the sixteen friends invited by William Hawes, or Thomas Cogan, to found the **Royal Humane Society**, an institution dedicated to "affording immediate relief to persons apparently dead from drowning." Another such was **Lettsom** (qv). Drownings in large numbers were an everyday occurrence on the busy Thames.

The March of the Medical Militants to the Siege of Warwick Lane Castle in the year 1767. Engraved by J. June 1768. (© Royal College of Physicians of London)

The Siege of Warwick Castle; or The Battle between the Fellows and Licentiates. The artist is unknown. (© Royal College of Physicians of London)

In 1782, Heberden, by now a ripe old 72 years of age, and his family were settled in their newly acquired summer residence in Windsor. The following year, **Dr. Samuel Johnson** suffered a stroke. He lost his power of speech, and wrote seeking Heberden's assistance. He had many symptoms, including "a painful, or more properly an oppressive, constriction of my chest.." which he could relieve by opiates. He also suffered from the dropsy, which was treated with squill. He died on 13th December 1784. Withering's publication on treatment of the dropsy was to appear the following year. Although Lettsom had been trying Digitalis since 1778, he had not found it of much value, and when in 1787 he wrote to Withering for advice, he was treated to a riposte detailed elsewhere. Heberden does not appear to have been aware of the value of digitalis treatment, since it does not appear in his seminal work "Commentaries on the History and Cure of Diseases." If he had, he might have been able to have helped Dr. Johnson. It is possible that Johnson had atrial fibrillation (a quivering action of the small chambers of the heart, carrying an increased risk of stroke, and oedema due to cardiac failure - dropsy).

Like some doctors, even those of great eminence, Heberden perhaps failed on another occasion, to achieve that duty of care that one would have expected. This was in relation to the case of the famous artist, **Thomas Gainsborough** (qv), who "caught a cold which caused a tumour to inflame." Heberden "treated it lightly and said it would pass away with the cold." Gainsborough then applied to John Hunter "who advised salt water poultices which greatly increased the inflammation & a suppuration followed. There seems to be a strange neglect both in Heberden and Hunter." Thus wrote Kenneth Garlick and Angus Macintyre, editors of "The Diary of Joseph Farington" (Yale University Press, 1978, Vol.1, p.256). It is interesting to ponder what actually happened. Perhaps Gainsborough was merely suffering an acute common cold of viral origin, with an enlarged neck gland, a fairly common occurrence. The application of poultices and salt and general meddling at the site of the swollen gland may have caused a secondary bacterial infection. Further efforts may have compounded the problem, as a result of which poor old Gainsborough may have developed septicaemia (blood poisoning), from which he died. In the absence of antibiotics, the result comes as no surprise. On the other hand, was Heberden actually ahead of his time in recommending no interference for the common cold, (a thing some people even nowadays do not realise, with the not unusual plea for an antibiotic?). Heberden also attended **George III**, who was afflicted with episodes of insanity, generally attributed to acute intermittent porphyria.

This doyen of English medicine advanced knowledge of angina, arthritis and night blindness, and in his Commentaries on the **History and Cure of Diseases (1802)** left clinical descriptions of lasting lucidity. He was the master of wisdom at the patient's bedside. In 1794 he wrote to his friend **Thomas Percival** (qv):

"I please myself with thinking that the method of teaching the art of healing is becoming every day more conformable to what good reason and nature require; that the errors introduced by superstition and false philosophy are gradually retreating; and that medical knowledge, as well as all other dependent upon observation, and experience, is continually increasing in the world. The present race of physicians is possessed of

George III. Portrait by the studio of Allan Ramsay.
(Reproduced with permission of the National Portrait Gallery, London).

several most important rules of practice, utterly unknown to the ablest in former ages, not excepting Hippocrates himself, or even Aesculapius."

His commentaries contain many illuminating observations. In the Preface to the History and Cure of Diseases he states:

"Plutarch says, that the life of a vestal virgin was divided into three portions; in the first of which she learned the duties of her profession, in the second she practised them, and in the third she taught them to others. This is no bad model for the life of a physician......"

On the subject of **constipation** (Alvus):

"A very great difference is observable in different constitutions in regard to the evacuation by stool. One man never went but once in a month: another had twelve stools every day for thirty years, afterwards seven in a day for seven years, and in the mean time did not fall away, but rather grew fat....

The inner coat of the rectum is sometimes so relaxed as to come out after every stool, and in riding, and will not go up again without the assistance of the hand..."

(a reference to rectal prolapse).

The Malignant Sore Throat (Diphtheria):

"....The younger the patients are, the greater is their danger; which is contrary to what happens in the measles and smallpox. In a child who died on the sixth day of this distemper, and was opened, the velum pendulum was putrid; the tonsils were outwardly blackish, and livid within; the uvula was covered with a thick mucus resembling a membrane; the epiglottis was sound, and so was the oesophagus: but that mucous covering descended down the trachea quite to its division, in the upper part of which it appeared like a membrane.......

There may be more use in determining, whether this fever, like the small-pox, be incapable of infecting the same person more than once. According to my experience, some children have beyond all doubt been afflicted a second time with this disease: but it is evident that this happens very seldom....."

Arthritis:

"The gout most usually begins with a pain in the first joint of the great toe, which soon looks very red, and after a little while begins to swell. The violence of the first pain seldom lasts twenty-four hours; but before it has quite ceased, another begins in the same, or some other part, where it continues as long. A succession of similar pains makes up a whole fit of the gout. These will be renewed every day, or with intervals of two, three, or more days, for a few days, or several weeks.....

The gout is derived from gouty ancestors, or is created by intemperance..... Women are less subject to it than men; yet examples of gouty women are by no means rare.... and I have known a female who suffered by the gout to the degree of having numerous sores from chalkstones...

Violent fits, frequently repeated, usually produce chalkstones and chalky sores, and by these, or in consequence of numerous inflammations, make the joints stiff and almost useless. The cramp may also be reckoned one of the certain attendants upon the gout. Flatulencies, heart-burn, indigestion, loss of appetite, sickness, vomiting, acidities, with pains of the stomach and bowels, giddiness, confusion and noises in the head, numbness of the limbs, epilepsies, palsies, apoplexies, inquietude, universal aches, wastings of the flesh and strength, and lowness of spirits, are symptoms, some of which often attend the fit, and some follow it; and most of them are the lot of old gouty patients, who have moreover the prospect of entailing all these upon their posterity.

Though at first the gout returns but rarely, yet at length it becomes familiar, returning oftener, and staying longer, and by the uncertainty of the fits interrupting all business, and disappointing all pleasures. During its presence the patient is helpless as an infant, and without those circumstances which make an infant so easily and cheerfully assisted. It can hardly be considered one of the disadvantages of the gout, that after destroying all the comforts of living, by this weight of misery, or by bringing on a palsy or apoplexy, it immaturely extinguishes the powers of life. Yet people are neither ashamed, nor afraid of it; but are rather ambitious of supposing that every complaint arises from a gouty cause, and support themselves with the hopes that they shall one day have the gout, and use variety of means for this purpose, which happily for them are generally ineffectual.

Various distempers in certain ages and countries have had the fashion on their side, and have been thought reputable and desirable: others, on the contrary, have been reckoned scandalous and dreadful; not from any circumstances in which they are contracted, but from some prejudice or fancy not easily to be accounted for. Epilepsies seem to have been held in particular abomination by the ancient Romans; and ruptures, both with them and with the moderns, have been attended with as unmerited a shame. Some maladies have been esteemed honourable, because they have accidentally attacked the great, or because they usually belong to the wealthy, who live in plenty and ease. We have all heard of the courtiers who mimicked the wry neck of Alexander the Great: and when Louis XIV happened to have a fistula, the French surgeons of that time complain of their being incessantly teased by people, who pretended, whatever their complaints were, that they proceeded from a fistula: and if there had been in France a mineral water reputed capable of giving it them, they would perhaps have flocked thither as eagerly as Englishmen resort to Bath in order to get the gout. For this seems to be the favourite disease of the present age in England; wished for by those who have it not, and boasted of by those who fancy they have it, though very sincerely lamented by most who in reality suffer its tyranny. Hence, by a peculiar fate, more pains seem to be taken at present to breed or produce the gout, than to find out its remedy. For, so much respect hath been shown to this distemper, that all the other ails, except pain, which the real or supposed gouty patient ever feels, are imputed most commonly not to his having had too much of this disease, but to his wanting more: and the gout, far from being blamed as the cause, is looked up to as the expected deliverer from these evils.

The love of life, or fear of death, makes most men unwilling to allow that their constitution is breaking; and for this reason they are ready to impute to any other cause what in reality are the signs of approaching and unavoidable decay. Hence,in a beginning failure or languidness of the functions of life, they easily persuade themselves that their complaints are all owing to a lurking gout, and that nothing is wanting but a just fit, to the re-establishment of their health. Now to say nothing of the slight grounds upon which these fond hopes of a latent gout are generally founded, is it as certainly true as is commonly believed that this distemper, when it comes to a strong fit, clears the constitution from all others; and that by creating, or exciting it, we should not superadd one more evil to those which were suffered before? The itch is supposed to be wholesome in some countries, where it is endemial; and an ague has been considered as a minister of health, whose presence and stay ought by all means to be courted. These opinions are now pretty generally exploded in England; and I hope the time will come, when a specific for the gout, as certain as those which have been discovered for these two disorders, will ascertain the equal safety and advantage of immediately stopping its career and preventing its returns...........

But let the producing or maturing of a suppressed or unformed gout be ever so advantageous, still all physicians must allow the criteria of it to be very obscure, and that there are none by which we can know, and I think hardly any which give us ground to suspect this disease, where there is no pain, nor redness, nor swelling in the first joint of the great toe, or in any other part of the foot, and where the person never had the gout, nor has any hereditary right to it. Yet, notwithstanding the absence of all these circumstances, it is not uncommon to see it charged with being the cause of almost every beginning chronical disease, and of some acute ones..........

The gout affords a striking proof of the long experience and wary attention necessary to find out the nature of diseases and their remedies........

Strong wines, and in no small quantity, have the reputation of being highly beneficial to gouty persons; which notion they have very readily and generally received, not so much perhaps from a reasonable persuasion of its truth, as from a desire that it should be true, because they love wine........

Before I conclude this article, it may not be improper to lay down the distinguishing characteristics of what I would call gout, and rheumatism.

In the former of these disorders, the first attack, consisting perhaps of several ragings and remissions, is wholly confined to the first joint of the great toe, or however to some part of the foot; and the fit does not usually last above ten days or a fortnight.

The pains are sometimes preceded either by a considerable fever, or by slight feels of illness, which for a few days make the sleep less sound, or in a small degree abate the vigour of the appetite, digestion, spirits, and strength.

The part affected is coloured with a deep redness, and is so intensely pained as hardly to bear the gentlest pressure.

The pains are almost always found to return within a few years, and, after a few visits, to make their returns oftener, and their stay longer, extending themselves by degrees to every part of the body, which they enfeeble, or harass with chalky sores, or make useless by the effects of frequent inflammations in destroying the motion of the joints........"

Nowadays of course, gouty attacks can easily be treated with non-steroidal anti-inflammatory drugs ("NSAID's"), such as indomethacin (Indocid), naproxen (Naprosyn), and diclofenac (Voltarol). Colchicine, a traditional remedy derived from the meadow saffron syn. autumn crocus (Colchicum autumnale) is also very effective, and often preferred in the elderly where the side effects of NSAID's are frequently troublesome. Additionally, they can be prevented by a drug first introduced in the 1960's – allopurinol (Zyloric), which inhibits the production of uric acid, precipitation of which in joints is followed by the inflammatory response characteristic of the disease. (For a depiction of an attack, see Gillray).

Of the bath waters:
"The difficulty of ascertaining the powers of medicines, and of distinguishing their real effects from the changes wrought in the body by other causes, must have been felt by every physician: and no aphorism of Hippocrates holds truer to this day, than that in which he laments the length of time necessary to establish medical truths, and the danger, unless the utmost caution be used, of our being misled even by experience. This observation is fully verified in the uncertainty, under which we still remain, in regard to the virtues of the waters of Bath.............Such contrary decisions, so disreputable to physicians, and so perplexing to the sick, could never have happened after so long a trial, if a very small part of those, whose practice had afforded them frequent opportunities of observing the effects

of Bath waters, had told the public what in their judgement was to be hoped or feared from them. It is probable that in some cases it would have been almost unanimously determined they do good: in others, that they do no harm, though it might be doubtful whether they be of much use: in a third sort they would be generally condemmed: and in a fourth class of diseases, some might judge them to be beneficial, and others detrimental.

Wherever the generality of voices passed either of the first two sentences upon these waters, there the use of them might be advised, or permitted without any hesitation; and all should be cautioned against them, where a great majority agreed that they were hurtful......."

Here Heberden is clearly aware of the need for properly conducted trials, though none had yet been designed. It will be noted that spas, so colourful a feature of the Georgian era in England, have become far less popular here than in Europe. With the advent of the NHS, came cynicism for spas, and their cost implications. Yet it may be that for some people they would in fact be a cost-effective alternative to modern drugs with their side effect problems, particularly amongst the elderly.

Bronchocele:
"A SWELLING of the thyroidal gland is endemial in some parts of Derbyshire, Buckinghamshire and Surrey, and is sometimes seen in persons who live in other parts of England, where this disorder is not commonly known. It chiefly affects women, and the younger part of them; and is probably the same with the Alpine swelled throat, which, though so old a distemper, has not yet been found to endanger the life, or disorder the health, or to be worth regarding on any other account than that of its deformity: though I have seen some, who have complained of its giving them, in certain situations, a difficulty of fetching their breath. The cause of this malady is most probably to be found in the peculiar nature of the water in those places where it is common; a judicious examination of which is greatly wanted. I never saw this swelling come to suppuration. A course of sea water, or of solutions of any of the neutral salts, a removal from the place, or the drinking only of the Malvern, or distilled water, appear to be the most useful means of reducing the swelling, or of preventing its return.

We now know that these thyroidal swellings, or goitres, are due to iodine deficiency, a condition also referred to as "Derbyshire neck." Sea water is of course a good source of iodine (and unfortunately of a lot of other things, such as the disposal of untreated sewage).

Coxae Morbus et Exulceratio:
There is a disease near the hip very different from the sciatica, or rheumatism, of that part; and though less painful, it occasions greater lameness, and is far more dangerous. It is seated in the joint of the thigh, and is attended with a remarkable pain in the knee, but with any in the part affected, even after the swelling is become very great, and a fluctuation of matter is perceivable. The thigh wastes, and the foot of that side is unable to support any share of the weight of the body. The patients sometimes die hectic, and

wasted, before the swelling either breaks or is opened; but more commonly the ulcer of the joint makes a way for the purulent matter to discharge itself outwardly: yet this seldom saves their lives, and never prevents their lameness.

This disease will in some go on increasing for three years, before it becomes fatal. It is chiefly found from the sixth to the sixteenth year, during which time of life the joints and external parts of the body suffer most from scrofulous complaints; which, after this age, seem to be turned upon the lungs, or abdominal viscera. The hip-evil evidently belongs to the scrofula; and other scrofulous appearances are often joined with it. The Peruvian bark, and cicuta, opium, and eccoprotics, make up the whole of the medicines, which either aim at the cure, or can occasionally relieve this most difficult and dangerous distemper.

This is referring to tuberculosis of the hip. He makes the point, as every medical student now learns, that hip disease commonly results in pain referred to the knee.

Cutis vitia:

"There is a great variety of cutaneous disorders.........

The herpes, or shingles, has begun with a pain which has lasted in some for two or three days before the eruption appeared. It consists of a heap of watery bladders, itching at first, of which there are sometimes so many as nearly to surround the body, whence it has its name of shingles, from **cingulum**. This eruption is now and then attended with a fever......... But the greatest part of the misery is many times to come after they are perfectly well, and the skin has recovered its natural appearance; for I have known a most pungent burning pain left in the part, which has teased the patient for several months, or even for two or three years........In one person, in whom the herpes had broken out near the collar bone and shoulder, such an exquisite tenderness was left, that he dreaded to move his arm, and could hardly bear the application of any thing to the part, though made with the lightest feather......."

Here we have an excellent description of that most dreaded sequel of shingles - post-herpetic neuralgia, which can be so severe and incapacitating as to lead to suicide.

Digitorum nodi:

"What are those little hard knobs, about the size of a small pea, which are frequently seen upon the fingers, particularly a little below the top, near the joint? They have no connexion with the gout, being found in persons who never had it: they continue for life; and being hardly ever attended with pain, or disposed to become sores, are rather unsightly, than inconvenient, though they must be some hindrance to the free use of the fingers."

As every medical student well knows, osteoarthritis of the distal interphalangeal joints (the end joints of the fingers) is extremely common, particularly in post-menopausal women. These bony swellings, which often alarm their owners who fear they are going to become crippled, are nowadays called "Heberden's nodes," and are often found with a more generalised osteoarthritis. They have no connection with rheumatoid arthritis.

Hydrops:

"Swellings of the ankles or legs towards evening, which vanish, or are greatly lessened in the morning, are very common in women while they are breeding, and in hot weather;....."

Among the various causes of hydrops (dropsy), and treatments for same, no mention of digitalis is made. Perhaps its use is included only to be dismissed:

"...Many medicines have been delivered down from former physicians as possessed of this virtue (diuretic); but it must be owned that their effects are too uncertain, and often so slight, that whoever relies upon them, will in most cases be disappointed..."

Here Heberden is found wanting, since Withering's seminal work on digitalis was published 17 years earlier when Heberden was about 75 years old. Heberden had failed (in old age) to keep up with the literature. Today, continuing medical education (CME) is essential for those who continue to publish, as well as all practising doctors.

Pectoris Dolor:

"Beside the asthma, hysteric oppressions, the acute darting pains in pleurisies, and the chronical ones in consumptions, the breast is often the seat of pains, which are distressing, sometimes even from their vehemence........They have been called gouty, and rheumatic, and spasmodic........

But there is a disorder of the breast marked with strong and peculiar symptoms, considerable for the kind of danger belonging to it, and not extremely rare, which deserves to be mentioned more at length. The seat of it, and sense of strangling, and anxiety with which it is attended, may make it not improperly be called angina pectoris. They who are afflicted with it, are seized while they are walking, (more especially if it be up hill, and soon after eating) with a painful and most disagreeable sensation in the breast, which seems as if it would extinguish life, if it were to increase or to continue; but the moment they stand still, all this uneasiness vanishes.

In all other respects, the patients are, at the beginning of this disorder, perfectly well, and in particular have no shortness of breath, from which it is totally different. The pain is sometimes situated in the upper part, sometimes in the middle, sometimes at the bottom of the os sterni, and more often inclined to the left than to the right side. It likewise very frequently extends from the breast to the middle of the left arm..........

With respect to the treatment of this complaint, I have little or nothing to advance........ Quiet, and warmth, and spirituous liquors, help to restore patients who are nearly exhausted, and to dispel the effects of a fit when it does not soon go off. Opium taken at bed-time will prevent the attacks at night........"

This is the original and possibly the best description of **angina pectoris**, the consequence of a deficient blood supply (ischaemia) of the heart muscle, due to disease (narrowing) of the coronary arteries.

Phthisis Pulmonum:

"A CONSUMPTION appears by the London bills of mortality to be in that city the most destructive of all maladies to adults; one in four of those that grow up to manhood being reported to be carried off by this distemper. But all these must not be charged to the account of a pulmonary consumption; because whoever decline and waste away by any obscure, unnamed distemper, they are all charged to this article, though the lungs be not at all diseased.

The phthisis pulmonum usually begins with a dry cough, so slight and inconsiderable, that little or no notice is taken of it, till its continuance, and gradual increase, begin to make it regarded.............and after frequent recoveries and relapses the patient begins at last to find an accession of other symptoms, which in very bad cases will very soon follow the appearance of the first cough. These are shortness of breath, hoarseness, loss of appetite, wasting of the flesh and strength, pains in the breast, profuse sweats during sleep, spitting of blood and matter, shiverings succeeded by hot fits, ...

The state of the pulse is of great importance in acquainting us with the degree of danger in a cough, which on account of its duration, and of the bad symptoms with which it is accompanied, begins to be of a suspicious nature........

In England we have very little apprehensions of the contagious nature of consumptions; of which in other countries they are fully persuaded. I have not seen proof enough to say, that the breath of a consumptive person is infectious; and yet I have seen too much appearance of it to be sure it is not; for I have observed several die of consumptions, in whom infection seemed to be the most probable origin of their illness, from their having been the constant companions, or bed-fellows, of consumptive persons.

Our great experience of this distemper has hitherto availed but little in enabling us to find out an effectual remedy. The cure of a disease inherited from parents, or owing to such a vitiated habit of body, as that, which is called scrofulous, has proved at least as difficult as it might have been expected, and physicians have hardly advanced further towards it, than by being able to mitigate some of the symptoms. Asses' milk puts some check upon the tendency to emaciate. The dilute acid of vitriol in a decoction of bark is a very effectual remedy of the night sweats, and, as far as I have seen, is perfectly safe in all stages of this malady. A shortness of breath is no reason against using either this medicine, or an opiate at bed-time, which is the most certain soother of the cough, and saves the patient from being harassed with a restless night after a wearisome day........

Many medicines have been delivered down from former physicians, as remedies in strumous diseases; the efficacy of all which have upon trial appeared so dubious, that I cannot from experience recommend any of them as likely to correct the strumous habit, or to disperse the glandular swellings of the lungs which have not suppurated, or to heal those which are already ulcered, or to prevent any more from becoming scirrhous. In this case therefore, as in all others where the proper remedies have not yet been discovered, the patient must be content with instructions, which may enable him to avoid what has been found to aggravate the distemper, and by a proper regimen to put the general health into the best possible state; that the natural powers implanted in the body of re-adjusting any disordered part, may be able to exert themselves with the greatest vigour:........"

Regarding treatment:

"....the consumptive patient does not want encouragement to persevere steadily in a strict regimen, and a solicitous shunning of whatever may weaken the natural strength, or aggravate the distemper.

Cold weather, and bleak winds, will occasion coughs in the soundest lungs, and cannot be too easily avoided, where they are morbidly tender. Warm covering, as a flannel waistcoat, will have its use; but where removal to a warm climate is not impracticable, this will prove the most successful means. An island without any very high hills on it, and at a sufficient distance from the snowy mountains of the continent, and where the heat is from sixty to ninety degrees, is the most favourable situation........

In his diet he must abstain from all wine and spirituous liquors, and either wholly, or as he well can, from meat......The water which is used should be the purest that can be had, such as springs out of the Malvern hills, or distilled water.

Sailing, so as to be out at sea for some months, has been tried by some for whom I have been consulted, and they have thought it useful. However, it has failed in others......."

Though we have had effective drug therapies for tuberculosis for half a century, this disease is again becoming a major killer, due to the development of multi-drug resistant strains.

Pictonum colica (lead colic):

"THERE appear two species of this disorder, one of which may be called the acute, and the other the chronical. In the former, the pain of the stomach and bowels comes on suddenly, and is excessively great, joined with an obstinate costiveness, and sometimes with a stupor and loss of understanding, and ends in a palsy of the hands, if not in death. The chronical begins with dull pains of the bowels, not always accompanied with costiveness............

All the solutions and calxes of lead will certainly occasion this disease. The acute colic perhaps arises from a large quantity of this poison taken in a short time; and the chronical from very small quantities persisted in for a long time. Experience had taught mankind these singular effects of lead near two thousand years ago......It is remarkable, that the chronical Saturnine colichas often attacked only one person in a large family, all of which, as far as could be learned, lived in the same manner. But this must not be used as an argument, that it could not be produced by lead; because it would prove equally against any other external cause. The very small quantity of this poisonous metal, which is sufficient to produce the peculiar symptoms, makes it extremely difficult to trace its passage into the stomach. Three grains of sugar of lead, taken every day for four days, brought on colic, costiveness, inquietude, and loss of appetite. Thirty drops of the Saturnine tincture taken every day for a month created a colica Pictonum, which was long troublesome, though cured at last. It is hard to estimate the precise quantity of lead in those thirty drops, but I judge it can hardly exceed a grain. In the tinning of copper vessels much lead has generally been mixed with the tin, and if one of the family were to use a greater quantity of what had been boiled in such vessels, especially if he were fond of acid sauces prepared in them, this would afford the ready means of accounting for that person's being singled out as the only sufferer.. ....

The acute species of this distemper has never occurred to me, unless among plumbers, or painters, or those who had been exposed to the fumes of melted lead, the dust of old lead, or its calxes.

The unknown manner in which the lead is introduced into the stomach in the chronical colic makes probably the great, and often unconquerable difficulty of curing it. For if, from not being aware how they take this poison, they continue to take it on, no remedies can be of any avail; and accordingly most of these cases have proved incurable. Many children probably die of this distemper, (though confounded with their other bowel complaints) which they contract by having play-things painted with red or white lead, and by putting them, as they are apt to do, into their mouths. The painters of these play-things are liable to this illness; and I have had them under cure for it......."

Purpurae Maculae:
"SOME children, without any alteration of their health at the time, or before, or after, have had purple spots come out all over them, exactly the same as are seen in purple fevers.....In a few days they disappeared without the help of any medicines. It was remarkable, that in one of these the slightest pressure was sufficient to extravasate the blood, and make the part appear as it usually does from a bruise.

A boy four years old for several days had swellings rise on his knees, legs, thighs, buttocks, or scrotum. The part affected was not discoloured, and when at rest, was easy, but could not be moved without some degree of pain. Together with these swellings there appeared red spots sometimes round, sometimes angular, a quarter of half an inch broad, which on the second day became purple, and afterwards yellow, just as it happens from a bruise. The child continued perfectly well in all other respects. These swellings ceased to appear in about ten days; but the red spots continued coming out a few days longer.

Another boy, five years old, was seized with pains and swellings in various parts........He had sometimes pains in his belly with vomiting, and at that time some streaks of blood were observed in his stools, and the urine was tinged with blood. When the pain attacked his leg, he was unable to walk....After a truce of three or four days the swellings returned, and the bloody dots as before........The child struggled with this uncommon disorder for a considerable time, before he was entirely freed from it."

The description of the condition **Henoch-Schonlein purpura** is credited to **Schonlein**, who, in 1837 described a patient with a purpuric rash, arthritis and an abnormal urine sediment, and to **Henoch**, who in 1868 described 4 patients with a purpuric rash, colicy abdominal pain and bloody diarrhoea. Heberden's writing was published in 1802, and it would appear likely that his description was of the same, or if not, a very similar condition to that described by Henoch and Schonlein.

Rheumatismus:

"THE rheumatism is a common name for many aches and pains, which have yet got no peculiar appelation, though owing to very different causes. It is besides often hard to be distinguished from some, which have a certain name and class assigned them: it being in many instances doubtful, whether the pains be gouty, or Venereal, or strumous and tending to an ulcer of the part affected. There are two different appearances of the rheumatism, one of which may be called the acute, and the other the chronical.

The acute is attended with a sense of great restlessness, and intolerable pain upon motion, succeeded by a swelling, which in the very first fit attacks various parts of the body, one after another, seldom remaining long in any..........The degree of fever denoted by the quickness of the pulse does less injury to all the powers of the body, and mind, in the rheumatism, than in any other distemper;........The pain upon motion, and the swelling, have (unlike the gout) kept wandering in their first visit from one part to another for many weeks, and even for some months..........

Such a rheumatism as this has in more than one or two patients returned once or twice a year for several years.......A rheumatic pain in the shoulder of a woman gradually weakened the arm, till it became almost paralytic and useless: in six or seven months the motion of the arm began to return.........

The chronical differs from the acute rheumatism in being joined with little or no fever, in having a duller pain, and commonly no redness, but the swellings are more permanent, and the disease of much longer duration.........

The rheumatism has appeared so early as in a child only four years old, and I have seen several afflicted with it at the age of nine years: in which it differs from the gout, which I never have observed before the years of puberty.........."

Heberden is here likely to be describing several diseases, including acute rheumatic fever. Frozen shoulder, cervical disc prolapse and neuralgic amyotrophy are possible diagnoses for the woman with the shoulder problem. The chronic disease described could have been rheumatoid arthritis, though this disease was first authoritatively described by Landré-Beauvais in 1800. With regard to the 9 years old child, this could have been a case of Still's disease, (nowadays called juvenile chronic arthritis).

Variolae Pusillae. The Chicken-Pox:

"The chicken-pox and swine-pox differ, I believe, only in name; they occasion so little danger or trouble to the patients, that physicians are seldom sent for to them, and have therefore very few opportunities of seeing this distemper. Hence it happens that the name of it is met with in very few books, and hardly any pretend to say a word of its history. But though it be so insignificant an illness, that an acquaintance with it is not of much use for its own sake, yet it is of importance on account of the small-pox, with which it may otherwise be confounded, and so deceive the persons, who have had it, into a false security, which may prevent them from keeping out of the way of the small-pox, or from being inoculated. For this reason I have judged it might be useful to contribute, what I have learned from experience, towards its description.

These pocks break out in many without any illness or previous sign; in others they are preceded by a little degree of chillness, lassitude, cough, broken sleep, wandering pains, loss of appetite, and feverishness for three days.

In some patients I have observed them to make their first appearance on the back, but this perhaps is not constant. Most of them are of the common size of the small-pox, but some are less. I never saw them confluent, nor very numerous. The greatest number, which I ever observed, was about twelve in the face, and two hundred over the rest of the body.............

The principal marks, by which the chicken-pox may be distinguished from the small-pox, are,

1. The appearance on the second or third day from the eruption of that vesicle full of serum upon the top of the pock.

2. The crust, which covers the pocks on the fifth day; at which time those of the small-pox are not at the height of their suppuration..........

.......these two distempers are surely totally different from one another, not only on account of their different appearances above mentioned, but because those, who have had the small-pox, are capable of being infected with the chicken-pox; but those who have once had the chicken-pox, are not capable of having it again, though to such, as have never had this distemper, it seems as infectious as the small-pox. I wetted a thread in the most concocted pus-like liquor of the chicken-pox, which I could find; and after making a slight incision, it was confined upon the arm of one who had formerly had it; the little wound healed up immediately, and showed no signs of any infection. From the great similitude between the two distempers it is probable, that, instead of the small-pox, some persons have been inoculated from the chicken-pox, and that the distemper which has succeeded, has been mistaken for the small-pox by hasty or inexperienced observers..........

Many foreigners seem so little to have attended to the peculiar characteristics of the small-pox, particularly the length of time, which it requires to its full maturation, that we may the less wonder at the prevailing opinion among them, that the same person is liable to have it several times........It would be no extravagant assertion to say, that here in England not above one in ten thousand patients is pretended to have had it twice; and wherever it is pretended, it will always be as likely that the persons about the patient were mistaken, and supposed that to be the small-pox, which was an eruption of a different nature, as that there was such an extraordinary exception to what we are sure is so general a law."

Vox:

"THE voice without any pain, or other disorder of the health, has been weakened so as never to rise above a whisper. In a slight degree of this complaint the persons are liable to laugh in the usual manner; but they are sometimes as incapable of laughing, as of speaking, loud. Those, who have once experienced such a failure of voice, have been very subject to relapses. They have lost their voices suddenly without any previous notice, and recovered them as quickly without any apparent cause. Nine out of ten of those, whom I have seen in this complaint, have been women, and most of them, but not all, have been young and puny, or hysteric, or old and infirm.......

The sudden weakness of voice, of which I have been speaking, is very different from that hoarseness, which belongs to bad coughs, asthmas, and catarrhs." This description clearly differentiates voice disorders due to local physical abnormalities from hysteria.

Uterus:

"A PROLAPSUS of the vagina or womb is only to be relieved by a pessary: it is apt to be attended with an incontinence of urine....

The womb, as well as the breasts of women, is subject to scirrhous tumours, which slowly turn to incurable ulcers. This happens at the same time of life with similar disorders of the breasts, that is, generally after the age of forty. The first symptom is often a return of the menstrual discharge after it had long ceased...."

Post-menopausal bleeding, as any doctor knows, needs urgent investigation to exclude malignancy.

THE CONCLUSION

"It might be expected, that the experience of fifty years spent in the practice of Physic would have taught me more, than I here appear to have learned, of distempers, and their remedies. I readily confess my knowledge of them to be slight, and imperfect; and that a considerable share of this imperfection is chargeable upon my want of ability to make a better use of the opportunities I have had: but at the same time it must be allowed, that some part must be put down to the very great difficulty of making improvements in the medical art. This is too evident from the slow progress, which has been made, though men well qualified by their learning, experience, and abilities, have for above two thousand years been communicating to the world all they could add by just reasoning to the facts collected by attentive observation. Whoever applies himself to the study of nature, must own we are yet greatly in the dark in regard even to brute matter, and that we know but little of the properties and powers of the inanimate creation: but we have all this darkness to perplex us in studying animated nature, and a great deal more arising from the unknown peculiarities of life; for to living bodies belong many additional powers, the operations of which can never be accounted for by the laws of lifeless matter. The art of healing therefore has scarcely hitherto had any guide but the slow one of experience, and has yet made no illustrious advances by the help of reason; nor will it probably make any, **till Providence think fit to bless mankind by sending into the world some superior genius capable of contemplating the animated world with the sagacity shown by Newton in the inanimate, and of discovering that great principle of life, upon which its existence depends, and by which all its functions are governed and directed."**

The bold type is the author's addition for emphasis. Perhaps the discovery and understanding of the structure of DNA two centuries later by Watson and Crick and the explosion of genetics culminating in the elucidation of the human genome, was the kind of revolutionary discovery predicted by Heberden.

JOHN WESLEY (1703-1791)

He was the founder of Methodism, born the 15th child of Samuel and Susanna Wesley, at Epworth rectory on June 17th, 1703. At the age of five, he had a lucky escape when the rectory was burnt down. He was ordained a deacon in 1725. He preached frequently in the Oxford area. Eventually, he would travel up to 5,000 miles a year, preaching fifteen sermons a week. His writings included 'Appeals to Men of Reason and Religion,' which produced an extraordinary effect in allaying prejudice and winning respect.

The name 'Methodist' was intended as a derogatory term to identify a group of Oxford students who, together with the Wesleys (Charles and John), would meet for spiritual fellowship. Methodism began in a spirit of personal religion and its professed aim was to spread scriptural holiness over the land. Its doctrines were in no sense new. It was the manner in which they were taught (with zeal), and the distinction made between the profession of holiness, and the enjoyment of the power it gave, which attracted attention, distinction, ridicule and opposition. This opposition came from the Anglican church, which forbade entry of Methodists into church premises.Thereupon, the Methodists took to preaching outdoors. Methodism spread to the United States, where 16 distinct Methodist denominations sprang forth. They all agreed essentially in doctrine. The first Methodist chapel was opened in New York in October 1768.

Wesley verbally strove to bind his societies to the Church of England, yet by creating a separate ordination within the Methodist movement, succeeded in the opposite effect. Lord Mansfield stated 'ordination is separation.'

John Wesley. Portrait by Nathaniel Hone.
(Reproduced with permission of the National Portrait Gallery, London).

He constantly sought to educate his own people, strove to encourage good reading, and to provide books at the lowest prices. His writings were direct and to the point. He was a social reformer far in advance of his time who provided work, food and clothing for the poor. The profits on his cheap books allowed him to make donations of £1,400 a year. He established a fund from which to make loans to struggling business men, and did much to relieve debtors who had been thrown into prison. He opened dispensaries in London and Bristol, and was keenly interested in medicine.

In 1751, he married Mary Vazeille, a widow, but the union failed, and she left him. Wesley had hoped that **John Fletcher** (1729-1785), vicar of Madeley, a small parish a few miles from Withering's birthplace, would succeed him, but he died in 1785, (the year WW's account of the foxglove appeared). Born Jean de la Fléchière, he had become a tutor to a family in Shropshire in 1752. Here, although he came under the influence of the new Methodist preachers, he took orders, being ordained by the Bishop of Bangor in 1757. He often preached with John Wesley, and was vicar of Madeley from 1760 till the time of his death. He was one of the few parish clergy who understood Wesley and his work, yet he never wrote or said anything inconsistent with his own Anglican position. He manifested a transparent simplicity and saintliness of spirit. **Voltaire**, when challenged to produce a character as perfect as that of Christ, is reputed to have cited Fletcher of Madeley, though it is unlikely he ever met him. It is more likely he was told of him by Wesley. Wesley preached his funeral sermon from the words 'Mark the perfect man.'

During the last three years of his life, John Wesley was welcomed everywhere. His visits were public holidays.

SAMUEL JOHNSON (1709-1784) (SJ)

SJ was an English writer and lexicographer, born in Lichfield, the son of a bookseller and magistrate. It was felt that he had the scrofula (TB), and was taken to London at the age of three to be touched by the monarch (Queen Anne). It did not help, and his face remained badly scarred. He suffered temporary loss of the vision of one eye, and had poor vision in the other. Despite being a lazy pupil, he excelled at both schools he attended, in Lichfield and Stourbridge. Whilst at home between the ages of 16 and 18 he read everything he could lay his hands on, particularly Latin works. Unfortunately, his family were sinking into hopeless poverty, his father being more scholarly than commercially minded. Nevertheless, SJ went to Pembroke College, Oxford, where unfortunately his poverty and strange appearance made him an object of mirth and ridicule. He established a reputation as a mutineer against discipline, and using his Latin skills, translated Pope's "Messiah" into Latin. He missed his Bachelor of Arts degree because he could not pay his fees. For the next thirty years he remained poverty stricken. He suffered hypochondriasis, and a condition characterised by grimaces, gestures, and mutterings. This sometimes terrified people who did not know him. One wonders if he had Tourette's syndrome, as well as the aforementioned TB. His posts included being an usher at a grammar school in Leicestershire, and literary drudge in Birmingham. He fell in love with a widow twenty one years his senior, described as a short, fat coarse woman, heavily made up, dressed in

Portrait by Sir Joshua Reynolds.
(Reproduced with permission of the National Portrait Gallery, London).

gaudy colours, and possessed of many airs and graces. SJ not being possessed of gimlet vision, nevertheless thought the world of her. He tried to provide for her by his teaching, but was unsuccessful. He then went to London to seek his fortune as a writer. Times were very hard, he was often seen in his shabby coats and dirty shirts, with the manners of a savage. Hunger drove him to eat with ravenous haste, and he gorged himself disgustingly whenever the opportunity presented itself. At the age of twenty-nine he obtained a post on the Gentleman's Magazine. His job was to report speeches from parliament, under the disguise of "Reports of the debates of the Senate of Lilliput," freedom of the press not yet having become manifest (vid. the Gordon riots).

In May 1738, he anonymously wrote a poem called "London," based on an adaptation of Juvenal's account of life in the tottering garrets of the pigeon nest infested roofs of Rome, and which paralleled SJ's early days in London. This work was very successful. A second edition was required within a week. It was about this time that SJ became friends with Richard Savage, the son of an earl. He was a failed writer, driven to begging, but whenever in possession of funds, would spend them extravagantly. There were certain similarities between these two, except that SJ possessed enormous talents, and eventually, after Savage died heartbroken and penniless in Bristol Gaol in 1743, SJ wrote (again anonymously), the "Life of Savage." Lord Macaulay (1800-1859) English historian, essayist and politician, later hailed this as the finest specimen of literary biography existing in any language, living or dead. SJ's reputation was on the ascendancy, and in 1747, he was commissioned to prepare the "Dictionary of the English Language," in two folio volumes. The agreed fee was fifteen hundred guineas, from which he was to have paid assistants for carrying out the more mundane parts of this work. Macaulay had gone on to say:

"The prospectus of the Dictionary he addressed to the earl of Chesterfield. Chesterfield had long been celebrated for the politeness of his manners, the brilliancy of his wit and the delicacy of his taste. He was acknowledged to be the finest speaker in the House of Lords. He had recently governed Ireland, at a momentous conjecture, with eminent firmness, wisdom and humanity; and he had since become secretary of state. He received Johnson's homage with the most winning affability, and requited it with a few guineas, bestowed doubtless in a very graceful manner, but was by no means desirous to see all his carpets blackened with the London mud, and his soups and wines thrown to right and left over the gowns of fine ladies and the waistcoats of fine gentlemen, by an absent minded scholar, who gave strange starts and uttered strange growls, who dressed like a scarecrow and ate like a cormorant. During some time Johnson continued to call on his patron, but, after being repeatedly told by the porter that his lordship was not at home, took the hint and ceased to present himself at the inhospitable door."

The Dictionary was completed in 1755, after seven years of drudgery. Prior to its publication, it was anticipated that it would include a dedication to the earl of Chesterfield. In fact, the same person had in two successive numbers of 'World' praised SJ's writings warmly, perhaps to the extent, if that were possible, of flattery. In the event, the Dictionary appeared without a dedication, instead, a declaration in the preface that the author owed nothing to the great, and described the difficulties with which he had been left to struggle so forcibly and pathetically.

The work was hailed enthusiastically, and made very pleasurable reading. It exhibited two weaknesses, one being his lack of grasp of etymology, the other his unconcealed Jacobite prejudice. He received honours from the university of Oxford, the Royal Academy, and an interview with the king.

From now on, he wrote less, but was renowned for his powers of conversation. As Macaulay stated,

"He had strong sense, quick discernment, wit, humour, immense knowledge of literature and of life, and an infinite store of curious anecdotes."

Now he found himself in the celebrated company of men of letters: **Burke, Goldsmith, Reynolds, Gibbon,** and **Garrick,** who formed themselves into a club in 1764. To this club, after much effort, was admitted **James Boswell**, a young Scots lawyer, described as a coxcomb and a bore, weak, vain, pushing, curious, and garrulous. Boswell glued himself to SJ, as disciple to master.

Theirs was a curious relationship, SJ frequently scolding and sneering at his disciple, yet having for him a deep affection.

In August 1773, SJ and Boswell went on their celebrated journey to the Hebrides, about which SJ wrote in 1775 ('**Journey to the Hebrides**'). In 1779, and 1781, appeared possibly his best work, the "Lives of the Poets," in ten volumes. In 1783, SJ's health was bad, he had a 'paralytic attack,' (? stroke), by September 1784, his asthma was very bad, day and night (?cardiac asthma,) and dropsical signs appeared (?congestive cardiac failure). That winter was to be his last. His dropsy was treated by incisions, to drain the oedema. He was attended by the ablest physicians and surgeons. To no avail, because at 7.15 p.m. on 13th December, he died, in his seventy sixth year. He was buried in Westminster Abbey.

WW's account of the foxglove and some of its medical uses did not appear until the following year. It is quite possible that Samuel Johnson's condition might have responded for a while to treatment with digitalis leaf.

SIR JOSHUA REYNOLDS (1723-1792)

He was born at Plympton Earl in Devonshire, on July 16th 1723. His father was a clergyman and master of the free grammar school. At the age of seventeen, he was apprenticed to Thomas Hudson, in London, a painter of no great talent, yet popular as a portraitist. Hudson introduced Reynolds to the artist's club that met in St. Martin's Lane. It was Reynold's portrait of Captain the Hon. John Hamilton that first brought him to any notice. Reynolds travelled to Italy where he arrived in 1750, and stayed for over two years. After visiting Parma, Florence, Venice and other cities, he returned to London, and established himself in St. Martin's Lane as a portrait painter. He was very successful in

Self-portrait of Sir Joshua Reynolds.
(Reproduced with permission of the National Portrait Gallery, London).

society, and Lord Edgcumbe was his patron who also helped obtain commissions for his protege. Reynolds met Dr. Johnson, who was his friend for life, and he also befriended Burke, Goldsmith, Garrick, Sterne and Bishop Percy. They were members of "The (Literary) Club" which was established at Reynold's suggestion in 1764. With the patronage of George III, the **Royal Academy** was founded in 1768, and Reynolds was the first president. Within a few months he was knighted. In 1784, he was appointed painter to the king.

He has become generally admired for his portraits of women and children, of which the Althorp portraits of the Spencer family are classics. He died in 1792, and was buried in St. Paul's Cathedral.

THOMAS GAINSBOROUGH (1727-1788)

He was born in Sudbury, the son of a woolencrape maker, and the youngest of nine children. He studied at St.Martin's Lane in London. In 1745 he returned to Sudbury, and from 1750 began painting portraits and landscapes from his house in Ipswich. In 1759 he went to Bath which was at its fashionable height and there established a studio. By 1774, he was very prosperous, and returned to London, where he resided in Pall Mall. He was commissioned to paint the king, queen, and other members of the royal family. He also painted Sheridan, Burke, Johnson, Franklin, Canning, Pitt, Lady Mary Wortley

Self-portrait of Thomas Gainsborough.
(Reproduced with permission of the National Portrait Gallery, London).

Montagu, Mrs. Siddons, Clive and others. In 1768, he was elected one of the original 36 members of the Royal Academy.

His work differed from that of Reynolds in that Reynolds was more influenced by the Italian school, having spent two years there. Gainsborough had led a more secluded life early on, and his early landscapes reflected the Dutch school. Once in London, his landscapes were painted from memory.

He died on August 2nd 1788, and was buried at Kew.

VOLTAIRE (1694-1778)

Born Francois Marie Arouet, in Paris. He was the fifth child, and his mother died when he was seven. His mother was almost certainly responsible for his introduction into society, being a good friend of the abbé de Chateauneuf (Voltaire's godfather). Up to the age of 18 years, he was educated by the Jesuits. His education, typical of the Jesuits, placed much emphasis upon acting, which undoubtedly influenced his lifelong devotion to the stage.

In 1711 aged 17, at his father's behest he grudgingly agreed to read Law, though his first love was literature. However, Voltaire at the age of 20 wrote several libellous poems which got him into trouble. As a consequence he was exiled. On his return further accusations relating to libels followed, and he was imprisoned in the Bastille at the ripe old age of 23 years. There, nothing daunted, he continued his writing. He changed his name after release to an abbreviated form, which is the name under which he is universally known - Voltaire. He revelled in stirring up foment, whether it be by books, plays or poems. He was also a very successful (and lucky - winning the French lottery) - financial speculator. He visited England from 1726 till 1729, where he made friends with George II, Queen Caroline, the Walpoles, Bolingbroke and others. (The English establishment were keen to make a fuss of this bête noir of the French, and no doubt Voltaire lapped it up).

In 1733 he wrote two very controversial books, which between them criticised French literature (especially that of Rousseau), plus the church and the state itself. Not surprisingly this led to trouble, the books were seized and burnt, and a warrant for Voltaire's arrest was issued. He didn't need to worry, since he was by now safe in the independent duchy of Lorraine. He was a close friend (probably very close) of Emilie de Breteuil, Marquise du Châtelet. They lived in the chateau of Cirey, occasionally visited by her (accommodating) husband. Emilie however was not renowned for her passivity, having a violent temper, (as well as a need for other lovers). Whilst at Cirey, Voltaire continued his writing. He came under constant criticism of his work by Madame du Châtelet. During this time, Voltaire began receiving invitations by Frederick of Prussia. These annoyed Madame, since she was never invited.

In 1746, Voltaire was elected to the Academy Française. He continued his writings, which as usual, were mischievous, and which stirred up his enemies. In 1749, Madame died after the birth of a child. In 1751, Voltaire at last agreed to move to Prussia at Frederick's behest. This offer came with a generous twenty thousand francs a year. He stayed for three eventful years, which were marked by the usual battles with rivals, plus a financial scandal, in which Voltaire was alleged to have forged a business document. In the end, and despite Frederick's amusement at his writings, he was arrested but allowed to leave the country. He then travelled to Colmar.

Eventually he wound up near Geneva, purchasing a very substantial property at Ferney, in 1758. He was a great philanthropist, and a statue stands in the village square bearing testament to his struggle for fairness, and his generosity.

Finally, he was permitted to return to Paris, where, in 1778, he was warmly greeted, not at court, but by the Academy. He attended the first performance of his work "Irene" and was crowned with a laurel in his box. Unfortunately, he fell ill, and died two months later, aged 84 years.

Throughout his life, he was very thin, never interested in sport, and drank coffee continually (much like Samuel Johnson was wont to drink tea).

It is very likely that Withering, who visited Paris in 1766, together with his ill-fated friend Townshend, would have heard tell of Voltaire, and the controversies surrounding him.

WILLIAM WORDSWORTH (1770-1850)

A great poet, he was born at Cockermouth, Cumberland, the son of an attorney. In 1787, he entered St. John's College, Cambridge and graduated B.A. in 1791. He did not feel that he benefited much from his time at Cambridge, being unimpressed by the manners of the

William Wordsworth. Portrait by Robert Hancock.
(Reproduced with permission of the National Portrait Gallery, London).

(male) students. Relatively little of his major work was completed during the lifetime of WW, though his first major work, "Guilt and Sorrow" was completed in 1794, and a portion of it, titled "The Female Vagrant" was printed in the **Lyrical Ballads** of 1798.

JOHANN ZOFFANY (1733-1810)

He was a painter, born in Frankfurt on Main, the son of an architect. At the age of 13 he ran away from home, and went to Rome where he studied art for 12 years. He came to England in 1758, and eventually obtained Royal patronage, and with it fame. In 1769, he was one of the founder members of the Royal Academy. In 1771 he painted a portrait of George III. He also painted a charming portrait of Lettsom and his family, (see Lettsom). He died in 1810, and was buried at Kew.

EDMUND BURKE (1729-1797)

He was a British statesman and political theorist, the son of an Irish lawyer. In 1743, he entered Trinity College, Dublin, where **Oliver Goldsmith** was also a student. Burke achieved no academic distinction whilst there.

He married the daughter of a Bath physician, Dr. Nugent, in 1756.

George III ascended to the throne in 1760, and the court determined to change the political system which, since the revolution of 1688, had placed power in the hands of a few wealthy families albeit provided with fairly enlightened principles and shrewd

Edmund Burke. Portrait by Sir Joshua Reynolds.
(Reproduced with permission of the National Portrait Gallery, London).

political sense. The first two kings of the house of Hanover had only been allowed to keep the crown over their heads by conciliating the Revolution families, and by espousing their principles. George III was not threatened in this way and consequently insisted on removing a measure of political power from the aristocratic politicians, and placing it in the hands of the monarchy. Ministers were to become answerable not to their colleagues, but to the king. This led to Prime Minister Bute's resignation in 1763. Grenville took over, and the Whigs proceeded to tax the American colonists, interfere with their trade, and withdraw freedom of the press. The nation was appaled, Grenville fell, to be succeeded by the Marquis of Rockingham, with Burke as his private secretary. Shortly afterwards he entered Parliament, representing the pocket borough of Wendover. He soon became recognised as a skillful debater. He was acutely aware of the penal laws against the Catholics, the iniquitous restrictions on Irish trade and industry, selfish facetiousness of parliament, corruption of administration, and absenteeism of landlords (though this was arguably less of a loss than the absence of her men of genius).

This government fell within a year, on account of lack of political connections, particularly by failing to obtain the collaboration of William Pitt. Burke became a friend of the future Prime Minister Charles Fox, but split with him over the French Revolution. He wrote "Reflections on the Revolution in France" and was regarded as controversial in that he denounced events there, regarding them as no more than mob rule. He supported reform through evolution, not revolution.

ROBERT BURNS (1759-1796)

He was the greatest of Scottish poets, and was born in a cottage about two miles from Ayr, the son of a farmer. He had to labour hard on the land, and wrote:

"This kind of life, the cheerless gloom of a hermit and the unceasing toil of a galley-slave brought me to my 16th year." He was a keen reader, especially of songs. By age 23, he had begun writing verse of note. At 27, being denied the hand of the one he loved, by her father, he resolved to go into exile in Jamaica. However, this was not necessary, as his work was recognised, the first volume being published in Kilmarnock in June 1786. His fame spread rapidly, and he joined the glittering literati of Edinburgh.

In 1788 Burns bought a farm at Ellisland on the Nith, where, settled and married, he wrote "Tam o'Shanter." He is credited with having written the words to "Auld Lang Syne" as well as the tune. However, although the words were written by Burns, the tune was probably not, and it has recently come to light (The Times, December 15th 1998), that the tune was probably composed in 1783 by the Gateshead born composer William Shield as part of his little known operetta "Rosina." Shield may also have composed "Coming Through The Rye." He was to become Master of the King's Music in 1817. In 1792, Burns was asked to contribute poems to George Thomson's "Select Collection of Original Scottish Airs with Symphonies and Accompaniments for the Piano-forte and Violin: the Poetry by Robert Burns." He also contributed about 100 songs.

As he grew older, he became more isolated from Society as a consequence of his revolutionary opinions and sour temper. He sought solace in the company of the common folk. In 1796 he was dying, of what we do not know. But it is said his hand shook, his pulse and appetite failed, his spirits sank into a uniform gloom, and within 3 months he was dead. He may have died of thyrotoxic heart failure, the clue being his irritability and bad temper, followed by the shaking hand and "failed pulse" whatever that meant. Alternatively, he might have suffered from Parkinson's disease, the frustration of which led to his irritability and depression.

It is very likely Withering knew of Burns, whose fame became established during the last twelve years of WW's life.

EDWARD GIBBON (1737-1794)

A celebrated historian, he was born at Putney. His father was member of parliament for Petersfield. Edward was the seventh child, and all his siblings died in childhood. After his mother died in 1747, his father moved to Hampshire, leaving Edward in the care of his aunt at his grandfather's house in Putney. The library was to be his fount of knowledge. He went to Magdalen College before he had turned fifteen, as a gentleman commoner. There was a mutual dislike between Gibbon and his tutors. As a result largely of his reading, he became a convert to the church of Rome, which grossly displeased his father. As a consequence, he was sent to Lausanne, to live with a Calvinist minister. Within two years he had returned to Protestantism. He studied the classics, philosophy and, for a while, mathematics. In 1757, he met Voltaire. The same year he

Edward Gibbon. Portrait by Henry Walton.
(Reproduced with permission of the National Portrait Gallery, London).

fell in love, but his choice (a pastor's daughter) displeased his father who, incidentally, had re-married at this time. He visited Rome in 1764 and stated:

"On the fifteenth of October 1764, as I sat musing amidst the ruins of the Capitol.....the idea of writing the decline and fall of the city first started in my mind." The first volume of his epic "History of the Decline and Fall of the Roman Empire" appeared after four years work, in 1776. It went rapidly to three editions. Between 1774 and 1782, he was in politics, initially as M.P. for Liskeard, losing his seat in 1780, but was returned for Lymington in a by-election in 1781. The same year, his second and third volumes appeared. After the fall of Lord North's ministry in the spring of 1782, he quit politics. Reflecting on his political career, he commented it had been "a school of civil prudence, the first and most essential virtue of an historian." He then sold up and moved to Lausanne, where the remaining three volumes were written, and published in London in 1788. He returned to England in 1793, where he died in 1794. He was buried at Flitching, Sussex.

Part Three

WITHERING'S LEGACY TO MEDICINE

Chapter 8

DIGITALIS TO DIGOXIN, PURPLE TO WOOLLY

(This section includes text largely written in technical language, describing the development of digitalis to its present form, known as digoxin).

SUBSEQUENT FINDINGS AND INDICATIONS FOR DIGITALIS
Although WW gave the first learned description of the use of digitalis for treating oedema, it had in fact been used previously as an attempted treatment for tuberculosis, epilepsy, syphilis, and many other diseases. It had probably been used in medicine for thousands of years, since squill, which also contains cardiac glycosides, certainly had. The foxglove was recorded as having been used for medicinal purposes in the Bury St. Edmunds herbal of 1120. Over the ensuing centuries, it was tried in wounds and for scrofula. In The Edinburgh New Dispensary of 1789 (The 2nd edition), Printed for Charles Elliott and for C. Elliott and T.Kay at Dr. Cullen's Head, Opposite Somerset Place, Strand, London, and priced at eight shillings (bound), we find:
"DIGITALIS [Lond.Ed.] Herbivorae
Digitalis purpurea Lin.
Fox glove; the plant.
.... (see original work)..........

Digitalis, however, has lately been employed with great success in other disease. A treatise has lately been published by Dr. Withering, professedly on the subject of its use in medicine; and containing many important and useful observations......"
Following WW's publication, the drug was introduced in America by **Dr. Hall Jackson**, (qv) in 1786, having written asking WW for some seeds. In 1790 he reported successfully treating seven out of eleven patients. During the 19th century, digitalis was tried (with little effect) in a wide variety of conditions. It was used in inflammation, infection, mania, "erotomania", and nymphomania! In Trousseau's Lectures on Clinical Medicine delivered at the Hôtel-Dieu, Paris, 1869, the translated version of which was published by the New Sydenham Society in London in 1872, we see that digitalis was recommended for the treatment of: epilepsy, exophthalmic goitre, haemoptysis associated with disease of the heart, with antimony in pneumonia, in spermatorrhoea, and together with colchicine in gout. Specifically for the treatment of dropsy it states:
"When it is, as usual, connected with disease of the heart, decided benefit is obtained by very moderate bleedings, the preparation of digitalis in full doses, acids and rhatany."
In the "Principles and Practice of Medicine, by the late Charles Hilton Fagge M.D. F.R.C.P, Physician to, and lecturer on pathology at, Guy's Hospital, Examiner in medicine in the University of London" published by J.& A. Churchill in 1886, we read on the treatment of cardiac disease:

"This is of two kinds or has two objects, the one directed against the perverted action of the heart and the other against the effects of the obstructed circulation. For the former great object we have in our hands one of the most remarkable medicines in the Pharmacopoeia, one which if given opportunely may truly snatch the patient from the jaws of death. He may, for example, be the subject of mitral disease and all its attendant consequences, and may be approaching his end, when digitalis – for this is the remedy referred to – is administered; the heart becomes quiet, contracts with more energy, and with this improved action, all the symptoms depart and the patient is restored to comparative health. There is no such striking effect seen from the influence of any other drug. A pill consisting of digitalis, squill, and mercury had long been known as a most valuable medicine in cardiac dropsy, but formerly its administrators scarcely understood that it had any other than a diuretic action; it is evident, however, that the digitalis was influencing the heart in a very direct and specific manner, and in this way its action was beneficial. .....Digitalis gives tone and regularity to the heart, it has been called therefore the tonic and opiate of the heart.....Just as digitalis is the true remedy in the weak, irregularly acting heart in order to steady and strengthen it, so it is almost valueless when the organ is hypertrophied and acting steadily." This statement has stood the test of time – it is now regarded generally as only being of value in rapid atrial fibrillation and particularly when accompanied by congestive cardiac failure ("dropsy"). When the heart is beating normally –"sinus rhythm"- its value is far less certain.

Early in the 20th century, the drug was put back on a firmer footing by **Dr. James Mackenzie** who published the first description of atrial fibrillation in 1902, and in 1905, the effect of digitalis in slowing the ventricular rate.

By 1921, the Wellcome Medical Diary listed the following:
"Digitalin (amorphous) gr 1/100, crystalline gr 1/250, also hypodermic 1/640 gr
Digitalis Tincture min.1, min.5, and (1 in 10), 0.1gm.
Digitalinum (Amorph.) 1/100 – 1/30 gr. and (cryst.) 1/500 – 1/130 gr.
Also Hypodermic product.
Digitalis, B.P., Tincture of 'Wellcome' Brand (*Physiologically Standardised*)
(Also five times B.P. strength as a concentrated tincture)."

For the following information which includes the **discovery of digoxin**, without doubt the most significant event subsequent to the discovery of digitalis, I am greatly indebted to **Dr. John Reader**, lately retired Manager, Natural Plant Products Dept., The Wellcome Foundation Ltd., Dartford, who fortuitously managed to salvage the original laboratory notes of the person responsible, **Sydney Smith** see figure. Smith was working at the Wellcome Chemical Works in Dartford, and in 1930 published his seminal paper:

"**Digoxin, a new Digitalis Glucoside.**" It appeared in the Journal of the Chemical Society. It commenced thus:

"In recent years it has been shown that the leaves of Digitalis lanata have a greater physiological activity than those of Digitalis purpurea, the species used in medicine; e.g., Wokes (Quart. J. Pharm. Pharmacol., 1929, 2, 292) found the potency of a specimen of Digitalis lanata to be 3.5-4 times that of the international standard leaf."

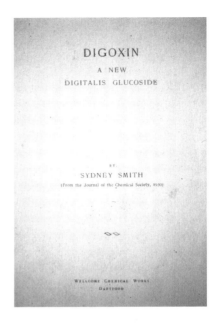

Portrait of Sydney Smith.
(With permission of GlaxoSmithKline)

Cover of Sydney Smith's manuscript.
(With permission of GlaxoSmithKline)

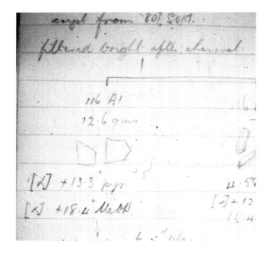

(Left & right) Sydney Smith's manuscript regarding the isolation and description of digoxin, obtained from Digitalis lanata (With permission of GlaxoSmithKline).

The total glucosides of the leaves of this species were therefore isolated and fractionated in order to separate the glucosides and compare them with those from the official species. This part of the work is not yet completed, but during the differentiation a glucoside was obtained in small amount differing from those hitherto known. This new glucoside, which has been named **digoxin**, resembles gitoxin in its sparing solubility in chloroform, but is readily distinguished from it by giving an olive brown colour completely free from red when dissolved in acetic acid containing a trace of ferric chloride and treated with sulphuric acid (Keller reaction). In the latter respect it is similar to pure digitoxin. Digoxin is optically active. It is very easily hydrolysed and gives a crystalline genin and only one sugar, digitoxose. The results of combustion and the molecular weight determinations of the genin suggest the empirical formula $C_{41}H_{64}O_{14}$ and $C_{23}H_{34}O_5$ for digoxin and digoxygenin respectively......."

By way of acknowledgement, Smith states that he is indebted to Dr. Hill, Director of the Royal Botanical Gardens, Kew, for the botanical verification of the material used and to Mr. A. Bennett for the micro-analyses.

There are several foxgloves under the Digitalis genus, order Scrophulariaceae. The species are listed below:

D. dubia, ferruginea, grandiflora, laevigata, lanata, leucophaea, lutea, obscura, parviflora, purpurea, thapsi. The purple foxglove, D. purpurea, is a biennial (rarely perennial). There are three subspecies, purpurea, mariana, and heywoodii.

Cardiac glysosides are substances with a characteristic structure and action. The foxglove is only one of many sources, though clearly the best known. A list is shown in the table overleaf.

The leaves of the foxglove contain several cardiac glycosides with similar actions. Other plants including squill, lily of the valley, and oleander produce similar substances. Therapeutically important are digoxin, digitoxin, strophanthin and ouabain. Their chemical structure consists of a lactone and steroid component with a sugar moiety attached to the steroid, see accompanying figure over page.

The methyl and hydroxyl groups on the steroid vary, and the sugar residues consist of 1-4 monosaccharides (digitoxose). Sugar free derivatives are known as aglycones or genins, e.g. **digoxygenin**, which are relatively insoluble and short acting, and therefore are not clinically useful. The lactone ring is essential for activity and is capable of retaining this even when the steroid is removed.

The important differences between the glycosides mentioned involves their absorption and duration of action. Ouabain is short acting and more rapid in onset than the others given intravenously. The time to peak effect is about one hour and thus it is of value when a rapid response is required. The others are much longer lasting, the time to peak effect being four to six hours after an oral dose, and are used for long term therapy. Digitoxin is 90% plasma protein bound, whereas digoxin is only weakly bound.

Their current clinical use is only for cardiac disease, the main applications being cardiac failure, and atrial dysrhythmias. However, it is of great interest that cytotoxic activities of some plant extracts have been reported. Thevetoside has been shown

CARDIAC GLYCOSIDES AND THEIR SOURCE

(from Aronson 1985)

CARDIAC GLYCOSIDE	SOURCE
Adonitoxin	Adonis vernalis (false hellbore)
Antiarin	Antiaris toxicaria (upas tree)
Convallatoxin	Convallaria majalis (lily of the valley)
Cymarin	Apogynum cannabinum
Deslanoside*	Digitalis lanata (woolly foxglove)
Digoxin*	" "
Digitoxin*	Digitalis purpurea (purple foxglove)
Hellebrin	Helleborus niger (hellebore)
Helveticoside (Erysimin)	Erysimum helveticum
Lanatoside C*	Digitalis lanata
Neriantin (Oleandrin)	Nerium oleander (oleander)
Ouabain (strophanthin-G)*	Strophanthus gratus Acokanthera schimperi Acokanthera oubaio
Periplocin	Periploca graeca Strophanthus preussii
Peruvoside*	Thevetia nereifolia
Proscillaridin*	Urginea (Scilla) maritima (squill)
Sarveroside	Strophanthus sarmentosus
Strophanthin-K	Strophanthus kombe
Tanghinin	Tanghinia venenifera
Thevetin	Thevetia nereifolia

*Glycosides with clinical application

Chemical structure of cardiac glycosides.
Individual compounds vary in respect of (1) methyl and
hydroxyl groups on steroid nucleus; (2) sugar residues.

experimentally to inhibit certain tumours in mice, alone and in combination (Zhang et al 1994). From the Solanaceae family, extracts from Nierembergia aristrata have shown significant toxicity to cancer cell lines (Gil et al 1995). It is also of considerable interest that ouabain-like immunoreactive substances have been demonstrated in the hypothalamus and adrenal medulla in rats (Takahashi et al 1994), and have been extracted from mammalian tissue using acid extraction plus reverse phase high pressure liquid chromatography (Qazzaz & Valdes 1996).

Two aspects of the digitalis/digoxin story not generally appreciated are
(i) That **digoxin is not present in Digitalis purpurea (purple foxglove)**, though digitoxin is.
(ii) Digoxin is part of **Lanatoside C**, which is found in **Digitalis lanata (woolly foxglove)**.

WW initially used a decoction of D.purpurea (a decoction involves the treating of leaves with boiling water). This method was replaced by the use of an infusion (seeping of the leaves in hot, or cold water), and later, by using digitalis powder, obtained by grinding the dried leaves. WW also mentions use of foxglove tea, and of decoctions made using a wine and water mix.

AR Cushny (Proc. Roy Soc Lond viii 1914-15) (Sect Hist Med pp 85-93) has written: "At first the leaves were made into a decoction, later an infusion, and sometimes they were used as a powder. The doses prescribed were very large, for example the decoction from 9 gr. of the leaves every two hours, until vomiting followed. Our British Pharmacopoiea suggests as a maximal dose the decoction from ? gr. These doses proved a sovereign remedy in the numerous cases of dropsy which he gives.————

————the use of digitalis quickly spread among Withering's friends in the profession and especially in Edinburgh where Hope₃ was its sponsor, and in 1783 it made its first official appearance in the Edinburgh Pharmacopoiea. It is interesting to meet the name of Charles Darwin, brother of Robert as recommending its use on the ground that it had proved valuable in the hands of his father Erasmus; this Charles Darwin was the uncle of the great naturalist of the same name who was the son of Robert Darwin."

In a late edition of Withering's Botany, lines by "S.H."

'The foxglove's leaves, with caution given,
Another proof of favouring Heav'n
Will happily display;
The rapid pulse it can abate;
The hectic flush can moderate
And, blest by Him whose will is fate,
May give a lengthen'd day.'

The D.purpurea plants contain lanatosides A and B and these compounds would have been included by WW when using the dried leaves. Degradation products of the lanatosides are hardly present in either the growing plant or the dried leaves. The appropriate enzymes, responsible for degrading the lanatosides, contained in the same plant tissue but in different cells do not gain access to the lanatosides until the tissue is destroyed. The enzyme splits the glucose residue from the lanatoside to give the acetyl derivative, e.g. acetyl-digitoxin is obtained from lanatoside A. In the modern process to isolate digoxin from D. lanata, the maceration stage of the process when the dried leaves are treated with a solution of aqueous alcohol, lanatoside C yields acetyl-digoxin. The lanatosides can be isolated without degradation from the leaves, and lanatoside C is prepared and marketed. Mild alkali treatment of the acetylated products yields digitoxin (in the case of lanatoside A), and digoxin (in the case of lanatoside C). As a point of interest, alkali treatment of lanatoside C (in the absence of enzyme), yields desacetyl-lanatoside C (Deslanoside in Aronson's list, vid. page 225 et seq.)

The active substances in older preparations of D.purpurea are slowly absorbed, so that the effects of overdosage may not be apparent until a considerable excess of the drug has accumulated. They are also slowly excreted. Digoxin by contrast, with its rapid absorption and excretion allowed clinicians a more accurate and sensitive control of cardiac arrhythmias.

The cultivation and selection of D. lanata plants followed the work of Dr. Sydney Smith in 1929, described above. In the 30's leaf from Canada and Central Europe was used, the latter being replaced by leaf grown in the UK due to the outbreak of the second World War. German prisoners of war worked here on some of the farms. After the war, leaf was again imported from Europe and Marshall Aid funds were used to establish a cooperative organisation for growing, drying and selling Digitalis lanata amongst other medicinal herbs in the Netherlands. This is because it is cheaper for the pharmaceutical industry to extract digoxin from the dried leaves of the plant than to synthesise the drug chemically. Digitalis lanata is called woolly foxglove because the calyx of the flower is thickly covered with white glistening slightly sticky hairs, see the accompanying figure.

The inherited properties of the species have been steadily improved. These improvements including the digoxin content are considerable. It is necessary to select plants and grow the seeds continually in order to prevent the resumption of the wild form (Mastenbroek 1985).

In order to obtain an improved and uniformly high yielding crop, compatible with the chemical processing plant, research was carried out on the cell culture and cloning of individual plants. Analyses of a large number of plants in a crop had revealed a digoxin content varying between 0.08% and 0.4%.

Seeds are drilled in mid-April, seedlings appear two months later, and rapid growth takes place between July and August. Harvesting is carried out between the end of September and the middle of November depending on the weather, and transported to drying centres. Thereafter the leaves are thoroughly washed in water and carefully dried in hot air to avoid digoxin loss.

Resistance to disease is important, the major commercial problem being caused by the fungus **Septoria digitalis** which causes leaf spot, and diminishes the number of seeds. Therefore spraying is carried out twice during the growing season. Resistance to bolting is also important, bolting meaning the formation of flowers and fruits within the first year, and thus a digoxin depleted leaf. Bolters are therefore removed. Because Digitalis lanata can include up to 63 different glycosides, the products from individual plants are assessed by paper chromatography, and more recently using thin layer chromatography. Selection of plants is then made.

The breeding procedure takes seven years, selecting for all the desired characteristics.

Digitalis lanata
(Woolly foxglove)
(from whence digoxin).

Digitalis purpurea
(Purple foxglove)
(from whence digitalis, and digitoxin).

(With permission of the Royal Botanical Gardens, Kew).

Harvesting D purpurea at Dartford c. 1926 for products of digitalis leaf.

Harvesting D. lanata in Holland, 1984 for extraction of digoxin.

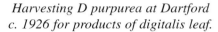

(With permission of GlaxoSmithKline).

Bales of dried leaf are stored in cool, airy warehouses, under which conditions they can be kept for several years without loss of digoxin. Warmth and humidity are to be avoided.

The chemical manufacture involves several stages.

Stage 1. Preparation of total glycoside extract.
The process is simple and straightforward but attention to detail is imperative if digoxin loss is to be avoided.

The leaves are macerated at a controlled temperature for a limited time with a solution of alcohol in water to allow the enzymic action to remove the glucose molecule from the lanatoside. This action can be undertaken with water alone but the conditions are different and much carbon dioxide is released during the process.

The "total glycosides" are then extracted from this mixture, together with other plant substances, by the use of more aqueous alcohol. There is argument for both percolation and batchwise extraction methods for obtaining the total glycosides.

Stage 2. Deacetylation
Treatment of this solution with dilute alkali, under very tightly controlled conditions, allows the conversion of acetyl-digoxin to digoxin.

Stage 3. Purification of the total glycosides.
The total glycosides are transferred from one solvent to another by means of countercurrent liquid/liquid extraction.

Stage 4. The chromatographic separation of digoxin from the total glycosides.
In the early days, digoxin was obtained by dissolving the dried total glycoside extract in acetone from which crude digoxin crystallised. Further recrystallisations afforded 'pure' digoxin.

The invention of chromatography in the 40's allowed many substances to be purified much more easily and this included digoxin.
Stage 5. The recrystallisation of digoxin.
This is carried out in such a way as to make it suitable for use in therapeutics. This stage of the process and the manufacture of tablets are critical for the final product which has to pass demanding tests of bioavailability.

Preparations currently in routine use are limited to:
1. **Digoxin (Lanoxin - Glaxo-Wellcome).** Tablets, elixir and injection for intravenous use. This preparation is generally satisfactory for all purposes. Indications: heart failure, supraventricular arrythmias particularly atrial fibrillation. Dose: 62.5-500mcg daily.
2. **Digitoxin.** Tablet and oral solution. This may be chosen in patients with renal impairment, and in those who vomit on small doses of digoxin. Indications: As for digoxin. Dose: 100 mcg on alternate days. Maximum dose 200 mcg daily.
The following are no longer in common use:
3. **Lanatoside C.** Tablet
4. **Medigoxin (Lanitop).** Methylated form of digoxin, more completely absorbed, and more rapidly effective. Half life 60 hours.
5. **Ouabain** injection. When a particularly rapid onset of effect is required. Given intravenously.

CURRENT VIEWS ON THE USE OF CARDIAC GLYCOSIDES

Cardiac glycosides in common use are shown in the table.

PREPARATION	INDICATIONS	PHARMACOKINETICS
Digoxin	Heart failure Most supraventricular arrhythmias, atrial fibrillation	Half-life 36 hrs. Excreted by kidney. 20-40% bound to plasma proteins
Digitoxin	Heart failure, chronic atrial fibrillation	Half-life 6-7 days. Largely metabolised by the liver and excreted in the gut. Some undergoes reabsorbtion >90% bound to plasma proteins

The chief effect of digoxin is to slow nerve conduction from atrium to ventricle by an indirect effect on the vagus nerve, resulting in an increase in the refractory period of the atrio-ventricular node.

Its main clinical use is in controlling (reducing) ventricular rate in atrial fibrillation (AF). Whilst it will not per se restore sinus rhythm, if the AF is of recent onset, by slowing the ventricular rate digoxin increases the likelihood of spontaneous reversion to sinus rhythm.

As a consequence of these properties, it is still widely used in the management of heart failure, particularly in the presence of AF. Its place in management of heart disease with sinus rhythm is more debatable. Many continued to prescribe it under these circumstances, as a consequence of perceived familiarity with one of our most tried and tested drugs.

Digoxin inhibits sodium potassium adenosine triphosphatase, which is found in cell membranes, including the heart muscle cells (myocytes), and which regulates the active transport of sodium and potassium across them. Indirectly, this also affects intra-cellular calcium, raising its concentration within heart muscle, and increasing the amount of work done (positive inotropy). This was the all pervading view of its mechanism of action in the 40's, 50's and 60's.

The paradigm was that the ventricles were unable to receive or eject sufficient volumes of blood in a given period of time. The **inotropic effect** was thought to increase cardiac output and consequently improve renal perfusion leading to a diuresis (with a little help from co-prescribed diuretics).

From the 60's to the 80's, the emphasis switched to the importance of the peripheral vasculature, and the anticipated benefit by **counteracting peripheral vasoconstriction** (associated with fatigue and shortness of breath), by vaso-dilator drugs such as hydralazine. The results of this approach were not encouraging with worsened heart failure, worse symptoms, and increased mortality (Franciosa & Cohn 1981).

It was in the 90's that the **neurohormonal** involvement in heart failure was recognized, and this forms the mainstay of current attitudes. It involves the **renin-angiotensin-aldosterone system**, and the sympathetic nervous system. This paradigm change led to the use of angiotensin converting enzyme **(ACE) inhibitors**, which interrupt the neurohormonal activation involved in congestive heart failure. This group of drugs has been shown to increase survival, as well as reduce symptoms (Michael & Parnell 1998).

Where does this leave digitalis, and latter day digoxin?

There have been a number of clinical trials which have sought to elucidate the place of digoxin in patients with varying degrees of heart failure, some on, some not on ACE inhibitors, and in sinus rhythm. One such was the Randomised Assessment of Digoxin on Inhibitors of the Angiotensin-Converting Enzyme **(RADIANCE) trial** (Packer et al 1993). This looked at the effect of withdrawing digoxin and substituting placebo in 178 patients on ACE inhibitors and with New York Heart Association class II or III heart failure. All had an ejection fraction of 35% or less. Withdrawal of digoxin resulted in a 5.9 times greater chance of worsening heart failure, mean serum digoxin concentrations being 1.2 ng/ml.

The Prospective Randomized Study of Ventricular Failure and the Efficacy of Digoxin **(PROVED) trial** was a similar trial in 88 patients, the difference being that they were not on ACE inhibitors (Uretsky et al 1993). Patients fared significantly worse when digoxin was withdrawn, again the mean serum digoxin level being 1.2ng/ml.

A retrospective analysis of the PROVED and RADIANCE trials has yielded some interesting facts. Subgroups of patients whose serum digoxin levels were low (0.5-0.9ng/l), medium >0.9-≤1.2ng/l), or high (>1.2ng/ml) were found not to differ in their propensity to worsening heart failure in contrast to those on placebo. At lower doses, side effects were less, and yet the drug was as efficacious. It emerges therefore, that the beneficial effect is being achieved at serum levels less likely to be capable of positive inotropy, but quite capable of neurohormonal modulation or effects on parasympathetic tone. In favour of this is the observation that digoxin improves heart rate variability, lack of which is a symptom of disturbance of parasympathetic tone due to heart failure (Gramstad & Lilleaasen 1982).

It was therefore somewhat disturbing when excess mortality in cardiac infarction cases receiving digitalis was reported (Ryan et al 1983; Bigger et al 1985; Banerjee & Campbell 1996). However, a major study in 1997, by the **Digitalis Investigation Group (DIG)**, looked at a large number of patients with heart failure, who received either digitalis or placebo, in double blind fashion. **The conclusion was that digoxin did not reduce overall mortality, but it reduced the rate of hospitalisation for all reasons by 6% and for heart failure by 7.9%.** The graph below shows the incidence of death or hospitalisation in the two groups over a four year period. The risk associated with the combined outcome of death due to worsening heart failure or hospitalisation related to that diagnosis was lower in the digoxin group (1041 patients) than in the placebo group (1291 patients), the risk ratio being 0.75, and P<0.001.

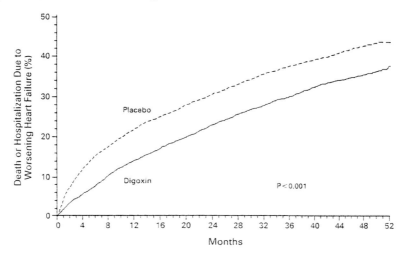

Figure (from the DIG study) Incidence of death or hospitalisation due to worsening heart failure in the digoxin and placebo groups.

The reduction in hospital admissions would suggest that patients tolerated their disease better, and since the drug is cheap and readily available, it has secured a place in the management of heart failure patients in sinus rhythm, as well as in those with AF. How long these patients should stay on digoxin is debatable. So is the dosage, there being evidence that dosing tends to be more aggressive in France and the USA than in Britain, where the median dose in the DIG study was 0.25 milligrams per day. A dose-related relationship to mortality has been reported (Leor et al 1995).

For an up to date assessment of atrial fibrillation, the reader is referred to a review of all work published between 1966 and 2001 (Peters et al 2002). In regard to the use of digoxin it states,

"Digoxin is the most frequently used agent to control ventricular rate during atrial fibrillation. Unlike most other agents, it has weak inotropic properties, making many physicians comfortable with its use, even in patients with impaired ventricular function...

...Combinations of digoxin with calcium-channel blockers or beta blockers might not only improve control of ventricular rate, both at rest and during exercise, but also improve exercise capacity, even in patients with underlying ventricular dysfunction..."

All in all, it appears to be beneficial in heart failure from the point of view of symptom relief, and allowing patients to remain at home, but does not appear to decrease mortality. Doses required for benefit are lowish, increased doses having a tendency to shorten life without symptomatic gain.

Withering wrote (in 1785):

"——it was moreover of consequence not to repeat the doses too quickly, but to allow sufficient time for the effects of each to take place, as it was found very possible to pour in an injurious quantity of the medicine, before any of the signals for forbearance appeared.——"

Its positive inotropic effect, alluded to above, is generally regarded as being a weak one, and has led to a search for more potent inotropic preparations. Unfortunately, these agents as they have entered the therapeutic arena, have performed badly in respect of effects on survival. In this context therefore, digitalis stands proud and untainted, together with its economic advantages both from the standpoint of the cost itself (approximately 30 pence per month for a 500 mcg daily dose), and the reduction in need for hospitalisation. Purchasers of health care in 2000 along with contributors to hospital formularies, still recognise the role of digoxin despite its more recent rivals.

The author (centre) visiting the production plant for digoxin, at Glaxo-Wellcome,
(Dartford) in the company of Dr. John Reader, 14th May 1998.
(With kind permission of GlaxoSmithKline)

An interesting incident which in a sense takes Withering's detection of the effect of digitalis in the legendary Old Mother Hutton's recipe full circle, was reported in the New England Journal of Medicine, on September 17th 1998 (Slifman et al).

Contrary to the requirement for drugs by the **Food and Drug Administration (FDA)** (the United States regulatory authority), dietary supplements now come under the less stringent **Dietary Supplement Health and Education Act of 1994.** No longer are dietary supplements regulated as strictly as food additives or drugs. Drugs have to be shown to be safe and effective for a particular indication before approval for marketing, not so dietary supplements.

Two cases were described of patients who developed digitalis toxicity after ingestion of botanical dietary supplements in 1997. The first was a 23 year old female who presented with nausea, vomiting, lethargy and a sensation of irregular heartbeats. She had been taking an oral regimen of dietary supplements for the purpose of "internal cleansing" starting one week before admission. The course consisted of two different tablets, each containing a variety of herbs, plus capsules consisting of various harmless bacteria, in a formulation to be taken as a drink. 24 hours after taking this, the patient felt lethargic, and experienced nausea and severe vomiting. She continued for a total of three days, then stopped on account of vomiting, but then restarted at a lower dosage two days prior to admission. However the nausea persisted together with irregular heartbeats and hot flushes. An electrocardiogram revealed complete heart block. The admitting doctor to his or her credit, suspected digoxin poisoning so requested a serum digoxin level. This was found to be 3.66 nanograms per millilitre, whereas the range for patients intentionally prescribed digoxin was 0.9 to 2.0. The case was reported to the FDA.

One month later another case was reported to the FDA, on this occasion a 46 year old female taking the same "cleansing preparation." She developed visual disturbances described as "yellow scintillations," together with nausea, vomiting, shortness of breath, palpitations and "chest pressure." Analysis of her serum revealed the presence of digoxin at a concentration of 0.9 nanograms per millilitre. Over the next 36 hours, ECG monitoring revealed brief episodes of first and second-degree atrio-ventricular heart block, from which she made a spontaneous recovery.

Next, the investigators tested each of the components comprising the product as taken by the first patient for the presence of digitalis, and one of them was positive. Samples of the raw material of each of the ingredients was obtained from the manufacturer and analysed. The presence of cardiac glycosides was confirmed by thin layer chromatography and mass spectrometry. Microscopical examination showed the typical epidermal hairs found in Digitalis lanata. This was in the raw material as supplied under the name 'plantain.' The detective work actually showed that the lot numbers used in the manufacture of the product consumed by the patient matched the contaminated batch. Analyses carried out by the FDA on further samples of plantain showed that 150 manufacturers, distributors and retailers, received potentially contaminated plantain.

So, whereas Withering was able to surmise that the only active ingredient against the dropsy in the old Shropshire lady's cure was the foxglove, so the latter day physicians presented with two patients manifesting certain toxic effects, were suspicious of digitalis toxicity, the effects all having been originally documented by Withering. In like manner when doctors and pharmacists responsible for determining the contents of drug formularies in the nineteenth century began the task of assiduously removing preparations of doubtful efficacy, so these products began returning via the health food industry in the twentieth and twenty first centuries. The general public have not yet been educated to understand the vast difference in standards of safety testing as applied to ethical products, compared with dietary supplements. On the other hand, should some latter-day Withering choose to study in depth an alleged health cure for some condition incurable using standard approved medicine, then the scene might be set for the discovery of another useful drug. But even then, it would be an uphill struggle with the stringent regulations now in force.

MODERN MANAGEMENT OF DIGOXIN TOXICITY

WW was well aware of the problems of digoxin toxicity, and described them in great detail (qv). Research into providing an antidote to digoxin or digitoxin overdosage began in 1967, when Dr. Vincent Butler and Dr. J.P. Chen at Columbia University produced an antibody in rabbits that could bind digoxin, rendering it harmless. Three major problems arose:

1. The antibody was recognised as a foreign antigen by the patient's immune system, resulting in an allergic reaction.

2. Being a whole immunoglobulin (protein) molecule it would not be excreted in the urine until broken down.

3. Degradation of the protein would risk release of attached digoxin.

The answer was provided by **Dr. Tom Smith**, a cardiologist in the USA in 1976. It will be recalled that antibody molecules have two main functions, subserved by opposite ends of the molecule. The end which binds to antigen (in this case digoxin), is known as the F(ab) end (= <u>f</u>ragment <u>a</u>ntigen <u>b</u>inding), whereas the other end is used for attachment to phagocytic cells and activating complement. Monovalent F(ab) was the answer to the earlier problems associated with whole antibody molecules, and Wellcome Research laboratories in Beckenham, Kent took on the commercial production aspect. Subsequent development and use in clinical trials led to its general incorporation in national formularies. Currently it is marketed as **'Digibind'**, by Wellcome UK.

A report of its use in counteracting the cardiotoxicity of yellow oleander has recently appeared (Eddleston 2000). The report came from Sri Lanka where deliberate self-poisoning with yellow oleander is a recent phenomenon. Common (Nerium oleander) and yellow (Thevetia peruviana) ingestion can produce a syndrome similar to digoxin poisoning (Langford 1996; Pearn 1989).

Nerium oleander (L) (Source: Sibthorp J. Flora Graeca, Vol 3, London, 1819).

The study was a randomised controlled trial in which 34 patients received anti-digoxin-Fab, and 32 patients placebo. The presenting arrythmia resolved completely after 2 hours in 15 test patients compared to 2 controls (p<0.001). Withering would have approved.

Appendix (v)

THE WILLIAM WITHERING LECTURES AT
THE UNIVERSITY OF BIRMINGHAM

(I am indebted for this information to Dr. S.R. Jenkins, Retired Faculty Archivist, University of Birmingham).

The minutes of the Faculty of Medicine of the University of Birmingham, indicate that in 1919 a letter was read stating that a **Mr.Charles Hyde** was offering the University "a sum not exceeding £100 to provide a lectureship in psycho-therapy for a term of years. The Vice-Chancellor will be glad if the Faculty of Medicine will take the matter into its consideration with a view to reporting to the Council the best method of making the gift effective." It was resolved that a committee be appointed to report to the Faculty on the proposed lectureship.

Charles Hyde (1876-1942) was a proprietor of the Birmingham Post and other local newspapers. He was a philanthropist and gave considerable sums of money to local charities, in particular hospitals and the University. He gave £5000 to the Medical School for a dissecting room, as a memorial to **Sir Bertram Windle**, first Professor of Anatomy and first Dean of the Medical School. £10,000 was donated for the Medical School museum, as a memorial to **Joseph Chamberlain**. Donations were also made towards Chancellor's Hall, a Hall of Residence, and the Students' Union. In all he gave £150,000. Why he specified psychotherapy has not been established.

The Committee reported back to the Faculty the following month that in the first instance the lectureship should be for one year only, that it should be given by a medically qualified person experienced in psychiatry and that clinical demonstrations should take place at the two general hospitals where the clinical teaching of the university was carried out. Mr. Bernard Hart MD MRCS LRCP should be invited to give the first series of lectures.

Subsequent minutes make it clear that the Faculty were not very happy about the arrangement, in November 1920 the Committee were "of the opinion that the time has not yet arrived when a permanent appointment in connection with this lectureship should be considered." It recommended Dr. William HR Rivers MA MD DSc LLD FRCP FRS, Fellow of St. John's College, Cambridge, be invited to accept the lectureship for the year 1921.

A year passed and a further list of proposed lecturers was constructed, though the minutes give no clue as to whether any lecture had been given. In March 1922, a letter from the Vice-Chancellor, **Gilbert Barling** to the Dean was read to the meeting. This letter proposed that a Diploma in Psychological Medicine be offered as in other universities, and that Sir Frederick Mott be made the Lecturer in Psychotherapy. Two months later a committee appointed to consider this, recommended that the decision be postponed because of envisaged difficulties in preparing candidates for the examination. In regard to the lectureship, it was felt that the scope should be widened to include treatment and pathology of organic as well as functional nervous disease, and Sir Frederick Mott was nominated as lecturer. In June 1922 the Vice-Chancellor replied to the extent that he had conversed with Sir Charles Hyde who was willing for the lectureship to be modified to anything thought advisable by the Vice-Chancellor, who now wished to know exactly what the Faculty wanted. In October 1922, it was agreed to change the title of the lectureship to "Applied Psychology." By November, it had evolved into Psychology in Medicine. Sir Frederick meanwhile had intimated that he would not accept this lectureship for only one year, and it was proposed to appoint him for three. By February 1923, correspondence from the Vice-Chancellor to the Dean, described the lecturer elect as "the lecturer on morbid anatomy" and "director of research." The reason for this is not clear. By October 1925 a letter to the Vice-Chancellor from (the by now surely patience-exhausted) Sir Charles stated that he was willing for his funds to be used by the Faculty of Medicine "for any useful purpose." Sir Charles did not wish his name to be attached to the lectureship and in December it was agreed to call it the "Sands Cox Postgraduate Lectureship." In January 1926, Sir Charles suggested the word "memorial" be inserted, but the Council referred this back to Faculty for further discussion. It was agreed to attach the name "Dr. Withering" to the lectureship, and in March 1926, the Chairman reported that the Council had decided to name the lectureship the "William Withering Memorial Lectureship."

List of William Withering Lecturers, and lecture titles, or, subjects on which lecturers were invited to speak.

(Where more than one name appears, it is likely that all were to be approached to give the lecture, though who actually did so has not been recorded).

1926   **Mott.** The biological aspects of normal and morbid psychology. The evolution of the brain as an organ of the mind, with a special reference to normal and abnormal psychology

1927   **FAE Crew.** Organic inheritance in man

1928   **Sir Thomas Legge.** Factory diseases

1929   **Charles Singer.** Epochs of medical history

1930   **WE Dixon.** Specific therapy

1931   **Sir Charles Hubert Bond.** Correlations between general and psychological medicine

1932   **Charles John Bond.** Some aspects of human biology. 5 lectures:
Lecture 1. On the genetic significance of hemilateral asymmetry in the vertebrate organism.
Lecture 2. On the making of use acquirements; the neuro-psychic and other responses.
Lecture 3. Genetics in relation to public health and preventive medicine.
Lecture 4. On the influence of environmental conditions on the shape and constitution of the red blood cell.
Lecture 5. On the clinical and biological significance of the above observations.

1933   **Lancelot Hogben.** Nature and nurture: The methods of clinical genetics
1934   **ED Adrian.** Social biology
       JBS Haldane. Contributions of genetics to medical science
1935   **Edward Hindle.** Filtrable viruses
       E Weston Hurst. Filtrable viruses
1936   **WWC Topley.** The mechanisms of immunity
       P Hartley. The chemical aspects of immunology
1937   **WN Haworth.**
       JC Drummond. Nutrition and nutritional disorders
       LG Parsons.
1938   **Sir Henry Dale.** Chemical transmission of nerve impulses
1939   **Peyton Rous.** Cancer research
1940   **F Verzar.**
       Lennox Ross Broster. The suprarenal gland in health and disease
       S Levy Simpson.
       S Zuckerman.
1941
       No lectures arranged
1942
1943   **JA Gunn.**
       HW Florey.
       LEH Whitby. Chemotherapy (probably shared by all four lecturers)
       RS Pilcher.
1944   **BA McSwiney.** Physiological basis of pain
       JR Learmonth. Clinical aspects of pain
1945   **JR Rees.** Health and disease: social medicine and salvage. Finding the right
       work. Selection, morale, and mental health
1946   **Guy Crowden.**
       Macdonald Critchley. The effects of the extremes of heat and cold on the body
1947   **A Szent-Györgi.** The nature of life
1948   **JF Fulton.** Functional localization in the frontal lobes and cerebellum with
       particular reference to the operation of frontal leucotomy
1949   **EB Verney.** The excretion of water by the kidney, with special reference to its
       neurohypophyseal control
1950   **HM Evans.** The internal secretions of the anterior lobe of the pituitary body
1951   **Sir Edward Mellanby.** Some nutritional aspects on bone and the nervous system
1952   **Boris Ephrussi.** Nucleus and cytoplasm in the genetics of microorganisms
1953   No lecture given
1954   Lecture cancelled through the illness of **KS Lashley**
1955   No lecture given
1956   **PB Medawar.** Transplantation and immunology
1958   **JS Mitchell.** Studies in radiotherapeutics

1960   **JZ Young.** Mechanisms of learning and form discrimination: A model of the brain

1962   **J McMichael.** Digitalis and heart failure today

1964   **EB Chain.** The biochemical effects of insulin. Some recent contributions from chemical microbiology to medicine

1966   **WS Feldberg.** A new concept of temperature control in the hypothalamus

1968   **Sir Hans Krebs.** The effects of alcohol on liver metabolism

1970   **JL Gowans.** The origin and fate of lymphocytes. Lymphocyte heterogeneity and immune response

1971   **D Michie.** Mirrors for man. The coming symbiosis

1974   **ASV Burge.** Selectivity and specificity in drug action

1976   **DC Gajdusek.** The origin and disappearance of kuru. Unconventional viruses

1978   **Sir Richard Doll.** Preventive medicine: a strategy for the future. Nutrition and the incidence of cancer

1980   **S Brenner.** Genetic analysis of complex biological systems. The molecular genetics of higher organisms

1982   **WF Bodmer.** The HLA system: genetics and biochemistry
The HLA system: function and evolution

1986   **DJ Weatherall.** The application of recombinant DNA technology to the prevention and treatment of genetic disease

1990   **Leonardo Mata.** Control of infection as a means to eradicate malnutrition

1992   **M Shepperd.** Epidemiological aspects of insanity

Appendix (vi)

THE WILLIAM WITHERING CHAIR OF MEDICINE
AT THE UNIVERSITY OF BIRMINGHAM

At the end of World War II, the University of Birmingham made its four full-time appointments to clinical chairs: medicine, surgery, paediatrics, obstetrics and gynaecology. The chairs, according to the recollection of Stanley Jenkins, Faculty Archivist, were titled the **Barling chair of Surgery**, the **Leonard Parsons chair of Paediatrics**, the **Lawson Tait chair of Obstetrics and Gynaecology**, and the **William Withering chair of Medicine.** The William Withering chairholders and their terms of office were as follows:

W. Melville Arnott (later Sir Melville), 1948 - 1971
Raymond Hoffenburg (later Sir Raymond), 1972 - 1985
Michael J. S. Langman, 1987 - 2000
Michael Sheppard, 2000 -

Appendix (vii)

THE WILLIAM WITHERING PRIZE
OF THE ROYAL COLLEGE OF PHYSICIANS OF LONDON

Founded by a gift from the World Conference on Clinical Pharmacology and Therapeutics, received in 1981 – in memory of William Withering FRS (1741-99): £20,000 to endow a prize in recognition of distinguished contributions to the science and practice of clinical pharmacology and therapeutics. The prize is awarded triennially, or at such times as the Royal College shall decide, --------. Prizewinners receive a medal and are invited to deliver a lecture.

Lecturers.

1983	**Sir James Black**	The heart as a pharmacological target.
1985	**Dr. C.T. Dollery**	Drug treatment of heart failure.
1988	**Dr. M. J. S. Langman**	Drugs – consideration of safety and efficacy.
1991	**Sir John Vane**	Control of the circulation by mediators from the endothelium.
1994	**Prof. M. D. Rawlins**	Pharmacovigilance: Paradise lost, gained or postponed.
1997	**Prof. P. J. Barnes**	How glucocorticoids control inflammation.
2000	**Prof. P. D. Wall F.R.S.**	Changes in the understanding of pain.

Appendix (viii)

THE BICENTENNIAL CELEBRATION OF WITHERING'S TREATISE

Below are seen the chairman and speakers at the William Withering commemoration meeting, organised jointly by the Association of Physicians and the British Cardiac Society, on 18th April 1985 in Birmingham. The William Withering lecture of the Royal College of Physicians, was given by Dr. C. Dollery, and published in the British Heart Journal the same year. Some of the comments made are of considerable interest:

"Future prospects

Despite the success of diuretics, it is a sobering thought that other advances in therapeutics over the last 200 years such as the discovery of penicillin and the treatment of tuberculosis would impress a physician of Withering's era far more than our use of vasodilators and inotropes for chronic heart failure. Indeed Withering himself, a forward thinking member of the Lunar Society, would probably be dismayed to find that we are still using digitalis, a drug which he recognised to be highly toxic and of limited efficacy. Perhaps only the angiotensin converting enzyme inhibitors and the modern management of hypertension would provide him with some faith in our progress in the treatment of heart failure——"

After the Scientific Proceedings, participants gathered at Edgbaston Old Church, (where Withering's body had been laid to rest), for an address by Dr. George Whitfield (a physician fondly remembered by this author when a medical student). He gave a resume of Withering's life and, by contrast to the opinions of Withering expressed in Peck and Wilkinson's book, was highly critical of Withering the man. He described him as being spoilt during childhood, a writer of petulant letters, quarrelsome with colleagues, and perhaps "imbued with a desire for greater wealth."

One wonders whether those gathered had come to bury rather than to praise. In any event, seventeen years later digitalis still remains an important part of the armamentarium, though its range of indications is becoming ever more narrow.

Bicentennial celebration of Withering's treatise. From left to right are seen: CT Dollery, SV Perry, Sir Raymond Hoffenburg, PRCP, DG Gibson, WA Littler, Sir Melville Arnott, D Noble, DM Krikler, A Guz, FL Meijler, MF Oliver, HB Burchell, and TW Smith. Following the address, a reception was held at Edgbaston Hall, Withering's leased home until a week before his death at Fairhill (Sparkbrook). (With permission from the B.M.J. Group).

Appendix (ix)

THE BICENTENNIAL OF WITHERING'S DEATH
- WELLINGTON REMEMBERS ITS MOST FAMOUS DOCTOR

Report from the Telford Journal. Wellington Mayor,Councillor Mrs. Mary Lewis, on behalf of the Wellington Civic Society, presenting a picture to the manageress of the Three Cooks Bakery, Margaret Williams, around the time of the bicentenary of Withering's death.The bakery occupies the site thought possibly to be where Withering lived. The Civic Society had chosen William Withering as its "Man of the Millennium." The picture shows foxgloves, together with an image of Withering, and hangs in the shop window. Councillor Davies is seen on the left, and George Evans, local historian, on the right of the picture.

(Reproduced with permission of the Telford Journal).

Bibliography

The Encyclopedia Britannica, 1950 edition.

J.K.Aronson. An account of the Foxglove and its Medical Uses 1785-1985. Oxford University Press 1985.

R M Baxter A history of Wellington. 1949. In Wellington library.

Anthony Blackwall Historical Bridges of Shropshire. Shropshire Libraries and Highways & Transport Department, Shropshire County Council, 1985.

Erasmus Darwin, "An account of the Successful Use of Foxglove in Some Dropsies, and in the Pulmonary Consumption." Medical Transactions of the Royal College of Physicians of London, 3 (1785), 255-286.

Jessie Dobson John Hunter. Published by E. & S. Livingstone Ltd. 1969.

Richard B. Fisher Edward Jenner 1749-1823. Published by Andre Deutsch 1991.

Abraham Flexner Medical Education in the United States and Canada. A report to the Carnegie Foundation for the Advancement of Teaching. Bulletin no. Four. 576 Fifth Avenue, New York City 1910. DB Updike, The Merrymont Press, Boston.

Fielding H. Garrison AB MD An introduction to the History of Medicine Philadelphia and London. W.B. Saunders Company, 2nd Ed. 1917.

Ernest Heberden. "EPONYMISTS IN MEDICINE. William Heberden. Physician of the Age of Reason." Royal Society of Medicine Services Ltd. 1989.

William Heberden MD London. Commentaries on the the History and Cure of Diseases,. London. Printed for T. Payne, Mews-Gate, 1802.

DG Julian, AJ Camm, KM Fox, RJC Hall, PA Poole Wilson Diseases of the Heart. WB Saunders Publishers, 1996.

G.A. Lindeboom. Herman Böerhaave. The Man and his Work. Methuen & Co. Ltd, London 1968.

G.A. Lindeboom (ed). Böerhaave and his time. Leiden. E.J. Brill 1970.

Marjorie McCrea, A history of the Parish Church of All Saints, Wellington, Shropshire 1991. Parish Church publication.

Ronald D. Mann; with collaboration of Helen Townsend and Joanna Townsend. William Withering and the foxglove: a bicentennial selection of letters from the Osler bequest to the Royal Society of Medicine, together with a transcription of "An account of the foxglove" and an introductory essay. Lancaster; Boston; MTP Press 1986 178p Medical reports of the effects of arsenic, in the cure of agues, remitting fevers, and periodic headachs (sic)..Together with a letter from Dr. Arnold.. and another from Dr. Withering London: Printed for J. Johnson & W. Brown, 1786.

Thomas W. Peck & K.D. Wilkinson William Withering of Birmingham, John Wright, Bristol, 1950.

Thomas Percival MD Manchester. Medical Ethics; or, A Code of Institutes and Precepts, Adapted to the Professional Conduct of Physicians and Surgeons. Printed by S. Russell for J. Johnson, St. Paul's Church Yard, and R. Bickerstaff, Strand, London, 1803.

Roy Porter. The Greatest Benefit to Mankind. A Medical History of Humanity from Antiquity to the Present. 1997 Harper Collins.

Arthur Raistrick. Dynasty of the Iron Founders. Sessions Book Trust, in association with the Ironbridge Gorge Museums Trust, 1989. vid. p. 149.

Benjamin Rush An Account of the Bilious remitting Yellow Fever, As It Appeared in the City of Philadelphia in the Year 1793.. Philadelphia, Printed by Thomas Dobson, 1794.

Fredrick A. Willius, and Thomas E. Keys. Cardiac Classics. A collection of classic works on the heart and circulation with comprehensive biographic accounts of the authors. London, Henry Kimpton, 1941.

George B. Wood. A Treatise on Therapeutics and Pharmacology. 2nd ed. (Philadelphia, J.B. Lippincott, 1860), pp. 118-119.

J. Worth Estes Hall Jackson and the purple foxglove. Medical Practice and research in revolutionary America 1760-1820. University Press of New England, Hanover, New Hampshire 1979.

W.H. Wynn: William Withering, a memoir, 1926.

References

1930 Smith S. Digoxin, a new digitalis glucoside. J Chem Soc 1930 i: 508-510.

1940 Musser R & Krantz JC. The Friendship of WW and Erasmus Darwin. Bull. Hist. Med 1940 Vol 8 No.6.

1965 Horn DB The Anatomy Classrooms in the present Old College, 1725-1880. University of Edinburgh Journal Vol 22: 65-71.

1975 Posner E. William Withering versus the Darwins. History of Medicine 6(1):51-57. Based on a paper read to the British Society for the History of Science, January 1974.

1981 Franciosa JA & Cohn JN. Effects of minoxidil on haemodynamics in patients with congestive heart failure. Circulation 63: 652-657.

1982 Gramstad L & Lilleaasen P. Dose-response relation for atracuronium, Org NC45, and pancuronium. Br J Anaest 54: 647-51.

1983 Ryan TJ, Bailey KR, McCabe CH, Luk S, Fisher LD, Mock MB, Killip T. The effects of digitalis on survival in high-risk patients with coronary artery disease. The Coronary Artery Surgery Study (CASS). Circulation 67(4): 735-42.

1985 Bigger JJ Jnr, Fleiss JL, Rolnitzky LM, Merab JP, Ferrick KJ. Effect of digitalis treatment on survival after acute myocardial infarction. Am J Cardiol 55(6): 623-30.

1985 Dollery CT & Corr L. Drug treatment of heart failure. Br Heart J 54: 234-42. (the William Withering lecture of the Royal College of Physicians 1985).

1985 Krikler DM. Withering and the foxglove: the making of a myth. Br Heart J 54: 256-7.

1985 Mastenbroek C. Cultivation and breeding of Digitalis lanata in the Netherlands. Br Heart J 1985; 54: 262-8.

1985 Whitfield AGW. Bicentenary of An Account of the Foxglove. Historical address given at Edgbaston Parish Church, Birmingham on 18th April 1985 as part of the William Withering commemoration meeting. Br Heart J 54: 253-5.

1989 Pearn J. Oleander poisoning. In: Covacevich J, Davine P, Pearn J, eds. Toxic plants and animals: a guide for Australia, 2nd edn. Brisbane, Queensland: William Brooks, 37-50.

1993 Packer MP, Gheorghiade M, Young JB et al. Withdrawal of digoxin from patients with chronic heart failure treated with angiotensin-converting enzyme inhibitors. N Eng J Med 329: 1-7.

1993 Uretsky BF, Young JB, Shahidi E, Yellen LG, Harrison MC, Jolly MK. Randomised study assessing the effect of digoxin withdrawal in patients with mild to moderate chronic congestive heart failure: results of the PROVED trial. J Am Coll Cardiol 22: 955-62.

1994 Takahashi H, Ihara N, Terano Y et al. Ouabain-like immunoreactive substances exist in the hypothalamus and adrenal medulla in rats. Pathophysiology 1994. 1 (1): 25-28.

1994 Zhang XW, Huang ZQ, Li CC. Antitumour activity of thevatoside alone and in combination with chlormethine in vivo. Acta Pharmacologica Sinica 1994. 15 (3): 285-288.

1995 Gil RR, Lin LZ, Chi HB et al. Cardenolides from Nierembergia aristrata. Journal of Natural Products (Lloydia) 1995. 58 (6): 848-856.

1995 Leor J, Goldbourt U, Behar S. Is it safe to prescribe digoxin after acute myocardial infarction? Update on continued controversy (editorial). Am Heart J 130 (6): 1322-6.

1996 Quazzaz HMAM, Valdes Jr. Simultaneous isolation of endogenous digoxin-like immunoreactive factor, ouabain-like factor, and deglycosylated congeners from mammalian tissues. Archives of Biochemistry and Biophysics 1996. 328 (1): 193-200.

1996 Langford SD, Bloor PJ. Oleander toxicity; an examination of human and animal toxic exposures. Toxicology 109: 1-13.

1996 Banerjee AK & Campbell RW. Digoxin therapy and survival in heart failure in sinus rhythm. Int J Cardiol 55 (1): 9-13.

1997 The Digitalis Investigation Group. The effect of digoxin on mortality and morbidity in patients with heart failure. New Eng J Med 1997 336 (8): 525-532.

1997 RWF Campbell. Whither digitalis? Lancet 1997 349: 1854-1855.

1998 Slifman NR, Obermeyer WR, Musser S, Correll WA, Cichowicz BS, Betz J & Love LA. Contamination of botanical dietary supplements by Digitalis lanata. New England Journal of Medicine 1998 339 (12): 806-810.

1998 Michael KA & Parnell KJ. Innovations in the pharmacologic management of heart failure. AACN Issues, 9 (2): 172-191.

1998 Soler-Soler J & Permanyer-Miralda G. Should we still prescribe digoxin in mild to moderate heart failure? Eur Heart J 19(Suppl P): 26-31.

1999 Terra SG, Washam JB, Dunham GD, Gattis WA. Therapeutic range of digoxin's efficacy in heart failure: what is the evidence? Pharmacotherapy 19(10): 1123-6.

2000 Eddleston M, Rajapakse S, Rajakanthan, Jayalath S, Sjostrom L, Santharaj W, Thenabadu PN, Sheriff NHR, Warrell DA. Anti-digoxin Fab fragments in cardiotoxicity induced by ingestion of yellow oleander: a randomised controlled trial. Lancet 355: 967-972.

2000 Hackenbruck HA. From digoxin to angiotensin-converting enzyme inhibitors: Issues in pharmacotherapy for congestive heart failure. Cli Exc for Nurse Practitioners 4(4): 197-204.

2002 Peters NS, Schilling RJ, Kanagaratnam P, & Markides V. Atrial fibrillation: strategies to control, combat, and cure. Lancet 359: 593-603.

Index